★ UNCOMMON VALOR SERIES ★

MISSION ISRM
"I SHALL RETURN, MACARTHUR"

Al Hernandez and Guerilla Operations
in the Central Philippines

As told by Captain Al Hernandez to Dixon Earle

Foreword by General Douglas MacArthur
and with a new Preface by Steve W. Chadde

Dedicated to
GENERAL DOUGLAS MACARTHUR
by one who served under him
and like the millions of
others who waited, knew
the true meaning of
"I SHALL RETURN"
A. H.

Mission ISRM—I Shall Return, MacArthur
Al Hernandez and Guerilla Operations in the Central Philippines

Captain Al Hernandez as told to Dixon Earle
Foreword by General Douglas MacArthur

with a new Preface by Steve W. Chadde

Preface copyright © 2014 by Steve W. Chadde
Printed in the United States of America.

ISBN: 978-1951682774

Mission ISRM, by Dixon Earle, was first published in 1961 as *Bahala Na...Come What May: The Story of Mission ISRM, An Army-Navy Intelligence Mission in the Pacific,* by Howell-North Books, Berkeley, California. The original book is now in the public domain.

TYPEFACE: Athelas 10/12.5

PREFACE

MISSION ISRM, originally entitled, *Bahala Na* (a Tagalog expression translated as "Come what may"), details the intelligence gathering and reporting operations of a hardy group of American and Filipino soldiers on the island of Mindoro during World War II. The mission's code-name, "ISRM," was derived from the famous slogan of General MacArthur, "I shall return," his promise to liberate the Philippines from the Japanese.

The objective of Mission ISRM was primarily to provide intelligence on enemy movements—on ground, sea and air—in and around Manila and the Manila Bay region. Members of the mission and their equipment were transported secretly by submarine to Mindoro, where they went about the dangerous task of establishing observation posts and radio transmission sites in enemy-held territory. Information was transmitted to allied headquarters in Australia, and would prove invaluable in planning for the coming invasion of Philippines by the allies. A secondary objective was the harassment of the enemy and sabotage of Japanese supply and communication lines.

ABOUT CAPTAIN HERNANDEZ

The story of Mission ISRM is related by Captain Al Hernandez, the executive officer of the operation, and widely respected by those in his command. Hernandez was born in Iloilo City, in the Philippines on June 25, 1909. Hernandez was the son of a Spanish lawyer and publisher and led a privileged life, attending the finest schools in the Philippines and in California. Al was a nephew of Spanish-American War hero Gen. Adriano Hernandez.

In his 1920s, Hernandez went to work in Hollywood as a stage director and film producer. He was half of the popular pre-war dance team of Hernandez and Carmelita, and one of the dance sequence producers for the hit 1933 musical motion picture '42nd Street' with Ginger Rogers. Of interest is that his offspring followed in his footsteps: a son and grandson were both producers in Hollywood.

At the outbreak of World War II, he produced military instruction films but later was commissioned as a second lieutenant and was sent to intelligence school. He served in the U.S. Army's 5217th Reconnaissance Battalion, and for his outstanding service on Mindoro, received two Bronze Stars and the Legion of Merit (see page 243). The jacket he wore while plotting strategies in the Philippine jungles today hangs in the Hernandez Museum in Iloilo.

Following the war, Hernandez worked as editor of the monthly Hollywood magazine, 'Movie News.' Later, while in the Army Reserves, Hernandez became a member of the 6312th Logistical Command at Nellis Air Force Base, where he retired as a major.

In the mid-1960s, Hernandez began a 13-year stint as a host at the popular Las Vegas club 'Don the Beachcomber' and became a prominent booster of Las Vegas during its rapid growth in the 1960s. He remained in Las Vegas for nearly 40 years before passing away in March 2001 at the age of 91.

UNCOMMON VALOR SERIES

Mission ISRM is part of a series entitled *Uncommon Valor,* taken from the quote by Admiral Chester W. Nimitz, U.S. Navy:
"Uncommon valor was a common virtue,"
referring to the hard-won victory by U.S. Marines on Iwo Jima. The intent of the series is to keep alive a number of largely forgotten books, written by or about men and women who survived extreme hardship and deprivation during immensely trying historical times.

Steve W. Chadde
SERIES EDITOR

ACKNOWLEDGMENTS
To Smythe for his faith and assistance,
to Charlotte,
to Paul and Susan for being quiet,
to June and Ann for their help when
the going got rough.
D. E.

FOREWORD

The resistance movement in the Philippines during the period of Japanese occupation has few parallels in military history. It was based fundamentally upon a whole people's unshakeable loyalty to and faith in the United States. There were armed guerilla bands, composed of both Americans and Filipinos, which denied large sections of the country to enemy penetration, and units of carefully selected and highly trained volunteers sent in by submarine with the mission of establishing radio communication with my headquarters and developing and reporting on such military intelligence as might bear upon our operations.

These forces, spiritual and physical, were coordinated, supplied and welded into an effective element of my command by Major General (then Colonel) Courtney Whitney of my staff.

The unit, whose activities this book chronicles, was given the vital task of secretly penetrating into the Philippines to secure and report, from a base in Northern Mindoro, information on enemy positions and movements in the Manila and Manila Bay areas. Its personnel, ably commanded by a young Naval officer, Lieutenant Commander George Rowe, fulfilled its assigned tasks with courage, devotion and resourcefulness and made an effective contribution toward the liberation of the Philippines.

Douglas MacArthur

16 November 1960.

American troops arrive in the Philippines; shown here in Cebu, March 1945.

CONTENTS

Chapter		Page
	Preface	iii
	Foreword	v
	Introduction	ix
1	Mission ISRM	1
2	The Penetration	12
3	First Reconnaissance	20
4	Smugglers Deluxe	25
5	Fifteen Tons Ashore	31
6	The Long Arm	38
7	I Pledge Allegiance	48
8	Combat Reconnaissance	52
9	Enemy Occupied Territory	61
10	Wrong River	72
11	Asis Outpost	83
12	To the Rim of the World	90
13	The Tower of ISRM	94
14	Undercurrents	105
15	Mission to Manila	115
16	"How" Party Periled by Informers	122
17	Hernandez Escapes	129
18	A Second Try	138
19	Return from the City	146
20	Life at ISRM	156
21	The Tower Position Is Compromised	160

22	Operation Riverboat	170
23	Top Secrets Afloat	176
24	Jungle City	186
25	Capture of a Treasure Ship	195
26	The Coconut Patrol	201
27	The Q-Boat Menace	210
28	Eyes and Ears of GHQ	215
29	Landing on Mindoro	222
30	Mission Accomplished	233
	Citation for Legion of Merit	243

INTRODUCTION

This is the story of a joint Army-Navy Intelligence mission in the Pacific. The Commanding Officer was an American stockbroker from Manila ... whose heart was still there. The Exec ... an American mestizo ... a choreographer from Hollywood who danced his way from a popular night club and a Chicago Draft Board into the hearts of the people of the Philippines, the military secrets of the Japanese and a Citation for the Legion of Merit. The top kick was an American master sergeant with 18 years of Regular Army, most of which had been spent in the Intramuros, the old Walled City in Manila.

From the time they pushed off in a little yellow life raft from the U. S. Submarine *Nautilus,* until they joined the invasion force at Nasugbu, Luzon, P. I., almost a year later, the word "uniform" might mean anything from the white sharkskin suit and Panama hat of the tropical trader to the picturesque costume of strolling troubador^s and dancing "girls," the drab garments of a sailing copra trader in his small *batel* (sailboat), a bellhop or *calesa* (horse-drawn taxi) driver, or the rags and tatters of a band of roving beggars.

The supplies they took into the jungle were as incongruous as their professions and ranged from needles and thread to weather balloons ... from lipsticks to hydrogen tanks. Even their money was counterfeit. It had to be! When operating supplies and equipment ran out they were replenished from time to time by what they chose to call lend-lease from the enemy.

On a lonely mountain peak on the Island of Mindoro, where they established their first main radio station, their means of communication ranged from "runners" from the Mangyan tribesmen, tiny, nude Pygmies indigenous to that wild, mountain region, to the most advanced electronics devices known. They worked at crude bamboo tables with instruments newer than tomorrow ... tuned to feel the pulsebeat of the Orient.

Their theme song, an old Tagalog phrase, BAHALA NA, translates Come What May ... and plenty came. If it didn't ... they went after it.

DIXON EARLE

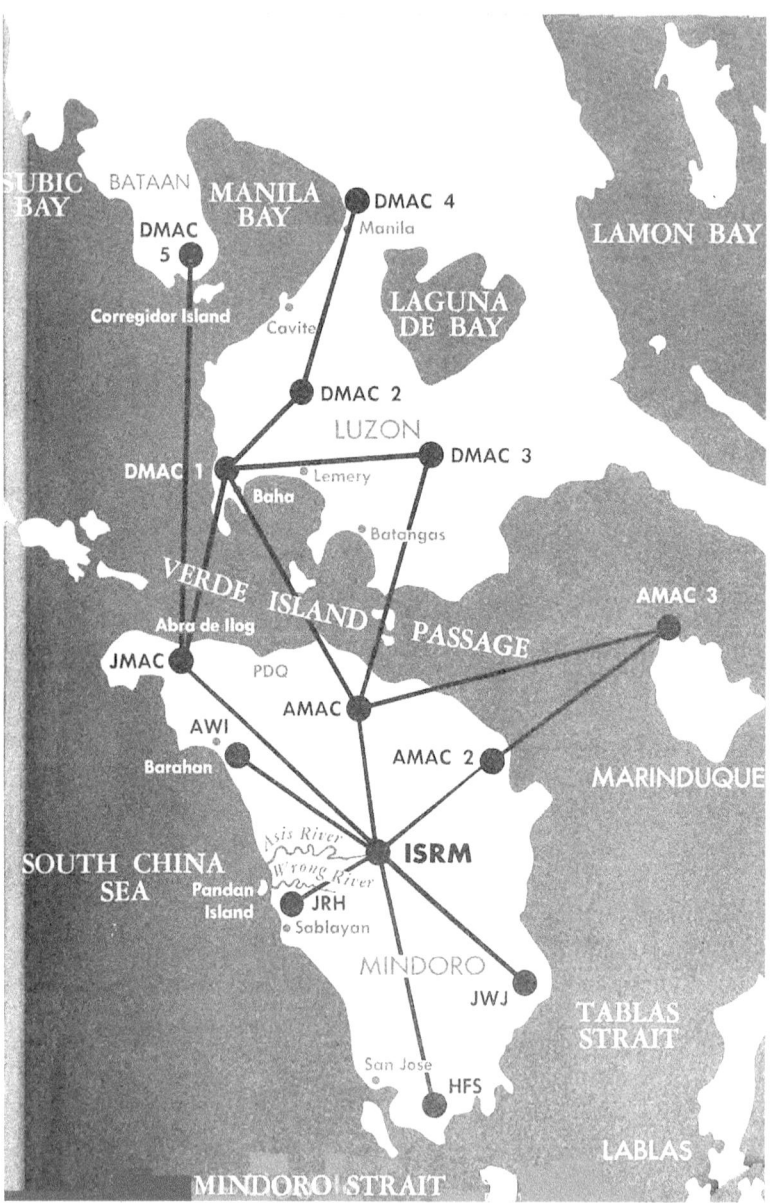

Location of ISRM and other radio stations on Mindoro, Luzon and Marinduque.

Lieutenant Commander George F. Rowe, commanding officer of Mission ISRM.

Lieutenant Al Hernandez, executive officer of Mission ISRM.

Master Sergeant Gerald Berg.

Willie Hernandez, cousin of Al Hernandez, and hero of the most daring guerilla exploits.

Our Mangyan helpers distributing rations.

Guerilla detachment ISRM standing retreat.

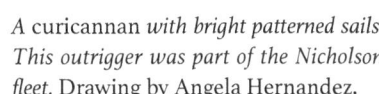

A curicannan with bright patterned sails. This outrigger was part of the Nicholson fleet. Drawing by Angela Hernandez.

Headquarters building at Camp Nimitz.

Rescued American flyers with Al Hernandez (center).

Daily "march route" Camp Nimitz—nurses, technicians and office force.

Official Record
ADVANCE INTELLIGENCE ECHELON
BASE HQS. MINDORO
SWPA

1ST LT. AL HERNANDEZ
TRP. COMDR.

JUNE 1944 · MARCH 1945

3 · PLANES

1 · SUBCHASER captured and sunk

5 · LAUNCHES

ENEMY CASUALTIES
R. I. H. Y. B.
495

27 · PRISONERS

Pilots, Crewmembers and P.O.W.S. evacuated from enemy territory

NAVAL AVIATORS

NAVAL CREWMEN

SIGHTINGS AND TARGETS
REPORTED TO U.S. NAVY & U.S. AIR·CORPS

- BATTLESHIPS 6
- HEAVY CRUISERS 19
- AIRCRAFT CARRIERS . . . 7
- LIGHT CRUISERS 34
- DESTROYERS 62
- FOX TARE DIVISION . 49
- FOX DIVISION 41
- TARE DIVISION 37
- SUGAR DIVISION . . 137
- LAUNCHES 129
- PATROL CRAFT 67
- PLANES 1,122
- MOSQUITO CRAFT . . 420

ARMY AIR CORPS

PRISONERS OF WAR
CHIEF RADIOMAN

COAST ARTILLERY

MEDICAL CORPS

PHIL. AIR CORPS

Record of Mission ISRM activities, June 1944–March 1945.

Mrs. Virginia Rowe and son George Earl (1940–1941).

Dr. Legarda, Señora Legarda and Lt. Hernandez. They were active in relaying information to ISRM.

Angela Hernandez' drawing of a calesa (horse-drawn taxi).

Little Town Cathedral.

Lieutenant Al Hernandz poses below Hernandez Park sign.

Camp mascot and kitchen police. Drawing by Angela Hernandez.

Manila in ruins following the war.

This two-color edition of the newspaper heralds peace.

Carabao, *the Philippine beast of burden.* Drawing by Angela Hernandez.

Captain Bill Dodson and his constant helper Pablo.

1
» » MISSION ISRM

On the dusky side of evening on 9 July 1944, the U. S. Submarine *Nautilus* moved stealthily northward below the surface of the Sulu Sea and pushed in under the waters of Mindoro Strait. She had zigged and zagged her way from Darwin through the Timor Sea, then right to the Arafura Sea, up past the Moluccas, the Spice Islands, the search for which had changed the course of history four hundred years before. She had veered left again almost to Borneo, on through the Celebes Sea to the heart of the Philippines. The course was not new to the *Nautilus*. She was running the Jap blockade!

Young men in regulation shipboard suntans sat at the wardroom tables with the practiced casualness of those accustomed to being often in danger, always on the alert. Most of them were drinking coffee. Some were reading, others playing cards. Two men occasionally moved ornately carved ivory and black chessmen silently from one square to another on the board.

One man in his middle thirties sat alone, reading. He was a slight, handsome man with fine, regular features, clear olive skin, deep, intense, dark eyes and black hair which lay back from a high forehead in deep, shiny waves. Accurate identification as to his nationality might have been difficult but one thing was certain. Somewhere in the past, the men of Old Spain had been among his forebears. He was a shade below medium height by American military standards, and the slimness of his body was not concealed by the faded, tropical shirt and the washed out, shapeless cotton pants he wore, together with heavy, brown leather boots and a completely incongruous gold wrist watch of excellent quality.

Obviously this man was not of the ship's crew. He was, in fact, returning to the land of his birth where, had he chosen to remain and take his rightful place as the head of his family and guardian of its holdings, he would have been known as Don Alfredo Eufronio Guillermo Omez de Hernandez.

The intercom clicked on and a voice said, "Calling Lieutenant Hernandez. Lieutenant Hernandez, report to the captain's quarters."

Instantly the man in the faded, tropical shirt looked up and closed his magazine. He had read that last paragraph three times and still could not have told a word that was in it. There was unmistakable precision in the way his slim, brown hands placed the magazine on the shelf before he started down the passageway—and in his walk, in spite of the too-heavy boots. That precision was a characteristic which was to serve him well in the months to come.

He found his commanding officer, Lieutenant Commander George F. Rowe USN (NavAir), in conversation with the ship's captain. The commander also wore faded, threadbare, civilian clothing but in sharp contrast to the lieutenant, he was tall, broad-shouldered and blond. Somewhere around his mouth—or maybe it was in the set of his jaw, was an expression of rugged determination and a zest for the life he lived. In his clear, blue eyes was the look of a man accustomed to looking DOWN at the setting sun or the shadow of his craft streaking across verdant island mountains or the open sea.

As Hernandez stepped over the coaming Rowe said, "We're getting close, Lieutenant. The captain says we should reach Pandan some time tonight. Probably between 0100 and 0300, assuming of course, that we don't have to wait out some kind of enemy activity the ship's instruments might pick up."

The captain turned to a map posted on the bulkhead and began tracing their course along the west Mindoro coast. "It's impossible to maintain an exact timetable in these waters," he said. "From here on up to where you're going ashore has been hot water for a long time." He pointed to a narrow passage in Cuyo Pass. "The Japs found out too late that MacArthur's party had slipped through their fingers about here. They also know that the area where you've landed, maybe a little farther north, was a rendezvous point for submarines supplying Major Philipps' expedition and picking up his reports for GHQ. Still farther to the north, in Verde Island Passage, General Lim and several other Philippine Army men were surprised by an enemy patrol and never heard from again."

Hernandez listened in silence. In a few hours he would head a small reconnaissance group in that hot water—probably the first since the Major Philipps party had been ambushed and slain.

Commander Rowe looked at the skipper and cut in with a trace of an edge to his voice. "I called you, Al, just to be sure that everything is squared away for the landing."

"I've taken care of the cameras, the film and the compasses and I'm picking up the radio," said Hernandez. Sergeant Berg and Sergeant Reyes have assembled the rest of the gear. They're below now making a final check of the weapons."

"Have you told the men yet, who you're taking with you?" "I didn't have to. Aguilar and Balleras, the two I wanted, asked to go."

"Good," said Rowe enthusiastically. "That's GOOD."

"If there's anything you want, Lieutenant, before you shove off, just say the word," said the skipper.

"Thank you, Captain," replied Hernandez. "I guess a good, dark night would be about all we could ask for."

The captain smiled and shook his head. They had surfaced momentarily in brilliant moonlight, several times the night before. "The moon will be almost full tonight," he said, "and if our timing turns out anything like we anticipate, it will be.. He stopped for a second, then said, "But we'll put in your requisition."

Commander Rowe was tense. His executive officer and two of his top technical men were starting on a dangerous reconnaissance mission. There was no way of knowing whether they would even reach the island and—if they did—what they might find or what might happen to them. "You're going to need everything you've got, Al, from the time that damn tub hits the water," he said. "Round up Aguilar and Balleras and all of you hit the sack as soon as possible."

"I sent the men below an hour ago," said Hernandez. "I figured we would reach there some time before dawn. Shall we check with Sergeant Berg?"

As they walked away from the captain's quarters Rowe said, "Al, something's bothering you."

"It's the damn radio set. They're insisting that we take one of the ship's sets instead of our own."

"So—what's the problem?"

"It's probably what I DON'T know that's bothering me. The radio man says theirs has a much longer range than our walkie-talkie, but dammit, we know what we can do with ours. He says if they have to lie any appreciable distance offshore, we won't be able to make contact with ours."

"Good God, Al, EVERYTHING depends on communication at this point. We've GOT to be sure."

"Right," said Hernandez, "and I'm probably all wet but . .

"Go on up and talk to them about it again, if you're not satisfied, but cut it short. Forget about checking with Berg. I'll take care of that." His hand rested for a moment
on the shoulder of the man who had been trained to think and act almost as his other self. "And then RELAX, fellow. Ill call you."

Hernandez went directly to the radio room. The ensign on duty had anticipated his coming. "Here you are, Lieutenant. It's all ready for you. I've put it in a waterproof cover, just in case you get in a hurry when you hit the beach and let it fall into the water."

"Thanks," said Hernandez, smiling. "We might do just that. But about the set—you know I haven't had any opportunity to try it out."

"I know how you feel," said the ensign, "but there's nothing to worry about. These sets are—well, there's just no better equipment made. This one's never been used. I unpacked it for you, myself."

"Fine," Hernandez persisted, "but I'd still like to get the feel of it before we shove off."

Just then a voice on the intercom said, "Calling Lieutenant Hernandez. Contact Sergeant Berg. URGENT."

"Excuse me," said Hernandez as he turned and started on the double toward the ladder which led below. If Sergeant Berg said urgent,' he meant urgent.

The ensign called after him, "Don't worry about the set, Lieutenant. We'll be ready and give it a quickie when we surface for the landing."

Hernandez entered the compartment where the two men had gone to check the weapons. He froze to the spot. Two seconds later, Commander Rowe appeared beside him. Sergeant Reyes was being strapped to a stretcher, and a white gauze pack on his leg suddenly turned crimson from the foot almost to the knee. A pharmacist's mate working over the wounded man quickly applied a tourniquet just above the knee.

Two or three men from the ship's crew and a few from the expedition looked on in silence. Sergeant Reyes, securely fastened to the stretcher, was hoisted up through the manhole to sick bay. Perspiration poured from his face. His shirt darkened and clung tight to his chest. One of their own men stepped aside to let the stretcher pass and muttered grimly as it passed out of earshot, "Two down—20 to go."

The supply officer assigned to the expedition had broken a hand during the final loading of supplies at Brisbane, too late to get a replacement. That was a loss Jerry Berg knew he would have to cover throughout THE MISSION—and now Sergeant Reyes!

Berg had stood grim-faced and silent, watching closely while the pharmacist's mate examined the wound. As the stretcher went out of sight, Rowe and Hernandez asked simultaneously, "What happened Sergeant?"

"I don't know exactly, Sir," said the sergeant, his teeth clamped tight, "but I'm sure as hell going to find out." He looked ominously about. "We had just finished our inspection, when some goddamned idiot must have DROPPED an automatic. The ankle is shattered!"

Hernandez looked at Rowe and Berg and said quickly, "Finish making your report to Commander Rowe. I'm going up to sick bay."

"Do that, Al," said Rowe. "They'll have to knock him out to treat a wound like that and there may be things he'll want to tell you before you shove off. But cut it short, and for God's sake, try to get some sleep."

Half an hour later, Hernandez started back to the quarters he had shared with Sergeant Reyes along the bulkhead in the torpedo room of the crowded submarine. His thoughts raced from the loss of a highly trained specialist to the hazardous reconnaissance mission before dawn, back to the questionable radio. As he passed the galley the steward called out, "Lieutenant, what do you want to take with you in the way of food, Sir?"

Suddenly sickened at the thought of food, Hernandez called back, "Throw in a can of peaches and a loaf of bread."

"That's ALL, Sir?" asked the man in amazement.

"That's all," answered Hernandez without stopping.

The steward stared after him and shook his head. "Well OK, you stupid bastard. That's the screwiest damn field rations I ever heard of, but you ought to know."

Sick at heart over the loss to the expedition of a skilled technician and the serious injury of a good, personal friend, Hernandez lay down and tried to relax. His temples throbbed and he could not sleep. If Senor Reyes, the sergeant's father, still operated his chain of men's hat stores, they might yet be able to use the stores for a front for certain of their operations, but establishing the contact would be much more difficult now.

Hernandez lay staring at the torpedo racks and the rows of flags of the Rising Sun painted on the bulkhead—one for every enemy ship the *Nautilus* had sent to the bottom.

Looking backward it seemed impossible that it had been less than six weeks since Sergeant Berg had taken him to the commander's office in Brisbane. That had been the first of June and specially picked and trained men were training at AIB (Allied Intelligence Bureau). They had crowded so much into so little time!

Stationed offshore on Fraser Island, they had just completed the first half of an intensive 3-month Commando Intelligence school. Several lean, tanned young officers were ready to take off on the first leave they had been able to wangle since their arrival on that side of the world. They were pushing back from the mess table when a voice on the PA speaker said, "Lieutenant Alan Hernandez, report to the Post Commandant. Lieutenant Hernandez, report to the Post Commandant."

Suddenly they were all talking at once, kidding him about what he'd been doing and speculating on whether he'd still be at liberty to go to Sydney after being called before the commandant. "Don't worry about me," said Hernandez, smiling. That was the call he had been waiting for. "You fellows have 72's for Sydney. I'm getting two weeks. Obviously my leave papers are ready. See you later."

The commandant, keen-eyed and direct, started off with, "Lieutenant Hernandez, orders have just come through for you to report at once to AIB at Brisbane."

"Brisbane?" said Hernandez, astonished and disappointed. "But we're only half way through this Commando Intelligence course."

"You've been in the Army long enough, Lieutenant, to know that orders are orders."

"Yes, Sir," said Hernandez quietly, trying to hide his disappointment.

"About your leave," the older man continued. "I noticed in looking through your records that this is your first in more than two years."

"That's right, Sir. I've been looking forward to it."

The commandant smiled. "That's why I've marked it NOT SUBJECT TO CANCELLATION. Of course I don't know exactly what your new assignment is, but at AIB, it's sure to be interesting."

Hernandez could close his eyes and see the tons of letters he had read and censored between directing shows in what seemed to him must have been every training camp between Ft. Benning, Georgia, and Australia. That had not been precisely what he had in mind when he volunteered for a special mission, more than a year before.

"They probably need a special services man," he said bitterly.

A half-smile flitted across the commandant's face. "I wouldn't be too sure of that. You might be going to—well, in any case, the landing barge leaves for the mainland at 0700. I'm afraid you'll have to be on it."

He leaned forward and handed a large manila envelope across the desk. "Whatever your assignment, Lieutenant, I'm sure you'll do a good job. I wish you luck."

The trip ashore in the bright, morning sunlight, over a smooth, blue sea brought Al Hernandez a feeling of elation. The train ride to Brisbane however, did something to dispel that feeling and as he climbed aboard the Army bus filling up with Military personnel for AIB, it disappeared altogether.

It was noon when the bus stopped in front of AIB mess hall. He sat at a table facing the main entrance. Glancing casually toward the door, he caught sight of an American master sergeant in conversation with the mess officer at the desk where he had signed in. They seemed to be looking straight at him. Then the officer looked down at something on the desk, looked up and nodded affirmatively to the stocky, square-shouldered sergeant.

The sergeant, immaculate from his short-cropped, light brown hair to the mirror-like toes of his GI shoes, turned and walked straight to the lieutenant's table. His gait, his set, unsmiling face, his whole bearing was so military it would have betrayed him in white tie or loin cloth. He hesitated just long enough for a mental salute which could be felt if not seen, and said, rather than asked, "Sir, you are Lieutenant Hernandez."

"Right," replied Hernandez.

"Sorry to interrupt your lunch, Sir. I'm Sergeant Berg from GHQ. My orders are to take you there as soon as you are ready."

"GHQ?" queried Hernandez, a little bewildered. He was still thinking of Special Services.

"Yes, Sir, GHQ," repeated the sergeant.

"I'll be with you as soon as I finish my coffee," said the lieutenant.

"I'll wait at the car, out front, Sir," said Berg and turning sharply on his heel, he strode away.

Hernandez looked after him and said to himself, "First it's AIB, then GHQ. I wish they'd make up their minds."

He took another swallow of his coffee. It had turned cold and bitter. He crushed his paper napkin into a tight little ball and dropped it into his plate. A moment later he slid his hat into place and walked outside.

"Here we are, Sir," said the sergeant from beside a long, low Army car at the curb. "Your gear is in back." Then to the corporal at the wheel he said, "GHQ Operations," and slid the glass partition together behind the driver's seat.

They rode in silence for a few moments. Then the sergeant said, "Do you know what your assignment is, Sir?" "Haven't the foggiest notion," replied Hernandez, not at all sure he liked this damned efficient fellow who seemed to know so much about his business. "Do you?"

"Not exactly," said Berg, and then with the first glimmer of a smile since they had met, "but I can tell you that you're reporting to Commander Rowe."

"Did you say COMMANDER Rower "That's right, Sir. Lieutenant Commander George F. Rowe USN—and he's eager as hell, Sir, to get you there." Now the NAVY was getting into the act. NOTHING made sense. "OK," he thought, "what have I got to lose?" Without waiting to hear more about the assignment he said, "Sergeant, you seem to know your way around, here." "I get along, Sir," replied the sergeant. His reply could have meant anything.

"If you were carrying furlough papers marked NOT SUBJECT TO CANCELLATION, how would you go about . . . ?"

The car turned abruptly and they were suddenly inside a subterranean entrance to a large building. Without a word the door opened, a corporal saluted and they stepped from the car into the lift. An operator in Australian Army uniform turned the hand lever. A green light came on and hurried along behind the row of numbers above the door. At the last number, the lift stopped and the door opened upon an immense area marked "OPERATIONS."

Certainly the interruption was no fault of the sergeant, but in Hernandez' state of mind at the moment, it might as well have been. As the door closed behind them, Berg said, "You were saying something, Lieutenant."

"Yes. I was saying 'if you were carrying furlough papers marked NOT SUBJECT TO CANCELLATION, and it looked to you as though they had just been cancelled, where would YOU go to get them UNcancelled'?"

"I take it you're speaking of a leave, Sir."

"Right," said Hernandez. How the hell did this fellow get so damned sure of himself?

"Well, Sir," replied the sergeant, "knowing the commander as I do, I'd say that just about ANYTHING that got in his way right now would be subject to cancellation."

"He MUST be eager," said Hernandez, and mentally abandoned his leave.

"You may have noticed, Sir, that the closer you get to this thing, the more serious the people are about it. I don't know what the commander's personal stake is, but the way he works, you'd think he owned the damn war and that beating the hell out of the Japs was his own personal responsibility. But don't get me wrong, Sir. He's a helluva swell Joe. Wait till you meet him."

Security police at every turn along the broad corridors stepped aside as they recognized Sergeant Berg. The last one, nearest the door, challenged but he too stepped aside when Berg said, "Lieutenant Al Hernandez and Sergeant Berg. Commander Rowe is expecting us."

The commander, tall, lean, and slim-waisted, was standing at a drawing board, working, when they entered. Maps lined the walls in front of him and at his left. Behind him was a table with neat stacks of papers. A large office safe completed his working area. As the door opened, his free hand quickly pushed back a blond curl that inevitably managed to get down on his forehead no matter how short he told the barber to cut his hair.

Sergeant Berg spoke. "Commander Rowe, this is Lieutenant Hernandez."

The commander laid his pen down and stood for a second appraising the newcomer, then said, "Come on in."

As the two men advanced he took in the lieutenant's slight, youthful build, his olive coloring and the precision of motion resulting from years of practice and working as a professional dancer. The smile which spread over his face as he thought of this man in the job ahead, gave an illusion of boyishness to his face as he said eagerly, "Perfect, Sergeant. Absolutely PERFECT. I couldn't have done better if I'd picked him myself."

Berg laughed. "I knew you'd say that, Sir."

Rowe thrust out his hand. "Glad to have you aboard, Lieutenant. This is our Sergeant Major, Gerald Berg. Sergeant, meet our new Exec."

Turning to the drawing board, he said, "I've just finished a rough sketch of our projected mission." Pointing to a circle on the sketch of the Island of Mindoro, he said, "We'll set up our transmitter here and . . . Turning away from the sketch, he reached for some gear under the table, saying, "This came in while you were gone, Sergeant. For our encampment in the wild country—the jungle, that is . . ." He stopped again and looked inquiringly at Sergeant Berg. "You didn't spill anything on the way over?"

Berg shook his head. "Not a word, Sir."

"And believe me he means NOT A WORD," said Hernandez. "For a while I thought he was an MP and I was on the way. He wasn't putting out a thing."

"Good," said Rowe. "I knew he wouldn't. But as I was saying, we have the latest of everything in jungle warfare equipment. Tents with steel nets to keep out snakes and small animals, and mosquito nets as big as houses to keep out those damned malaria-breeding she-anopheles. The Waldorf will have nothing on our accommodations."

"What kind of sleeping gear will we have in this Jungle Plaza?" asked Hernandez.

"Oh we have very swank jungle hammocks," said Berg, "with pocket compartments for everything—special papers, weapons, even your pillow. Jungle pullmans you might say." "OK," said Hernandez. "I'll buy that. NOW—what are we going to DO?"

"Good," said Rowe. "I'm glad to see we speak the same language. And speaking of languages, Lieutenant, I'm told you speak Spanish, Visayan, Tagalog, a little Japanese and God knows how many dialects."

"That's near enough," said Hernandez.

"You'll probably use all of them before we're through. You asked 'what are we going to do'."

The man's enthusiasm was amazing. Hernandez answered with a smile. "You might say you've aroused a mild curiosity." With a gravity in his voice not there before, the commander said, "Intelligence. Reconnaissance and espionage. Fourth District. Manila and the surrounding area—a place that's damned hard to get into, hard to get out of and nobody wants to stay."

He clapped his palms together and rubbing the heels of his hands together briskly, said, "OK. Let's get to work." Turning to the safe he twirled the combination a few turns to the right, then to the left and back again. Opening the heavy door, he took out a single sheet of paper and closed the door, whirling the knob again to lock it. "Here is a roster of the technical men assigned to THE MISSION. There are twenty-one of them—each a specialist in his own field. Every one except Jerry, here, who, incidentally, is our official photographer, was born in the Islands. Every one volunteered from some college or university in the States.

They are in the final stages of jungle warfare training at a secret intelligence training camp at Beaudesert. You'll go down there tomorrow and interview each of them personally. We'll go into that later, after dinner perhaps."

Hernandez listened now, his spine tingling. The commander continued. "THE MISSION—and I spell that with capitals—is to be called ISRM—I Shall Return, MacArthur.

I don't know how you, personally, feel about the general. That's not important. What IS important is that to the people of the Philippines he's—well, he may not be their God, but he certainly is their patron saint." He laughed. "I'm telling YOU about the people of the Philippines. But right here I might say that unless your identity, your family, and your acquaintances remain secret, and I mean SECRET by God, their very existence could become a tremendous hazard to you, to themselves, and to THE MISSION. Just remember that what a man doesn't know, can't be bayoneted out of him."

He paused for a moment as though to let that idea sink in before he continued. "As you've already guessed, this is to be a joint Army-Navy expedition. As executive officer, you'll be in command for the Army. I'll do the worrying for the Navy. The men in training at Beaudesert are all Army. Once in the field, I'm going to be completely outnumbered. So, just to keep the Navy touch out there we'll salute when we meet in the morning and no more until 'Good Night'."

"Aye, Aye, Sir," said Hernandez, clicking his heels in a sharp salute.

"Ha!—I knew you had some Navy blood in you," exclaimed Rowe, pleased at the rapport which had sprung up so easily.

"So it's going to be up to the top kick to keep the outfit REGULATION," said Sergeant Berg solemnly.

"And don't think he can't do it," said Rowe. "Just ask him for any Army Regulation or Article of War. He'll quote it and give the page and paragraph to boot. How long HAVE you been Regular Army, Sergeant?"

"Long as I can remember, Sir."

"I don't think it's been quite that long," said Rowe, "but he'd been a lone wolf around the Intramuros for eighteen years when Manila fell to the Japs."

At that moment a voice on the intercom brought Hernandez out of his reverie. Suddenly he was back in the present—and his bunk on the *Nautilus*. There were the torpedoes in the racks along the bulkhead and those flags of the Rising Sun. He glanced at his watch—0100. If the captain's calculations had been correct, and if the ship's instruments had not picked up too much enemy activity, in probably an hour he and his two volunteers would be shoving off in a little yellow life raft, heading for—his eyelids drooped and he was asleep.

Ten minutes later Commander Rowe laid a hand lightly on his shoulder and said, "Al, it's that time."

2
» » THE PENETRATION

For many months the skillful, nerveless crew of the *Nautilus* had maneuvered her in and out through the enemy blockade. She had smuggled medicine and supplies to our beleaguered troops on Bataan and Corregidor as long as the supplies had lasted. When Carlson's Marine Raiders were ready to make their stand on Makin Island, the *Nautilus* had set them down at their beachhead. She had evacuated hundreds of American and Philippine women and children from Manila and other areas.

Probably no other passengers had seemed more incongruous with the polished metal, spotless bulkheads and gleaming waxed linoleum in the wardroom than the men of that first reconnaissance party of MISSION ISRM, as they waited for the click of the intercom which would summon them topside. Their orders on leaving Brisbane had read:

PENETRATE ENEMY OCCUPIED TERRITORY AND REMAIN THERE UNTIL OUR FORCES ARRIVE.

The penetration was about to begin!

Peter Aguilar and Julio Balleras, the two sergeants who, with Lieutenant Hernandez were to make up the first reconnaissance party, also wore shabby, faded, cotton clothing. With black scarves deftly wound and tied about their heads and wicked-looking knives and bolos in their sturdy belts, they would have been the envy of the boldest pirates to sail the seas from Barataria Bay to the Caribbean.

Three things—heavy leather boots, weapons and identical gold watches—might have served to distinguish between these young men and the thousands of others roaming the jungle-covered hills and lowlands of the Philippines, jobless, homeless, and often hungry. Few people in the islands had the money to buy such shoes, even if they had been available for civilian use, and weapons of any kind had been forbidden (and confiscated by the enemy) from the time of the invasion. The watches had been brought to every member of the expedition from General MacArthur, by General (then Colonel) Courtney Whitney, G-2, in charge of secret missions in the Philippine Theatre, as they left for Darwin and their rendezvous with the *Nautilus*.

Major General Charles A. Willoughby, former G-2 chief for General MacArthur in the P.I.'s, and later at GHQ in Australia, had told them something of the success of our forces in the Pacific, the attack on the Marianas, and the impending invasion of Guam.

Dr. Joseph Ralston Hayden, patriot and educator of the Islands, then representing the Philippine government at GHQ, had come with the two military men to the blacked-out Aerodrome to see them off. It was he who had given them their theme song in the old familiar Tagalog phrase which translates, "Come what may!" The last to shake hands with Lieutenant Hernandez, he had said, "Good luck, my boy. BAHALA NA!"

The immediate assignment of this three-man task force was to paddle a small yellow life raft from the spot where they pushed off from the *Nautilus*, under a full moon riding high in a cloudless sky, across a brilliant expanse of enemy-patrolled, open sea, a distance of approximately a mile. Their destination, the island of Pandan, so infinitesimal that it failed to rate even a dot on most maps, lay three miles off the west coast of Mindoro. Specifically, it was their job to determine whether conditions there warranted landing the expedition with fifteen tons of radio, weather and photographic equipment and supplies, food, clothing, and all the other gear required for such a mission, and to relay that information to the *Nautilus*. Then, depending upon the conditions, they would wait there for the others to come ashore or try to make their escape and join the expedition at an alternate location later.

Technically theirs was not a combat unit, but the men of MISSION ISRM had spent many months in camps from the East Coast to California and again in Australia, in the grueling training for jungle warfare and commando tactics. They had been trained and equipped to protect themselves against the enemy, the elements, and the jungle. They were conditioned to the grim necessity of surprising an unsuspecting sentry who stood between them and the job they had to do, and dispose of him swiftly, surely and without a sound of struggle or the firing of a shot.

Lieutenant Hernandez had chosen Aguilar and Balleras for this first reconnaissance because between them, they possessed the necessary attributes for such a mission. Aguilar, the older of the two, had demonstrated outstanding ingenuity and resourcefulness and the ability to think clearly under almost any circumstances. Balleras had strength, courage, tremendous endurance, and a capacity for seeing through to the end, the most demanding task—and both had one thing more. Like the others, they had volunteered for this mission. They were not being sent into a strange land only because there was a job that had to be done there. They were going HOME!

As Sergeant Berg had said of Commander Rowe that day in Brisbane, every man had a personal stake in this struggle. Some had left parents, brothers and sisters or sweethearts behind. Others had children who, if they were still alive, probably were in need of money, food, clothing and medicine. These men had recognized and accepted the risks they would have to take—and the consequences. If they failed, they would not be likely to have a second chance.

A desire for education and a better way of life, economically impossible for most of them in their native land, together with a yearning for adventure, had taken these men away—across the Pacific. Many had gone on to the Atlantic coast. They had worked at any kind of job to finance their education, crowding in study time whenever and wherever they could, to make their dreams come true. Now they were coming back to aid their people in a life-and-death struggle against a powerful and merciless invading enemy. There had been no word from friends or relatives since the invasion, but somewhere amid the death and destruction of screaming bombs, burning homes and crumbling buildings were their families.

They had left Darwin on the last night in June and now, ten days and probably 4,000 miles later, Commander Rowe, Sergeant Berg, and two of the ship's crew stood with the landing party beside a small pile of gear and a deflated yellow life raft at the rail of the submarine barely above the surface of the sea.

The ship's captain and the ensign from the radio room were coming down from the tower. Lieutenant Hernandez hurried forward to meet the ensign who handed something to him and the two men started running in opposite directions. Reaching the spot where the others stood ready to put the gear over the side, the captain said, "I don't like lying out here in this bright..." Seeing Hernandez running away from the spot, he broke off and shouted sharply, "Lieutenant, your gear's right here." Turning to Rowe he said, "What's the matter with him? Doesn't he know we cant..."

Rowe interrupted, speaking calmly, "You probably know, Captain, that our men have had no opportunity to test the radio you are sending with them. It's important to us to KNOW that we'll be able to make contact."

"You know as well as I do, Mr. Rowe, that I can't lie here exposing my ship and my crew to try out a radio. If my man says it's OK, then you can depend on it." Turning again towards Hernandez, he called out, "All right, Lieutenant, let's GO!"

Hernandez came directly to the group and the captain said, "All right, Men, get them over the side and let's get out of here."

Rowe gripped Hernandez' hand firmly. "He's the skipper, Al. There's nothing I can do. We'll be listening for your call and the 'Storm Over China Sea' signal. Check your watches. We want to see that 'come ashore' signal at 1200 hours. Right now it's 0300 ex-ACT-ly. For God's sake, Men, be CAREFUL!"

At the sound of the rush of air inflating the raft as it hit the water, Sergeant Berg gripped Hernandez' hand hard. "It's not right, Lieutenant," he said. "I should be going with you."

"Positions, Men," said Hernandez. Then to Berg he said lightly, "You know I had to leave someone to keep the outfit regulation."

"And you know how I feel, Sir. WATCH it."

With a quick salute Hernandez turned and followed the others over the side. Aguilar and Balleras took air alert positions forming two points of a triangle. Hernandez sat aft, forming the third point and serving as a tiller in navigating the flimsy little craft. In sharp contrast to the shadows ahead, a full moon was doing a strip tease with a wisp of pale haze in a dome of midnight blue above and a blue-white phosphorescent wake stretched out longer and longer like a giant exclamation point toward the big, bright dot on the sea where their only shelter had already disappeared.

The three men knew what might lie ahead. Each of them, with an oar gripped in one hand, put out the other for a three-way handclasp and a simple BAHALA NA—an unspoken vow to meet the challenge—Come What May!

For the next several minutes they rowed swiftly in the brilliant moonlit silence of the night. Then Aguilar said, "I've NEVER seen the moon so bright."

"I guess the skipper doesn't carry much weight where the nights are dealt out," said Hernandez. "I ordered a dark one." Then turning to look toward the island for the first time, he said, almost breathlessly, "God, I'd forgotten how beautiful the nights here could be. Look at the moon glistening on those palms."

"Like a million goddam, glittering blades," said Balleras realistically.

Three quarters of the distance lay behind them and a long, narrow, white beach ahead contrasted sharply against the thousands of swaying, glistening palm trees and the black shadows underneath. There was nothing to mar the splendor of the night.

About three hundred yards offshore, Balleras said uneasily, "Do you feel a pull downshore?"

"Yes, I do," said Aguilar. "It began about fifty feet back."

"Me too," said Hernandez. "We must have hit a strong current."

He was right. Near the Pandan west shore and again, across the three-mile channel, off the Mindoro shore a deep, swift current flowed down from the South China Sea through Mindoro Strait.

They had expected to reach the island in a direct line from where they had left the *Nautilus,* but now, swept along by the swift current, they were powerless in the swirling, surging surf at high tide.

"We'll be heading back to Australia at this rate," said Hernandez.

"I hope we don't hit those goddam rocks ahead," said Aguilar.

"The way this tub's heading, we're sure as hell going to," Balleras finished with a shout.

At the same moment, Hernandez called out, "Watch it, Men. There's a BIG wave coming in."

A moment later, his shout, "Here comes a bigger one. Grab your GEAR," was lost in Balleras' cry, "HERE WE GO!" and they were thrown high on the crest of a wave that roared in, smashing them into the jagged rocks that lined the shore for two hundred feet along the beach.

Holding fast to the walkie-talkie, with his camera and other gear strapped to his shoulders, Hernandez looked back and saw Aguilar in the water, clutching wildly at the boat as it swirled out in the backwash of the wave. The man struggled for a moment, then dragged the fragile little craft clear of the water and past the rocks before he started forward.

Balleras had the second camera, a metal box of film and the rations. Passing out of the shadows cast by the rocks, the lieutenant dropped to the sand with, "Watch it, Men. Take care!"

Both men hit the sand and for a moment all three lay still. Then they started moving forward. In their minds were two thoughts—reaching the trees without being seen and—what they might find waiting in the black shadows underneath.

Each man was to take his turn at a signal from the lieutenant. In the bright moonlight no sound was necessary. They could see every move of his hand. A finger pointed at Balleras sent him forward on a low, crouching run to a position ten feet ahead. As he hit the sand, Aguilar saw the finger point his way and advanced, half-running, half-crawling, to his next position. With the two men probably fifteen feet from the water's edge, Hernandez crawled forward and started the advance over again. About twenty feet from the first line of trees—away from the sound of the surf, he said, almost in a whisper, "Now—ALL THE WAY."

Together they ran towards the shadows. Standing under the trees, they could hear nothing save the night sounds of the jungle, the pounding of the surf, not more than thirty yards away—and their own hearts. A quick look around indicated that the regular rows of tall coconut palms had been planted, but the thick undergrowth of plants and creepers told them that whatever had gone before, the jungle had taken over now.

There had been no way of knowing what to expect—no assurance that they would make it up that sandy beach. They might have picked a deserted island—or an enemy encampment. Anything could happen still, but there had been plenty of time for some kind of action if they had been spotted coming ashore.

While Hernandez opened up with the radio under a thin fringe of the overhanging trees, Aguilar and Balleras went back to the beach to clear the traces of the landing and to bring the raft in under cover. They would need that boat if they had to make a getaway and—few things could be worse for them now than having a U.S. life raft spotted there by an enemy patrol.

With the enemy activity being picked up by the ship's radar when they surfaced for the landing, there was a good chance that she had already gone beyond the five-mile range of the set. The lieutenant tuned in eagerly on the first frequency. Enemy communications came in loud and clear. "Thank God, it works," he said aloud, and tried the second—still Jap traffic. The third, the fourth and fifth were the same—all occupied. He was eager to get his landing report away as quickly as possible but cutting in on a busy frequency could be very dangerous. A message in English, even in code, might be a tip-off. He went over the dial again. This was taking time but he had no alternative.

He would have to take a chance on the frequency with the least traffic, Frequency C—and trust to luck. With a prayer and a BAHALA NA, he called the ship. "H to G—H to G. Storm over China Sea—Over."

They answered the first call! "G to H—Roger and out." It was done. If the Japs had picked up the message—but that wasn't likely. He actually had been on the air less than 60 seconds, and they couldn't have located him in that length of time, even if they'd been waiting for him with a direction finder.

While Hernandez had been busy with the radio the two men had gone farther back into the grove to make sure they had not landed on the perimeter of a sleeping enemy camp. In about twenty minutes Aguilar came back.

"The island is inhabited, Sir," he reported.

"How do you know?" asked Hernandez.

"I heard a rooster crow, Sir. If there are chickens, there must be people."

Hernandez smiled. "Seems logical," he said.

"And they must be natives," said Balleras, who had just finished his own reconnoitering. "Enemy troops would be unlikely to carry crowing roosters around with them."

"OK, fellows," said the lieutenant. He too was beginning to feel a little easier. "The rooster is encouraging. There must not be any hungry Japs around, but we have a full day ahead of us. We should all get some sleep before dawn." Looking at his watch, he said, "We'll break it up into three 35-minute watches. I'll take the first."

"Couldn't I take the first watch, Sir?" asked Aguilar.

"I'll take it," Hernandez answered quietly.

Now that he knew the radio to be adequate for his purpose, and that there seemed to be no immediate danger, he wanted this first hour in the Islands, alone. There in the warmth of the tropical night, thoughts of other, happier nights crowding one upon the other brought a nostalgic feeling so intense that it became more physical than emotional. It tightened the skin across his cheeks like a sudden cool breeze through an open door and sent wave on wave of a feeling akin to pain, out from his chest, creeping along his arms and down his legs, ending in a tingling, gone-to-sleep sensation.

He thought of his mother—how happy she had always been when he came home. He wondered if she were still at the island *hacienda* he had known as a boy. Then for the first time, he realized fully how dangerous her position had become in this last hour. She must be taken at once to a safe place, where enemy patrols could not find her. "God, let me find her—alive," he said fervently and got up and walked up and down the sandy beach under the fringe of the palms, calling to mind the many things they had learned at General Blarney's espionage school in Australia—enemy characteristics, his tactics and his torture methods.

Hernandez had seen no previous action in the war but he had seen the ugly side of one of the "incidents" that Japan was staging in the '30's to test out her incipient war machine and to serve as a barometer of world opinion. She was seeing just how far she could go in gobbling up smaller nations and invading and taking over the government of larger cities in China.

He had just arrived in Shanghai with a company of entertainers he had assembled in America for a tour of the Orient, when a squadron of Jap bombers roared in over the unsuspecting city, scoring a direct hit on the second of three cabs carrying the company to their hotel. Hernandez had been in the third cab, perhaps a block behind the others. By the time he regained consciousness in a hospital, several days later, he could find no trace of the others of his company in the panic-stricken, war-torn city. Eight months later, he met the only survivor of the group he was to see again, on a street in Hong Kong.

It was after his return to the States that he received the offer which took him back to Manila as Stage Director for the Philippine Exposition.

He glanced at the thin, luminous lines on the face of his watch. It was time to call one of the men for the second watch, but he was not ready yet. He sat down for a moment on a coconut log, thinking of that summer in Manila. The city had been so beautiful—so full of life and laughter. He could almost feel again the thrill of seeing the opening pageant as it became a beautiful, living thing. Symbolic of their progress in civilization, a thousand persons, each carrying a lighted candle, moved down from the darkness of a mountain in the background on the immense stage of the Exposition Building. As they assembled at the foot of the mountain, the light grew stronger, the tempo of the music increased and the dance began. Then, to the lieutenant, sitting there on a coconut log, alone in the jungle night, the music seemed to fade—farther and farther away. Suddenly he sprang to his feet, his heart pounding. This was no time to fall asleep!

The moon, now a deep coral, was sinking into the sea. Eight hours from now they would have finished their first reconnaissance. They would have to know the answers to a great many questions to signal the right instructions to the others. Hernandez called Aguilar to take over the watch. An hour later, he felt a touch on his shoulder. It was Sergeant Balleras, on the third watch. Few other words could have accomplished the sergeant's purpose so well as those he spoke in a low but excited voice, "Sir, JAPS!"

3
» » FIRST RECONNAISSANCE

 Thirty seconds after Aguilar's two-word reveille the two men were on their way to a wooded point jutting out into the sea probably 75 feet above sea level which the sergeant had discovered just before dawn.

 Pandan Island, three miles off the west shore of Mindoro, is approximately a mile and a half in length with an extreme width of half a mile, almost exactly midway north and south. There an east-west range of rocky, wooded, intersecting hills extends out on either side of the island and drops off abruptly into the sea. On the north a long, unbroken expanse of clean, white sand drops down gently from the green, jungle-covered hills to the blue waters of the South China Sea. To the south, in striking contrast to this barren, white sand, thousands of tall, graceful coconut palms in straight, even rows reach from the foot of the ridge to the southernmost tip of the island. They were camped at the edge of a richly bearing copra plantation, deserted by its owners early in the war.

 A rocky promontory where the ridge pushes out sharply to the west, served as an observation point for this, the first real reconnaissance of MISSION ISRM. About two hundred yards out beyond the surf, a native *banca* (small rowboat) drifted lazily in the rosy glow of the early morning, on an almost purple sea which, unlike the night before, now scarcely rippled in the breeze. The occupants of the *banca* apparently were fishing. There might be two—three of them at most. From where they stood it was impossible to tell.

 "Do you suppose they picked up the message, Sir?" asked Balleras.

 "They might," answered Hernandez, "but I'm sure their being out there now is pure coincidence."

 "They couldn't have picked up our location," said Aguilar. "Right," said

Hernandez. "We weren't on the air a minute."

Moving about to try to get a better view of the boat, he asked, "Did you see which way they came from, Sergeant?" "No, Sir." said Balleras, "They were sitting just about where they are now when I spotted them."

Balleras followed with, "What do you make of it, Sir?" "I'm not quite sure," Hernandez replied. "I think there are three of them. One seems to be thicker through the shoulders than the others. He could be a Jap, but he could just as well be a native out fishing for his breakfast."

"What are we going to do about them, Sir?" was Balleras' next and characteristic reaction.

"That depends entirely upon them," said Hernandez. "If they give any indication that they're looking for someone, then we'll have to . . ." He stopped.

"We'll have to WHAT, Sir?" insisted Balleras.

Hernandez looked him straight in the eyes and said, "Right now, Sergeant, I'm sure of only one thing. If they give us any reason to believe they're looking for us, we can't let them go back to the Mindoro mainland, if that's where they came from, and report our being here. I'll have to depend on you to see that they don't."

Then, as though the fishermen had heard the entire conversation, they turned about and began rowing toward the south shore. By cutting down to lower ground and running all the way around the bottom half of the island, just inside a fringe of the coconut trees, Balleras kept in range of the boat. Not until they beached their small craft in a sheltered cove on the east shore, and an old man and two little boys got out of the boat with a thin string of fish, did he put away his tommygun.

That was an hour which later, they were to know might have altered the story of MISSION ISRM.

The agreement with Commander Rowe was that at 1200 they were to raise a signal at the highest possible point on the western side of the island. If the signal indicated favorable conditions, the expedition would land that night, as soon as possible after dark. If they had to say "no," the landing party would proceed to a second prearranged island, do the necessary reconnaissance there, and the others would attempt to join them on the return trip of the *Nautilus* a week later.

With the first excitement of the morning over, Balleras went farther afield while Aguilar set about preparing mess. Lieutenant Hernandez was sitting on a coconut log, loading a camera, when Aguilar stepped up to him and with a great flourish, bowed low and held out to him a combination serving dish and tray—an expertly split coconut, still in its pale green coir, and said, "Sir, we have something delightfully different this morning—PEACHES with fresh, tender, young coconut on the half shell."

At the word "peaches," Hernandez dropped the camera. Retrieving it in mid-air, he looked up at the sergeant and said, "He DIDN'T—NOT peaches and bread?" At Aguilar's affirmative nod he finished, "That son-of-a-bitch."

Certain that in some way the lieutenant was responsible, inadvertently, for the situation, Aguilar could not resist pressing the point. "If you'll look right now, Sir, you can see some small white lumps over there on the ground. The bread was NOT in a can."

Hernandez motioned casually for Aguilar to set the food down while he finished with the camera, but the sergeant shook his head. "You'd better eat now, Sir. The way those damned red ants galloped through that loaf of bread, they'll be over here in a little while and take those peaches away from you. They're big as horses and twice as hungry."

As Hernandez snapped the camera shut, and looked up, he saw in the long, slanting rays of the early morning sun a shadow remarkably like that of a dinosaur. Not until then did he realize that they were also sharing their temporary quarters with a family of immense, sleek, green lizards. The head of that family, an excellent specimen fully two feet long, bent on a little reconnaissance of his own, had just emerged from the small mound of earth which had served Hernandez so comfortably as a pillow in the early morning darkness. Yes, they were back in the tropics.

There was a great deal of work to be done in order to know what word to pass along to the commander. They had to find out if there were enemy troops or indications that there had been—whether enemy Coast Watchers were active on the island—if there were native inhabitants other than this old man and the boys—if so, were they pro-American, enemy sympathizers or collaborators? They had to familiarize themselves with the terrain and photograph the area from many angles in order to check later for signs of enemy activity. Every minute of those next few hours had to count.

The steaming jungle heat pressed down upon them as they hurried from place to place, constantly on the alert for enemy patrols, land, sea, and air. They worked up and down the island several times from the hills to the southern tip and diagonally from NE to SW and reverse, with several crossings parallel to the rocky, intersecting ridge. In the rugged terrain of the hills they found many crevices and cave-like formations which would make excellent hideouts in the event of enemy patrols. However, the thought that only by point of view were they anything other than an enemy patrol, together with their too-recent Coast Watcher training dampened any enthusiasm they might have had about the hideouts. Even at that moment, those spots might be serving exactly that purpose. It would be impossible to search all of them in the short time they had, but they were constantly on the alert for evidence of a radio transmitter. Though they did not know it, the enemy had greatly simplified their task in that respect. Feeling himself in full control of that part of the world, he made no great effort to conceal his activities, but the purpose of their mission left no margin for uncertainty.

By 1100 they had determined that the old man and the two small boys were the only inhabitants on the island and that they occupied the sole habitation, a small *nipa* hut at the edge of the deserted plantation. There was no indication of enemy occupation past or present. By that time, also, their water was gone. Undoubtedly there would be water at the hut, but they could not go there in search of it, even if there had been time. Coconut milk would have to do, temporarily.

GHQ had made a fortunate choice in Pandan as the initial point of penetration. Nothing they had seen could be called unfavorable and they were eager to pass that word along to the others. With exactly an hour to go, they started back up to the spot they had chosen earlier as the signal point. The heavy growth of vines, bushes, and small trees was so low that they had to crawl or crouch to keep under cover after they left the coconut grove. Higher up, the jungle trees were taller, but penetration of the heavy underbrush left the men dripping with perspiration. Their clothing clung fast to wet, sticky bodies and their mosquito nets were tight against their necks and faces.

At the point where they had decided earlier to post the large white signal cloth, they had a full view of the China Sea approach and could not possibly be seen from the Mindoro mainland. "I believe this is the best possible place," said the lieutenant, "but let me take one more quick look from the other side."

"It will have to be quick, Sir, or well be late," said Balleras.

Hernandez looked at his watch. "My God, you're right, Sergeant," he said as he dashed around to survey the scene once more from the other side.

He came back saying confidently. "It's PERFECT. You can't see a thing from..."

His voice died in his throat. There was no sign of the signal—and only one man where he had left two, a few seconds before. Somehow he managed to say, "Where's Balleras?"

"Down over the ledge, Sir, looking for deeper soil. We're on solid rock here with only three or four inches of soil." Just then Balleras' head appeared from below and Lieutenant Hernandez put out a hand to steady himself against the strata of rock next to him and took a long, deep breath. Totally unaware that he had just given the lieutenant a very bad moment, Balleras said, "We can put it up about ten feet below here, but we'll sure as hell have to work fast. There's a lot of damn brush down there that could cut off the view from sea level."

Feverishly they hacked and slashed at the vines and saplings, remembering that every trace of their activity had to be hidden from passing air patrols. As they finished, Hernandez looked at his watch—1159—one minute to go. He took the binoculars hanging around his neck and started scanning the horizon. One of the men stood mopping his neck and forehead. The other held the white signal cloth with the sharp pointed poles thrust through the stitched casings at the edges. Posted as a narrow, vertical strip, it meant "safe to land." A wide, horizontal signal meant "see you next week."

"Do you see anything, Sir?" asked one of the men. "Nothing that looks like a periscope," Hernandez replied, "but we'll post the signal anyway. NOW!"

Quickly they thrust the sharp points into the soft, leaf-covered earth. Scanning the surface of the sea in the direction from which the *Nautilus* should come, Hernandez turned slowly to the north. "Drop it, men," he called out sharply. "QUICK! Back under the trees and keep that cloth DOWN." The two men wrenched the standards free and dashed to the shelter of the thick, tropical foliage. From out of nowhere a Jap patrol boat came steaming around the upper curve of the island, cruising along not more than five hundred yards off shore.

4
» » SMUGGLERS DELUXE

The three men stood motionless behind a thick, trailing vine overhanging a tall, broad-leafed plant. Hernandez watched every move on deck on the enemy patrol-boat through his binoculars, as it eased along to the south. There was nothing to indicate that their signal had been seen, but wait—they were slowing down—they were stopping!

No one seemed to be looking for anything in particular, at least not on the island side. "They don't seem to be putting anyone ashore," said Aguilar hopefully.

"Maybe they don't HAVE to come ashore," said Balleras, ever the realist. "Some goddam Jap Coast Watcher in one of these caves right here under our noses may be giving them a play-by-play report on what we're doing right now."

"I hope to God you're wrong," said Aguilar.

"I'll go along with you on that," said Balleras, "and what's more, I hope they aren't sitting out there because they spotted the periscope when it was raised for the commander to look for the signal."

"If that damned patrol boat that dropped ash cans on us for three hours is any criterion, they didn't," said Hernandez. "They'd be attacking by now."

The ash can incident had occurred when the *Nautilus* was about halfway up from Australia. The skipper had managed to maneuver his way around and out of combat with two exceptions on that long, hazardous trip. The first had been only a few hours out of Darwin, in the Timor Sea, when a squadron of what turned out to be American planes spotted her and took a few moments out to strafe and bomb the immediate area. Some of the bombs missed by less than a hundred feet.

The whole affair was over in a matter of minutes, but it took the men of MISSION ISRM much longer than that to regain their equilibrium after the crash dive that followed the cry, "Down periscope. Take her DOWN!" From 36 hours in the air, much of the time at 14,000 feet or more, to a crash dive in a submarine in a few hours' time was a rugged experience.

The attack days later, by the enemy patrol boat Hernandez mentioned, had been different. The crew and passengers of the *Nautilus* had just sat down to a real holiday dinner at evening mess on the Fourth of July, when they heard the "take her down" order, still devastating to the unseasoned submariners of THE MISSION. In less than sixty seconds from the first sound of the alert, one after the other of the crew had slithered lightning-like through the manhole, down the narrow, vertical, steel ladder and manned battle stations.

To stand beside the "Christmas tree" just once at such a time, and see the red lights on the board flash from red to green as valves and hatches closed, was all that was necessary to make anyone realize the responsibility and the importance of every member of the crew.

Down, down, down they went to what seemed to the newcomers to be the very bottom of the sea, while depth charges boomed overhead. "Absolute quiet" was the order. Engines were stopped. Batteries cut in. Around and around the attack boat went, dropping the "ash cans" fore and aft, to port and starboard. Every charge brought its rumbling, vibrating threat to the huge, silent, airtight ship. Closer and closer the ash cans came, even though they actually had submerged below the safety depth for the sub. Between the rumblings they could hear the crackling pressure of the sea as it crushed against the hull of the ship.

Idled air conditioning units mean NO CIGARETTES to help quiet taut nerves. An hour went by and muffled explosions alternated with violent vibrations that shook the ship like earthquakes. Tension left its mark on every face.

The second hour passed and seemed like three. The crew of the *Nautilus* had survived some of the toughest fighting in the war in the Pacific—in and out under the waters of Manila Bay to Bataan and Corregidor—at the Battle of Midway alongside the Argonaut—but now, hardened and nerveless as they were, action—any kind of action, would have been welcome. Compartments became intolerably hot. Men mopped their faces and stuffed sodden handkerchiefs back into already-wet shirt pockets. Then there was silence. It was over. Long breaths relaxed taut, aching chests. Men remained in their positions for no "at ease" command had been given.

NO! It was NOT over. The ash cans were coming down again. Another hour dragged slowly by. At the end of the third hour the rumblings stopped again. There were no more explosions—no more vibrations—just waiting, interminable waiting.

Finally came the order to proceed. Starting switches were thrown, but instead of the familiar throbbing of the engines, there was only heavy, sickening silence. Almost another hour passed while every point was inspected by an expert trained in that particular field. Still the engines would not start. The inspections started all over again. God! Had they endured all those hours of punishment at the hands of the sub-chaser to wait out eternity, untouched, at the bottom of the sea? One man took the St. Christopher's medal from the chain around his neck, and held it in his hands as his eyes closed and his lips moved.

Others sat in silence, thinking of things they might have done—or wished they hadn't. For some the only outward sign of the seriousness of the moment was a quick sign of the Cross as each one finished whatever solace he had sought. The tension in that particular group was broken by a joker who thought his number had just been drawn. "Hey, Julio," he said in a loud stage whisper, as he opened his wallet. "Here's the fin I filched you out of in that last poker game. Now don't go around up there telling them I didn't give it back to you."

Moments later came the sound that every ear was straining for—the hum of motors that brought the fans on with a rush of air and slipped smoothly into the rhythmic pulsing that took them up and forward, pale and spent as a result of the combined physical and emotional strain.

Remembering that experience, the men hiding in the jungle growth on the hill on Pandan were reasonably sure that the patrol boat out there had not spotted the periscope of the *Nautilus*.

Then, with a puff of smoke, the enemy craft started moving on down the shore. "There the dirty bastards go," said Balleras. "They've stuck there the exact forty-minute period we were to display the signal."

"Well, Coast Watchers or not, we're going to get that signal back up as soon as they're out of sight. Our men on watch may have seen them first and had to lie out there and wait. I just hope they haven't had to leave."

Thirty minutes later Hernandez and his men pulled up stakes, folded the signal cloth and started back to where their gear was hidden in the coconut grove.

As is true a good part of the time in intelligence work, there was nothing really reassuring in the entire situation. If the *Nautilus* had raised her periscope, they had not seen it. If she had not—what had happened? They were deep in enemy-occupied territory now and undersea warfare was one of the things the Japanese did best. In these waters, one submarine stalking another for hours far below the surface had become a weird and ghastly business.

With a casualness he certainly did not feel, Hernandez said, "Well, it won't be long now. It will take us till sundown to finish photographing the coast line and get places lined up for all that gear to be put away. We can't leave that to do in the dark."

"That's right, said Balleras. "Bright as the moon was last night, it was plenty dark back under those trees."

The sun was setting as they met back at their hideout in the grove, their reconnaissance activities completed. Another meal of Aguilar's fruit salad finished the peaches. However, there was scant prospect of actually going hungry, surrounded by thousands of coconut trees, each one heavy with its clusters of ripe fruit.

After mess Aguilar said, "Sir, what would you think of our taking one more look around for water?"

"We already KNOW where the only water on this island is, Sergeant," said Hernandez. They had been over almost every foot of the island by then, but they still had not had time to search the hills for CW's or other small units possibly under cover there. The lieutenant was not taking chances of losing a good man by letting him get separated from the party in the darkness, but he added lightly, "Go and pour yourself a coconut cocktail—and bring me one. No ice in mine, please."

Balleras had been lying stretched out on the ground with his hands behind his head. He turned over to one side and raised up on his elbow. "You know, I have a hunch that—well just suppose that—for ANY reason, we didn't get back with the others for, say a week. I'll bet you a fellow could get awfully damn tired of coconut."

"Don't forget," said Aguilar, deftly slashing the green coir from the coconut he had brought for the lieutenant's cocktail, "there's always my rooster."

"Listen to him, Sir," kidded Balleras. "Now it's HIS rooster. Last night it belonged to the natives."

"Well, we may be glad we know someone with a rooster, if that sub doesn't show up pretty soon," said Hernandez, looking at his watch. The luminous hands were just beginning to glow in the darkness. He picked up the walkie-talkie and walked out toward the beach. The time had come.

Cutting in on the frequency he had used in the early morning, he found it free. "What a break," he said. "No traffic at all." He began calling the ship. "How to George—Come in George—Come in George."

There was no answer. He tried the next frequency. Still no traffic. He began again, "How to George—Come in George—Come in George."

Still no answer!

Suddenly tense, he cut in quickly on the next frequency and the next, listening on each one. Up and down the dial he went, just listening. There was NO traffic. Here in the early evening which normally should have been a rush hour, was a complete reversal of the condition in the pre-dawn hours. It was not the set. It had been all right when he reported the landing and nothing had happened to it since. He said aloud, "I don't understand this radio silence."

RADIO SILENCE! The sound of those words raised the hair on his forearms and a chill ran down his spine. A paragraph from the CW Manual came into his mind. He could see every word of it.

"RADIO SILENCE:

"Make your transmissions as brief and as infrequent as possible at all times and when the enemy is least likely to be listening. When enemy activity endangers your post, shut down entirely. Don't take chances."

Right now whatever he did—calling—not calling, he would be taking chances. He decided to keep tuned in for a while and listen for a call from George.

"If they didn't see our signal, they've probably gone on," said one of the men.

"They wouldn't have done that," said Hernandez. "They're probably sweating out something we can't see. This NAVY radio doesn't pick up underwater activity you know."

The men laughed. They didn't know about the sleepless hours he had spent the night before worrying about that radio.

At 2000 he tried again to reach the *Nautilus* and followed up at 2015—at 2030 and 2045—again at 2100. By 2100 the enemy had broken radio silence, but the lieutenant kept tuned in hoping to pick up a call from the ship.

"I hope they make it in before the moon comes up," said Hernandez. "There's a lot of gear to unload out there in moonlight like we had last night."

"Fifteen tons is a helluva lot of gear to unload by hand, Sir, moonlight or not," said Balleras. "I helped load that gear at Brisbane."

The moon rose big and yellow from behind the coconut palms. Higher and higher she went, out over the sea, brighter and brighter. Came 2130—2200—2230, still no sign of the *Nautilus*. It was exactly 2300 when they heard the call that set their pulses throbbing—"George to How—Come in—Over."

Instantly Hernandez replied "H to G—Come in—Over."

5
» » FIFTEEN TONS ASHORE

Hernandez closed down the radio and stood there in the stillness of the tropic night, his heart pounding. They were coming in! "Thank God," he said, and a warm glow suffused his entire body.

It was a wonderful feeling. In a little while now MISSION ISRM would really be something more than a dotted-line-in-red on the map from Brisbane to Darwin and out across that wild expanse of enemy-controlled water, islands, and air from Australia to the Philippines.

Then they saw her—the *Nautilus,* Queen of the Jap Blockade runners, a veritable diving cruiser. She rose bravely out of the sea a scant 400 yards offshore, perhaps 1500 yards up from their landing of the previous night.

"Looks like they almost overshot the mark," said one of the men.

"That's good," said Hernandez. "That far up, they should miss the rocks if they get mixed up in that current as we did."

Soon Commander Rowe, who for security reasons was to be known from that hour forward as Commander Nicholson, came floating in on a calm sea with a party of men in five large, black rubber boats lashed together two and three, bringing with them several tons of equipment and supplies. As they drifted down-shore it was apparent that they were coming in well above the rocks.

The speed with which the men unloaded the gear justified all the dry runs they had made at Beaudesert. The job had been timed to the minute and they finished with seconds to spare. Every minute their gear lay out there on the beach and the sub on the surface of that moonlit sea, they were asking for trouble. As Rowe and Hernandez stood watching them work so efficiently, Al said, "I guess it was worth all of it."

"All of what?" asked Rowe.

"The time they spent loading and unloading the gear. Remember that Australian training officer and his rugged critiques?"

"Yeah," chuckled the commander, and then in a broad Australian accent, "I saiy, men, cawn't you remembah you're NOT running down the street? You're coming out of a SUBMARINE. She cawn't he out theah like a duck on a pond while you take youah jolly time. You theah, Sergeant, you with the generatah—the real one will be much heaviah than the dummy yo're carrying. You'll 'ave to get a move on y'know. Now let's try it again—and this time let's SNAP IT UP."

Hernandez laughed. "Well they're snapping it up now all right, but you missed your calling, George. You should have been on the stage."

George, feeling good over the way the landing was going, said, "The training was part of it, but standing out there first on one foot and then on the other for three hours waiting for those damn Jap ships to get out of the way, helped too."

Sergeant Berg had come in with the first contingent and was barking out orders the minute his boots scraped the sand. Now as the boats went back for the fourth and last load, the first landing party went along to get a hot meal. It had been almost 24 hours since the last one and they were hungry. Aguilar and Balleras went below at once. "Ask the cook to fix a plate for me too," said Hernandez. "I'll be right down."

He wanted to speak to the ensign, particularly to thank him for the waterproof cover on the walkie-talkie.

The tender roast beef, rich, brown gravy, crisp, bright-green and orange colored vegetables were hot and delicious. There was strong, fragrant coffee from the shiny coffee maker that bubbled cheerily in the comer of the wardroom day and night.

As the lieutenant picked up his fork the intercom snapped on. "Lieutenant Hernandez, report at once to the captain. Lieutenant Hernandez, report to the captain."

Hernandez took one longing look at his plate and swung his tired legs over the bench. Aguilar looked at him "You're not—you can't go without eating, Sir."

"He's the skipper, Sergeant."

"Well what the hell does he want that someone else can't do, Sir?" exploded Balleras, angered at what he considered a rank injustice. "You aren't even supposed to be on his damn ship now."

"But I'm here, Sergeant. I'll have to find out. If I don't get back before we're ready to shove off, bring me a sandwich—and thanks, Men."

Hernandez found the captain pacing the bridge. The boats were still being loaded alongside and a large sailboat was approaching from the north. In these waters she had to be regarded as enemy until identified as friend. As enemy, she could not be allowed to escape and possibly report the position of the submarine and a landing operation.

There was nothing to indicate that she was radioequipped—and the ship's guns could eliminate her with one blast. But it was not that simple. One shot from the ship could disclose her position and simultaneously compromise THE MISSION.

"Where do I come in, Captain?" asked Hernandez, frankly

"I want you to take one of the boats you brought back, and the two men who went with you last night; I can't spare any of the others from the unloading, and go after her."

"What could we do?"

"Find out who she is—what she's doing here—board her if necessary, but find out who her crew is."

"Well you goddamned stupid idiot," Hernandez said to himself angrily, but an instant later, his voice under perfect control, he said, "Captain, I admit I'm not much of a sailor and I don't know much about boats, but I DO know that a *curicannan* (large sail boat) of that size is FAST. We wouldn't stand a ghost of a chance playing pirate with her in one of those rubber boxcars we have."

"Those boats are OK," snapped the captain. "They have plenty of power, if they're handled right."

Then as if to help the lieutenant prove his point, at about 500 yards, the *curicannan* tacked abruptly to the right and skimmed away towards the open sea, her white sails billowing full over the black water. In a few moments she was gone and so was the skipper's idea of pursuit. Hernandez went wearily back to the wardroom to finish his meal.

The presence of the craft still constituted a hazard, for there was no way of knowing why she had come and when she might return.

Coming topside, ready to shove off, Hernandez realized that they had drifted about 2,000 yards offshore—and then with considerable alarm—that they were almost down to the point of departure of the night before, when they had crashed into the rocks. The sea was becoming very rough. As they went over the side, the captain said, "Goodbye and good luck." Before they had gone a hundred yards they knew they were going to need it.

A sudden wind had come rushing down through Mindoro Strait, whipping the sea into a roaring, thrashing monster. The last three rubber boats, lashed together, had been loaded to capacity to allow the *Nautilus* to get under way. Boxes stacked high in every available foot of space, swayed forward and back to the roller coaster action of the towering waves.

Pushed to their limit by the heavy load and the added burden of the rising, falling sea, the motors sputtered and died. The men took up the oars and fell into a steady, rhythmic heave-ho, only to have one powerful stroke of the oars slice through thin air on the crest of a mighty wave which fell away sharply from under them. Slapping down hard, they rose again to the crest of the next wave where, for an instant, the rope between No. 2 and No. 3 boats fell slack—then with a sickening, cracking sound, jerked taut and snapped in two.

Boxes of supplies and equipment had been piled high at the ends where the boats were joined and the men in No. 2 boat watched helplessly as the stacks tottered and fell into the sea which rolled about them as they wallowed in the trough of the wave. Then came the horrible thought of what was being lost—radios, batteries, tubes, weather equipment, supplies, rations, medical supplies, special devices they were to test for the Navy. Everything was vital—and the nearest replacement 4,000 miles away, by the route that had to be used to run the enemy blockade.

Two men in No. 3 boat unprepared for the snapping of the rope, their hands occupied with the oars, were thrown clear of the boat, into the water actually ahead of the others. The cry of "man overboard" was lost in the howling wind and it was seconds before the others realized that the men were floundering in the sea, eyes, ears, mouths, and noses full of salt water—and in the path of the next giant wave. Up they went and down again. Someone, spotting a length of rope left from tying the boats together, quickly looped it around the only life belt in sight and threw it to the man on the right, struggling to reach the boat. Two men on the left joined hands in an effort to reach the man who was nearer to the boat, but in serious difficulty. Twice their hands almost met. Once they touched and slipped apart. Finally, one man leaning far over the side, with the other man literally wrapped around his feet and legs to hold him steady, caught hold of the floundering man and pulled him aboard—icy cold, teeth chattering, unquestionably going into a state of shock.

By that time the boats had been pulled into the down-shore current they had hit the night before. Fearing that the No. 1 and No. 2 boats might also pull apart, the men did all they could to reduce the strain. Two men threw themselves along the ropes to try to hold them together and keep the losses from becoming even greater.

The commander and Sergeant Berg, together with several of the men, kept watch on the shore as the wind rose and tremendous waves came crashing in, where a few hours before they had floated in so easily and come to rest on the smooth sand. Seeing the lead boat of the original group of three, riding high on an incoming wave, a shout of joy went up from the men on shore. Noting its diagonal down-shore course, the watchers started down the beach. Once more the landing boats crashed into the rocks on the Pandan shore, spilling vital matériel into the sea.

Sergeant Berg called out to the man nearest him, "Get ALL the men, ON THE DOUBLE."

All rushed in to help retrieve the boxes still afloat in the shallow water and some of the oil-paper-wrapped contents of boxes splintered on the rocks. Shouting to make himself heard above the roaring surf, the commander cried out, "Get those boats ashore, Men. Try to clear the high water line. WAY UP now with the next wave."

The men pushed and pulled at the heavy boats, their hands blistered and bleeding, stinging with salt water, but making the most of the force of the next wave.

Failing to see the lieutenant in the half light of the fading moon, and realizing that he might have been hit by some of the floating gear or by the crash on the rocks, the commander called out anxiously, "Al, where are you?"

There was no answer. His voice had been lost on the wind. Suddenly he realized that there were only two boats where there should have been three. In utter panic he shouted again, "Al, where ARE you?"

From the center of the heave-ho operation not more than 15 feet away, Al raised up and called back, "Here, George. I'm helping the men with the boats," and walked back to where Rowe stood.

"God, Al, you gave me a hell of a scare—but the other boat—where is it?"

"It's gone, George, and everything in it."

"Oh my God NO!" groaned Rowe. "There must have been half to three-quarters of a ton of gear in it."

"Right, George, but the MEN are all safe."

"That's wonderful, Al, and I'm glad, but that much radio or weather gear—why my God, it could ruin us."

In the months to follow, insofar as weather reporting was concerned, it did almost that.

The two men stood together watching the boxes wash ashore and hoping for a sight of the boat. With the cargo which must be floating in the coastal waters, sighting that boat by a Jap sea or air patrol, undoubtedly would bring about a search of the entire area in a matter of hours. Finally George said, "Al, you've been on duty now for more than 24 hours. You've got to hit the sack."

Hernandez gave him no argument. He took Aguilar and Balleras and went back into the grove, leaving the earlier camp site for the others who were less familiar with the location.

The men on the beach had been divided into two details, one to transfer the material from the beach to places of safety marked by the landing party in the afternoon, back in the grove. The other, a salvage detail, was deployed along the beach to search for the lost boat and the packing cases which they fervently hoped would wash ashore before the dawn.

Sergeant Berg watched the commander walking up and down the beach and back again. He was burning up a tremendous amount of energy, but nothing out there was coming in any faster for it. On one trip he stopped near the sergeant. Without waiting for him to speak, Jerry said, "Sir, I could take over here if you would like to go and get some rest."

With a wave of his hand out toward the sea, Rowe said, "With all that gear floating out there, Sergeant?"

"The men are bringing it in as fast as it comes up to where they can get it. I can call you if anything changes and you know you're going to have a tough day ahead."

Rowe thought for a moment, then said, "OK, Sergeant, keep the salvage detail on the beach. When the others have finished moving the stuff, have them sweep the beach clear of all traces of the landing, and call me THE MINUTE it's light*"

"And the ones I don't need on those details, Sir?"

"Have them hit the sack. We'll make camp just inside the grove. Al and his men have gone farther in. We can't all be in one spot. You could use an hour's rest too. Try to get it." By dawn most of the boxes had washed ashore. A corporal from the salvage detail, standing in the shelter of a tree, scanning the surface of the sea for floating objects, saw a man walking up the beach in the pale grey dawn. Directly in front of him, not more than thirty yards away, a large wooden box rode in on a wave, drifted backward along the sand in the backwash and finally came to rest in shallow water.

His heart pounding till he thought the man must hear it too, the corporal stood there. He didn't dare to move but he couldn't let the man find out what was in that box. He watched as the man dragged the box from the shallow water and began examining it. Now he would HAVE to report it!

He started back through the trees on the double, stumbling over fallen logs and trailing vines. Dashing up to the scattered group of net-swathed men, he tried to identify the CO. Spotting a man on sentry duty he whispered loudly, "Where's the old man?"

Lieutenant Hernandez, on his way down for a dawn inspection of the area, appeared just as the sentry pointed silently to Commander Rowe and the corporal automatically threw a quick salute to the sleeping man. Then, seeing Hernandez, he blurted out the neither accurate nor original but never to become commonplace announcement of the sergeant on the previous morning, "Sir, JAPS!"

Hernandez assured the corporal that he had probably seen the man from the plantation (whom he had failed to hear about), and sent him back to pick up the floating cargo.

Sensing that someone had seen him and frightened of being seen with enemy property, the old man had looked around and then fled to the shelter of the trees.

6
» » THE LONG ARM

The Island of Mindoro was their next objective. It lay across a three-mile channel to the east of Pandan. Their only map of the area, furnished them at GHQ, showed the river by which they intended penetrating the larger island, emptying into the sea several miles to the north.

The move from the submarine to this, their first beachhead, which should have been relatively simple, now gave them an idea of the tremendous task ahead. The slow, hard-to-manage rubber boats, in which everything would have to be moved, were unlike anything seen in these waters. They could be used only at night. Nothing could change that.

The simple precaution of getting the matériel under cover—nothing more—had taken hours of backbreaking digging, dragging logs, moving boxes, cutting limbs from trees, and covering the traces of their activities. Those same things would have to be done over and over again. Also, to move the cargo on across the channel, they were almost certain to be battling the same high seas they had encountered the night before.

In addition, there was the old man of the plantation. He might be perfectly harmless, but they had no idea why he was there, how much he had seen, or what he would do with such information, if he had it. THEY HAD TO FIND OUT!

There was also the matter of reconnaissance and the selection of a beachhead on the larger and obviously more heavily populated island. Nothing else could be done until that had been accomplished and with the boats they had, that operation could not be started until after dark.

As for the actual move, it had taken four trips with all five boats to bring the matériel from the *Nautilus* to the beach at Pandan, a distance of 1800 yards. It was three times that far to Mindoro and almost certainly there would be a much longer haul to a place of safety after reaching the beach: because of the population and the attendant danger of discovery, plus the fact that the number of boats had been reduced to four. It was not going to be a one-night job.

The ideal situation might be to get everything to the larger island, to a more secure position. On the other hand, it might be better to risk a minimum setup on the initial penetration and leave the greater portion buried or camouflaged and under guard on Pandan. They could not afford to lose much more—but leaving a guard detail on Pandan would require men—and the entire expedition consisted of two officers and 18 men. More and more depended upon what they learned about the old man of the plantation.

Taking first things first, they assigned one detail to guard their position in the grove and one to keep a lookout for floating cargo and the lost boat, which might prove more of a hazard than all the rest.

Rowe and Hernandez set out with another detail through the tangled undergrowth of the coconut grove, to talk to the old man and the two little boys at the *nipa* hut.

In spite of the time he had spent stateside, Sergeant Pascua had retained the most natural-sounding native speech of all. He was, of course, the logical one to make the contact. "Don't forget your cover story when you start to talk to him," warned the commander. "What you say now may make a lot of difference later."

Pascua smiled. "Lieutenant Hernandez would send me to the firing squad if I forgot that cover story after all the hours he spent drilling me on it."

"He's right," said Hernandez, but he was not afraid. Sergeant Pascua would keep in character, and his Tagalog, the prevailing language of the area, was excellent.

The detail of men, concealed in the dense tropical growth around the place, surrounded the hut. Rowe, Hernandez, and Pascua stood in the deep shadows of a thick, luxuriant tropical plant from which they could see the front and sides of the hut. Sergeant Pascua called out, asking if there were anyone at home.

The old man, followed by the two small boys, came out at once. Looking about for the one who had spoken, the man said, *"Magandang umaga Po"* the Tagalog equivalent of "Good morning, Sir."

Hearing the man's greeting and seeing him full in the face without a hat was a relief to all of them. He was a Filipino. Now—about his sympathies... "OK, Sergeant," said Rowe. "Go on in and talk to him."

As Sergeant Pascua stepped out from the protection of the vines, the old man came forward, smiling, to greet him. He had few visitors here and this young man looked so pleasant and spoke his language too. HE could not be enemy.

Sergeant Pascua apologized for calling to him without letting himself be seen, but the man assured him that he understood. "No one takes chances nowadays—if he wants to live," he said. "That is why I bring my grandson and my nephew here to live. I think they have better chance of living, here."

Pascua nodded, understanding the problem.

"You are hungry, my friend?" asked the man. "I have very little to offer, but if you are hungry, I give you rice and fish."

Assured that his visitor was not hungry, the man asked how he had gotten there and if he knew anything about the box which had washed up on the shore. "I walk every morning around the island to see if anyone come during the night.

I see the box wash up in wave. I think I go see what it is—then I feel like someone watching me—so I run away. When I come out and look again, the box he is gone—but the tide is going out. Someone must have move the box."

"That's right," said Pascua. "I moved it. I wanted to know what was in it, too."

"You are not alone, Senor? You have someone with you?" "Yes, I have friends with me, but do not fear, they will do you no harm," said Pascua. "I will call them."

Realizing that his visitors were friendly and that they spoke his language, the old man was pathetic in his desire to show them that they were welcome in the house of old Pedro.

He began reminiscing as old men do—remembering when he was young, as they were now. He was a soldier when he was young—a Philippine Scout. How he wished he had been young enough to fight for General MacArthur! How long, he wondered, would it be until the general came back. Then he began telling of his scouting days.

Lieutenant Hernandez sat like one entranced. The man went on—and Hernandez felt a weird sensation, like someone trying to waken from a dream. A cold sensation passed over the top of his head. He felt as though the hair were standing on end and a noticeable quiver ran through his shoulders. Everything this man was telling, the names, the places, he had heard as a little boy.

Just as he had done so many times, one of the little boys said,

"Grandfather, tell them about the time you saved the general's brother, Don Julio from..."

"Yes," said the man patiently, putting his hand on the little fellow's head, "I will tell them when I come to that." Hernandez' pulse was pounding fast. There was nothing in the book that covered this!

Instinctively he felt that here was a man he could trust—but he remembered the commander's words—"Keep your identity a secret—and I mean SECRET, by God."

There was also the thought of Major Philipps and his party. They had trusted SOMEONE. For a moment he was so engrossed in his own conflicting thoughts that he did not hear what the man was saying. Then he heard, "I would give my life to save my Commandante, Don Julio..."

Hernandez' hands, now icy cold, began to tremble. There are 7000 islands in the Philippine Archipelago and probably a hundred thousand points where a rubber raft, hardly larger than a toy balloon, might have touched their shores. But by some strange fate—or what is sometimes called the long arm of coincidence—he had come halfway around the world to sit on the doorstep of a tiny *nipa* hut, and listen to an old man tell a story that, as a wide-eyed little boy, he had never tired of hearing told over and over by his uncle, General Don Adriano de Hernandez and his father, Don Julio. He realized that this man had served under both his uncle and his father and had saved his father's life.

Fully aware of the great responsibility he was taking, and without revealing their strength or their objective, he said, "Mang Pedro, I too have a duty to perform for your country and mine. If I told you that I am Don Alfredo Omez de Hernandez..." He stopped at the look on the old man's face.

Pedro stood looking at him, first in amazement, then recognizing the father-son resemblance, nodding, smiling, crying all at once, said, "Of course, Senor, of course! Is like seeing him again. You are JUST LIKE HIM—just like our handsome Commandante, Don Julio de Hernandez."

Tears ran down his cheeks unheeded, and standing as erect as his bent old shoulders would permit, he looked into the lieutenant's face, brought up his right hand in a smart salute, and said, "Sir, I am reporting for duty."

As Hernandez returned the salute, he thought guiltily, "And because of those staunch, old shoulders I almost took him to be a Jap."

Mang Pedro, they called him—as is the Philippine custom in addressing an older man of wisdom and experience, became an inexhaustible source of information and help, telling them much that they needed to know of local conditions and suggesting ways of cutting days from their expected time-consuming reconnaissance.

They had to know about the coastal village across the Strait—if there were enemy troops garrisoned there—and the sympathies of the people, especially the city government. He could tell them that there was no large concentration of troops there, but that was one of the things which would have to be checked every day. The city government was almost entirely in the hands of the mayor, a man loved and respected by his people, long known as a strong pro-American. But Mang Pedro did not seem to feel safe in giving his whole-hearted assurance that they could depend upon his help.

Finally the reason came out. It was understandable, Mang Pedro explained. The man had a family and for them he was afraid. He probably would do anything he could, if he could be sure of not being found out by the enemy. Less than a month before, the town had suffered cruelly at the hands of the enemy in retaliation for their aid to three escaping American POW's. The entire families of those involved had been rounded up and herded into the center of the town by enemy patrols. Their friends and neighbors had been assembled at the point of machine guns to witness the fiendish slaughter of their friends by what is known as the butterfly swing. Men, women, and children, had been hanged, heads down, feet up, their hands pegged to the ground with wooden pegs. Then, with one swift slash of a sabre, they were completely eviscerated and left to smother under their own vital organs falling over their faces as they bled to death. For that reason the mayor was loathe to take an active stand which might bring reprisals.

There was also the Kalibapi, an enemy spying system masquerading as a political society, with local citizens "enlisted" to serve in field work for the society. Suicides were not uncommon among the men chosen to serve as spies against their neighbors, and enemy agents checked frequently to be sure they performed their duties as assigned.

Mang Pedro assured them that there were other men who would stop at nothing to aid in undercover activities against the enemy. One in particular, Mang José, would take any risk. He had no fear—for he had no family left! Mang José was in contact with the Guerilla Fighters, being one of the few local members of the official Resistance Movement which in his report to President Roosevelt in 1942, General MacArthur had called FIGHTERS FOR FREEDOM. He could be depended upon for help in getting boats and men to help move their matériel. Already they could see many days cut from the labor involved in getting to the place where they would start their operations.

Among other things which Mang Pedro told them were the strict regulations governing travel. Crossing of provincial borders required a travel pass stating the holders name, residence, occupation, reason for making the trip, and other vital information. A travel pass was hard to come by, for it required the official Japanese Military stamp and was printed on one side in Japanese and on the other in English.

There was also the cedula, a card required of all civilians of any age or sex, bearing a thumbprint of the individual and serving as a sort of license, tax receipt and identification. Without these papers it would be impossible for them to move from place to place and to carry on the work they were to do. In this the mayor s assistance would be invaluable. He was, in fact, the only source of these very necessary papers known to Mang Pedro, who assured them that while he might be too cautious for their over-all requirements, he would certainly give them all the assistance he could in this respect. Being assured of the man's loyalty and needing desperately the one thing he could supply, they decided to contact him as soon as possible.

That being decided upon, Mang Pedro said, "Sir, you like to go now to see honorable Mayor?"

"Not until after dark," said Hernandez. "Our boats would be spotted by any kind of passing patrol."

"You no worry about boats, Sir," Mang Pedro replied. "Bring your men and come with me. We fix."

Within half an hour he had brought out from a perfectly camouflaged hiding place, two *batels* (small sailboats) used in better days at the plantation. In these boats they could start at once for the channel crossing.

In Mang Pedro's eyes the rubber boats were not their only problem, if they hoped to go strolling into an island town unnoticed—or—if they were stopped by a patrol boat on the way. "The boots, Sir," he said, "no one here have money to buy such fine boots—and if they did, no one could find the shoes. You have to go without them."

He chuckled in high glee at the grimaces they made when he insisted that they start running about like the native boys they might soon have to prove that they were.

Dipping in salt water and drying in the sun for an hour took the bright color from a neckerchief—and a frayed straw hat was more in character than a newer one. When his make-up job was complete, they were much more realistic natives than before. These were no longer the islands that any of these men had known a few years before, and certainly these men bore no resemblance to the men-without-a-country who had boarded the plane in Commando uniform that night in Brisbane.

With their weapons hidden under a pile of reeds, they had become a band of harmless native boys going to the town searching for work—anything to buy food.

Neither the commander nor the lieutenant wanted the other to go into the town without him. There was, of course, a risk in both officers going, but everything from now on would be a risk. They felt that in this first and somewhat dubious contact with the local undercover group, both should be there. They went in separate boats, with different time schedules.

Sergeant Berg was to remain on Pandan with the equipment and enough men to guard their position. They would attempt to contact him at 1300 with the walkie-talkie from the mayors *hacienda*, which Mang Pedro said was at the edge of the town. In the event that they ran into trouble or were in danger of jeopardizing the others by coming back, another island rendezvous was decided upon for contact later. Suddenly Mang Pedro's presence assumed new importance. He was a natural go-between if they should become separated now or later.

About halfway across the channel they had their first close-up of the enemy. An enemy patrol plane came in overhead and passed on over them. "You do not look up at him," said Mang Pedro. "Patrols not new to you. Long time now you see him every day—everywhere you go. He look over your boat when you go fishing. He watch you when you go trading. You no worry. You have nothing to hide." Casually he went on telling of life on the island with the two little boys as though nothing were happening, when the pilot, deciding to have another look at them, banked and flew in so low he almost skimmed the water alongside. "Don't hide your faces, Men, but don't let him get a good look at you. You don't want to be recognized later," said Hernandez, realizing what was happening. But the rush of air from the plane and the scramble to keep from losing their wide-brimmed hats took care of the situation with no apparent effort on their part.

After the second swing around, the pilot zoomed up and away and they went on in to tie up at a deserted pier without further incident. The loading platform of an empty warehouse furnished an excellent place for a poker game and a full view of the waterfront while they waited for the commander and his party. Several of the men got into the game, leaving others to keep watch on what went on in the area.

Interest in the poker game seemed to wane after a while and the first party moved on. About the same time another boat docked some distance away and the men came ashore, starting off by a devious route for the same destination, the mayors *hacienda*.

His Honor was in town when they arrived, but they were told that he would be coming home soon. If they had business with him they might wait. A number of the townspeople were waiting to see him also. Some were suffering with malaria and other tropical diseases and sores, causing much suffering. The civilian population had received little or no medical care since the invasion. Hospitals had been wantonly bombed and destroyed by the enemy and medical supplies burned during the first short-sighted days of the invasion. Most of the doctors had disappeared. Some thought they had been forced into service by the enemy. Others thought they had joined the guerillas hiding in the hills and jungles waiting for the opportunity to strike the enemy when they could do the most harm. No one seemed sure of anything but that they had no doctors and no medicine.

Soon after their arrival the mayor came home and Mang Pedro convinced him that they must speak to him immediately and in private. He was exactly as Mang Pedro had led them to expect. Being assured that none of the people present could be suspected of being disloyal, they took the opportunity to see and talk with the villagers and learn first hand how they had fared at the hands of the invaders and, what was most important at that point, how they felt toward the Americans.

It had been made very clear at GHQ what conditions in the islands were likely to be, so on this first step toward infiltration, they had not come unprepared. They had some of the sulfa drugs which could be administered without the aid of a doctor, together with aspirin and atabrin, which everyone seemed to need.

Recognizing this unexpected gathering of citizens as an excellent opportunity for a good public relations job, Commander Rowe took over and without revealing their identity or their mission, let it be known that they were friendly and had come "from the Americans." Among those things which had become luxuries were needles and thread. They brought out and distributed small sewing kits for the women and half-packs of American cigarettes for the men, each wrapped in small, bright posters bearing General MacArthur's picture, with his hand raised in a characteristic salute, to serve as bright reminders of his promise, "I SHALL RETURN."

Although ill and frightened by their recent tragic experience, most of these people still held fast to their faith that the war would be over soon. "Things will be different when he returns," they said. Then for reassurance, "How long do you think it will be?"

From that time forward they were to find that to the people of the Philippines, MacArthur had given his word of honor. Never did they doubt that he would honor his word.

The commander decided that as a morale builder, a demonstration of the magic power of the walkie-talkie might show the people what a superior force the Americans really were. Setting up for the pre-arranged call to Sergeant Berg, Lieutenant Hernandez carried on a conversation with men across the water, with no sign of wires or elaborate broadcasting set—just a small piece of hand equipment which, regardless of his doubts about it a few nights before, certainly was at that point, worth its weight in gold as a prestige builder.

The mayor urged the leaders to use extreme care in their operations in that vicinity. As Mang Pedro had thought, he could not find it in his heart to take the risk of trying to find boats. As he explained this to the commander, Mang Pedro said to Hernandez, "Do not worry, *Teniente*. We go to Mang José when we finish here."

The mayor explained, however, that he could do more good for them in the way of papers, which he set about preparing at once, together with instructions as to their use. He could also furnish extra sets to take care of changes in cover stories which might be necessary and loss of papers in an emergency.

Commander Nicholson and Sergeant Berg were to use the cover of German citizens, business men dealing in civilian necessities in the Islands, buying and selling in various provinces. Lieutenant Hernandez and some of the other men were to pose as collaborators, acting as Purchasing Agents for His Majesty's forces, buying cattle and other items, and Rice Inspectors, which involved visiting the producing areas as well as warehouses (*bodegas*) where the harvest was stored. Later there would be all the trades and odd jobs they would have to engage in to get where they needed to go.

Next Mang Pedro took them to Mang José. Both men were acquainted with the area around the mouth of the river and the loyal undercover workers living there.

The two local men agreed upon those they thought they should ask for boats and Mang José offered to arrange for guides to meet them at the river on Mindoro that night.

In that way, the men of THE MISSION would be able to put their boats under cover and also be warned of any enemy patrols known to be in the area.

If all plans went well, Mang José would come to Pandan that evening to help with the arrangements for boats for permanent use by the expedition.

Before the sun had set, the men of MISSION ISRM began to feel the strength of that brave, defiant band of men and women, the FIGHTERS FOR FREEDOM.

7
» » I PLEDGE ALLEGIANCE

Promptly at 1700, following the visit to the mainland of Mindoro, a motley group of *cargadorés* (transfer men, roustabouts) arrived by *batel* and *banca* at Pandan. Most of them were leathery-skinned old men or spindly-legged youngsters. Some who had wanted to come had remained in the town to avoid a suspicious absence of too many men, in the event of a visit from an enemy agent or a *Kalibapi* inspection.

They had come in response to a call for volunteers to move a large amount of heavy matériel and supplies for "the movement." News traveled fast in that loyal, undercover group and there was plenty of help to uncover and move the necessary equipment and supplies to set up a radio transmitter to contact GHQ.

Sergeant Berg and the men left in charge of the matériel had completed a very thorough camouflage job back under the sheltering palms, where the jungle had moved in fast to reclaim its own. Materiel to be taken to Mt. Bacó had to be unearthed, carried down through the tangled undergrowth to the waters edge and loaded into the rubber boats.

Rowe, Hernandez, and Berg agreed, after their devastating experience with the boats the previous night, that the hazard was tremendous, but they felt they had no choice. Mang Pedro was sure he could have native cargo boats available by the next morning, but they felt it was imperative that they get at least one setup off the smaller island under the cover of darkness. Even with the local boats, they could not move any appreciable amount of supplies by day with any degree of safety. In addition to that, there was the advantage of getting one day's start toward establishing radio contact with GHQ.

The group of volunteers was broken into working units, and each unit assigned to a sergeant. Commander Rowe thought that, having seen as much as they would by the time they had finished this job, the seriousness of what they were doing should be impressed upon them. He would swear them into the service, temporarily. Instructing the three sergeants to line their platoons up in formation, he asked Lieutenant Hernandez to take his place at the right and Sergeant Berg at the left. Then he instructed the men to stand at attention and repeat after him. Suddenly he realized that the words of both the Navy and the Army ceremonies had completely eluded him. His position might have been embarrassing to a less versatile man, but the commander's sense of humor was not to be denied. With a twinkle in his eye, he looked over the group and placing his hand over his heart, began, "I pledge allegiance to the Flag of the United States of America and the republic for which it stands . . ." and so on through the salute to the flag.

Berg and Hernandez stood speechless. WHAT was coming off now? Neither of them dared chance a look at the other as the commander went on through the only speech he could think of that seemed apropos of the situation. It turned out to be a very solemn and impressive ceremony and one which made every volunteer feel that though he might have been too old or too young for service in the Guerilla Fighters he would have liked to join—now he was serving directly with the *americanos.*

Before the hard work began, American cigarettes in the MacArthur posters were distributed. For many months the only cigarettes they had been able to buy at any price were made of crudely-cured, native tobacco, rolled in wrappers of cut newsprint. The acrid smoke of the paper "treated" with printer's ink would have destroyed any aroma the tobacco might have had—and they sold for $3.50 per pack in American money. Those clean, white tailormades brought smiles to the faces of the new recruits—and deep sighs of satisfaction as they smoked. It had been a long time!

While the native men were enjoying the luxury of the good cigarettes, the Americans learned much that had happened since the beginning of the war. The local men in turn were eager to hear news of the outside world—actual progress of the war, having received only enemy propaganda releases for many months. It was there in the quiet of the evening that the men of MISSION ISRM first heard the plaintive-voiced Filipino counterpart of Tokyo Rose. A girl turned traitor to her country— who knew why—now begged her people to stop fighting, to stop killing their brothers. She pleaded with them to give up what she said had long since become a lost cause—to be happy and prosperous under their Japanese liberators who had come to save them from ruin under

American rule.

In one short day they had learned a great deal about local conditions. Stories of relentless enemy searching details, once they were on the trail of someone they wanted, convinced the men of THE MISSION that getting their equipment as far inland as possible, was of paramount importance.

The original plan at AIB was to make a reconnaissance several miles up the Asis River, which met the sea a few miles to the north of their position, and to establish a series of outposts along the river as the rest of the equipment and supplies moved along to catch up with them.

They knew now that unless they were to spend months carrying equipment 40 miles up the trails, both river and mountain, to Mt. Bacó, they must acquire native boats of suitable types and sizes to meet their requirements. For the lighter hauls they would need several small *batels* and *bancas*. Small, fast *batels* and *bancas* would also be necessary for scouting operations and one or two large *curicannans* for channel crossings with the heavy equipment and for the long trips which would begin soon, into Manila.

Meanwhile, any delay in the removal of their equipment to the larger island seemed unnecessarily hazardous. However inadequate the rubber boats might be—THEY HAD THEM. Rowe and Hernandez decided to take the rubber boats and enough men to row them in the event of another motor failure, and start immediately after dark to try to complete at least one crossing before the moon rose. If possible they would return with one or two of the boats for a second load. In any case, they would try to keep them informed by the walkie-talkie of any change in plans.

The loading operation was well under way when several more helpers arrived in a large *curicannan*, a beautiful, long, sleek-lined craft with high white sails. Two of the men were able to identify themselves positively as couriers for the FIGHTERS FOR FREEDOM. The owner of the boat, a Mindoro trader, had come as soon as he had received word from the village undercover group that there was important work to be done. He made suggestions relative to the handling of their cargo and pointed out certain facts relative to penetration of the larger island which were very helpful. During the conversation, Lieutenant Hernandez said to him, "That's a fine boat you have there. Are there many like it around?"

"Oh no, Sir," said the owner proudly, "there isn't another like her anywhere—a-round."

He could hardly finish the sentence and his hands trembled. Reasonably sure that this was the skipper who had made for the open sea, and relieved him of an unpleasant duty the night before, Hernandez said, "The reason I asked—well, I almost had to play pirate with one very much like it last night."

"You did?" queried the boatman weakly.

"It wasn't my idea," Hernandez went on casually, "but while we were unloading our gear, just such a boat as yours came in from the north. The captain thought—"

The man interrupted. "That was my boat. I was coming back from a trading trip. I thought I would come up and see what was going on—maybe make friends. But I couldn't tell if you were a Jap or an American ship. Then I began thinking—it really didn't make much difference. Whoever had gone away out there for what they were doing didn't INTEND for anyone to see them. I didn't want to get mixed up in anything and lose my boat—or maybe get shot. Then I got scared. I couldn't think of anything but to get away." "You weren't any more scared than I was," said Hernandez, laughing a little. "I certainly wasn't eager to come aboard your boat, and we couldn't tell if you were radioequipped, but with all our gear lying out there, I would have had to if you hadn't taken off when you did."

Relaxing a little more, the man said, "I guess you can imagine how I felt when I came here and saw how many there were of you—and all with guns and ammunition. I'm still a little shaky. Guess I'm lucky to be alive."

The lieutenant shuddered as he thought, "How right you are!" The man might have done the perfectly natural thing—just started home—to Mindoro.

After some understandable hesitation the skipper offered them his *curicannan*, the *Doña Juana*, beginning the next morning. It was a sacrifice for he would greatly curtail his trading activities, temporarily at least, and there was also the possibility of the enemy agent responsible for his area, questioning him as to what had happened to his fine boat. It was agreed that he should be paid a fair price for the boat and it was to revert to him at the end of the emergency, without charge. He was to leave the boat at the dock and it was simply to disappear. He would take the chance of explaining its disappearance if questioned by the enemy.

8
» » COMBAT RECONNAISSANCE

The first consignment of matériel to be shipped to the Mindoro side that night was brought down to the edge of the grove in the fading light. As soon as it was really dark, a full set of radio gear, photographic reconnaissance and weather equipment to open an outpost and get into operation, were quickly loaded into the three rubber boats and once more lashed together. This time there were no stacks of gear to tumble into the sea.

In the early darkness, ahead of the rising moon Commander Nicholson, Lieutenant Hernandez, Mang Pedro and nine of the trained specialists from AIB, including Sergeants Balleras, Aguilar, Alvarez, Barcenas, Carillo, Logan, Pascua, Pascual, and Villalon, set out on the first lap of the trip en route to Mindoro and "the mountains." Naturally they could not tell all these people where they were going any more than they could tell them what was in the cargo they were helping to handle.

Sergeant Berg was left in charge of the supplies hidden on Pandan. He was also to make satisfactory arrangements with the owners of the boats Mang José had arranged for and was to man the newly acquired craft with competent crews which Mang José would help select.

By noon the next day a small but effective white-sailed fleet in the Pacific, named in honor of its commander, THE NICHOLSON LINES, had come into being. Though in the minds of his men he might sometimes be thought of as Rowe, never did the commander think of himself as anything but Nicholson. That was his only defense against some unguarded moment in which he might turn to look or unwittingly answer to the name of Rowe.

For the twelve men who had set out in the darkness in their rubber boats en route to Mindoro, things did not go so smoothly. Seldom, if ever, throughout THE MISSION was there a single night with so much heartbreaking disappointment and near-tragedy as that on which they set out to begin the penetration of Mindoro, toward their goal of establishing a main radio station, ISRM.

Mang Pedro warned at the start that the shore on the other side of the channel was very rough, the rocks big, and the current strong. "We stay way from shore till we near the river, then we go straight in."

In spite of the efforts of Sergeant Balleras, a pre-war master mechanic, and several of the other men in checking, oiling, and tuning up the motors of the rubber boats, the heavy load and the high waves they encountered almost immediately after leaving Pandan, taxed them to the limit. Less than halfway across the channel, like the night before, the motors sputtered and died. Once more the men took up the oars.

Probably halfway along the diagonal east-northeast course, a sudden tropical storm broke without warning. First, like the rushing of air along the surface of the sea came a weird, hissing sound. Then the wind bore down upon them, rolling up mountainous waves. The three big rubber boats hit the water hard after a sudden upswing on a gigantic wave. Suddenly Lieutenant Hernandez realized that he must have been rowing, asleep, for as the spray from the wave hit his face, he "came to" with the oars in his hands moving rhythmically with the others. Sleeping four hours out of forty had not been exactly ideal "crew training."

Over the roar of the sea, Sergeant Pascua shouted, "How high would you say that one was, Commander?"

"Did you ever look down from the Empire State Building?" was the commander's reply.

It was too dark to see his face, but there was none of the levity of his words in his voice. A few hundred yards farther the rain began. No one was asleep then. Everyone was rowing with everything he had and they seemed to be losing distance with every stroke. Desperately they tried to keep on toward their destination against the wind and the strong current separating them from it. They still had several hundred yards to go to the north before they could turn in toward the shore with safety, to find their way into the mouth of the river.

Feeling the pull of the downshore current, Mang Pedro called out over the noise of the wind and the sea, "*Teniente*, if we no stay way from the shore, we crash on rocks."

"Where does this current go?" shouted Hernandez.

"Out into . . ." The rest of his answer died on the howling wind.

They had come two thousand miles by air, and with all the zigging and zagging they had done, probably twenty-five hundred more by sea, from Australia, and now—with twenty-five hundred yards to go, they faced without any choice, two desperate alternatives—being dashed to bits on the coastal rocks of Mindoro or highjacked out into the wild, roaring South China Sea.

A moment later another wave flung them high into the air and after what seemed an interminable length of time, they felt the boats slowly turn over and, along with equipment and supplies, they were literally poured into the sea.

When Hernandez came up from under the water, he was under one of the boats which was bottom side up. For a moment he could not think where he was. Then he remembered. Seconds later he heard Mang Pedro call, "*Teniente—Teniente*, You all right, Sir?"

It was good to hear the old man's voice there in the darkness with their heads barely above the water, in that narrow space between the sea and the bottom of the boat—and for a moment, to be out of the howling wind.

"I'm fine, Mang Pedro," he answered, "but let's get out of here."

They ducked down and came up in the open sea and caught hold of the sides of the boat, which had broken away from the others. It was still too dark to see anything clearly but they could distinguish between the floating boxes and figures struggling in the water. The lieutenant called out, "George, are you OK?"

The commander's reply was a little hazy but a moment later he was calling the men by name. All were accounted for! A few pieces of lighter gear floating around them were picked up by some of the men and tossed onto the boat. In the darkness they did not see that the boat had capsized—but it would not have mattered if they had, for the next wave swept it far out of reach of any of them.

Now and then the wind subsided for a moment and in one such brief lull, the commander called out, "Al."

Al swam toward the direction of the voice and George shouted, "We've got to get out of here. We can't save anything. We'll do well to save ourselves."

Hernandez agreed with him but at that moment was totally inarticulate. He had looked at his wrist to check the direction—for he was completely disoriented—and HIS COMPASS WAS GONE!

"We can't be far from shore," Rowe was saying. "I think we can all make it, but we're wasting our strength." He caught his breath again and shouted, "All right, Men, according to my reckoning, we're facing due east.

It'll be rough going—but we can make it." He stopped again for breath. "Look out for the rocks—at the right. Keep bearing to the left and don't waste your energy talking unless you need help. Good luck, Men. Let's go!"

Without another word they were on their way—everyone hoping, praying that no man would have to call for help. They would be lucky if every man got ashore in that storm.

Mang Pedro was beside the lieutenant when they started. The younger man was certain he could make it—but he was by no means sure the brave old fellow beside him would survive.

Those gigantic waves that had snapped the ropes as if they had been twine, were now tossing the men around like puppets. No sooner did they come up from one wave until another rolled them down again. Just breathing was all but impossible, for as their heads came out of the water, gasping for breath, the wind whipped the breath away with almost suffocating force. Seeing Mang Pedro's head now and then, only to lose him in the next wave, Hernandez kept repeating over and over, somewhere between a hope and a prayer, "God, let him make it."

The lieutenant, young and in training, was tired and his heart was pounding hard when he felt the firm sand under his feet. But he had only to reach out his hand to steady Mang Pedro as he too got to his feet and waded ashore through the surf.

The clouds blew thin overhead. The moon cast a pale, cold light on the wet, sandy beach. They dropped down there to get their breath and to watch for the others to come ashore. As they shivered in the cold wind, Hernandez' thoughts went back to an orientation lecture at Beaudesert— "The night is the winter of the tropics," the lecturer had said. Now he knew what the man meant.

Lying there with his pulse throbbing, his ears pounding, he realized several things. His scant, wet clothing was no protection against the biting wind and not only was he cold and exhausted—but absolutely ravenous. Being cold, wet, and hungry was not pleasant but in the light of his next discovery, those things were suddenly unimportant. His automatic, his tommygun, and his bolo had joined his compass on the way to the bottom of Mindoro Strait.

The last man to be accounted for staggered up the beach and in answer to the shouts of joy that he was alive—that not one man had been lost—he gasped out, "How come some of you GOOD swimmers aren't out doing some scouting? There could have been Jap agents at that mayor's house. That goddam butterfly business ain't pretty."

With that, he collapsed on the sand, the nearest to a casualty they had from what was, in effect, a full-scale ship wreck. His stark reminder stirred them to action. While he was being given first aid, a reconnaissance detail went scouting into the wooded area nearby and a salvage detail was dispatched to search the beach. With such a quantity of cargo afloat, they were again begging for a search of the area by the enemy.

Along with the supplies, the rations, and a full set of equipment with which they had hoped to open the first outpost, they had lost the walkie-talkie AND THE BOATS!

There were four of them. They hadn't been very good boats for their purpose, but without them—or the radio—they had no means of contact with the men on Pandan who probably had the next load of matériel lying on the beach ready for loading.

As soon as Mang Pedro recovered from the long swim, he got up and with his unfailing salute, said, "Sir, I go now and look around. I find out where we are and come back very soon."

With Sergeant "Doc" Pascual and another first aider reporting satisfactory progress in their patient, the two details busy with their assignments, and Mang Pedro gone on his solo reconnaissance, Rowe and Hernandez, cold, wet, and hungry, settled down to consider what should be the next move. As Mang Pedro disappeared in the darkness, George said, "Well—we sure as hell haven't any transportation left, or communication either."

"Right now we haven't anything to transport," said Hernandez, "but we sure could use that damn Navy radio they gave me such a bad time over."

"Damn right," said Rowe. "About all we've got left now is—weapons and ammo belts. That's SOMETHING as long as we're wandering around in enemy occupied territory." "That WOULD be something," said Hernandez, "if you HAD them?"

"You don't mean . . . My God, Al, you haven't lost—?" "They're all gone. My compass too."

"Why you couldn't even . . ." Rowe stopped. There was no point in reminding his exec that he couldn't even defend himself if they should meet an enemy patrol.

"I wonder how many of the men are in the same shape," he continued. "We'd better call the roll and take inventory." They had just finished that very unsatisfactory operation when they heard Mang Pedro coming back. As he approached, Rowe said sharply, "Don't mention this."

The spirits of both men were really at low ebb when the old fellow returned from his walk along the beach. After looking around for perhaps twenty minutes, he had been quite satisfied as to their position. No one said anything, but their discouragement was obvious. He looked around the group and then, like an indulgent grandfather, said, "Come, follow me. We fix."

There had been no opportunity to check Sergeant Reyes list of matériel to know what had been lost the night before. Now with this additional loss, there was the horrible possibility that they might not have the necessary gear to set up even the first radio station and make contact with GHQ.

Mang Pedro was really enthusiastic after his "look around," but the others could hardly be said to share his enthusiasm. They were not much more than half a mile, a mile at most, down the coast from the mouth of the deep river by which they intended to proceed as far as it was navigable, toward the proposed mountain site of the main radio station.

He explained his mysterious "we fix" by saying, "Come, my friends, the rain has stopped and we have only short walk—maybe half mile, to the river."

"Why the river?" asked Rowe. "We have no boats—and very little to put into them if we did."

"But we have friends," said Mang Pedro, choosing to ignore the commander's tone of voice. "They will give us dry clothes and a place to sleep till morning. They will help us when it is light."

"Are you SURE they are friends," asked Hernandez—not doubting the man himself, but wondering, after all those warnings at AIB. This would bring more people into the knowledge that something was afoot, and that they wanted to go into the mountains.

"I am SURE, *Teniente*. VERY sure. They will help us get back boxes and find boats to take them up river."

In their miserable condition such an offer would have been accepted gladly if they had not known the fate of their predecessors. The commander and the lieutenant could not bring themselves to be led, at least without some consideration, to a place of which they knew nothing and not of their own choosing. Too much time and too many lives had been lost already, in establishing contact with our undercover people in Manila. Perhaps the ones responsible for that had seemed just as sincere and innocent as this old man.

The inventory of the remaining weapons was very disturbing. Four of the men had lost the same items as the lieutenant—their automatics, tommyguns, bolos and compasses. Most of them had lost something.

Some had lost everything. That left them vulnerable in any kind of emergency involving the enemy or his collaborators.

Hernandez realized the commanders responsibility to THE MISSION and to the men. The biting wind and their still-wet clothes chilled them through and through. He knew too that Rowe would be reluctant to refuse what might be a legitimate offer of help, but how could he know? Turning toward the men on the beach, Hernandez called out "Sergeant Pascua, have your men check the beach again." Then he said, "Mang Pedro, you try to get a little rest if you can. You must be very tired. We will be back in a little while." "Yes, Sir, I rest," replied Mang Pedro, and he sat down on a log to wait for their next move.

Rowe and Hernandez turned and walked away toward the beach. Rowe spoke first. "How the hell do we know where he's taking us, Al? And even if we did, we can't leave all that damn gear out there to flag down the first goddam Jap plane that flies over."

Standing there in cold, sodden garments on a windswept beach, the thought of warm, dry clothing and a place to rest until daylight had much to recommend it, and Mang Pedro's offer had included much more. He had said that his friends would also help in salvaging whatever they could—and in transporting their supplies on toward their objective.

"If that's the way it is, George, the harm's done now," said Hernandez. "He knows we're here. He knows our men and supplies are on Pandan. What can we lose?"

Then as was to happen many times in the future, once the facts were stated, no further discussion was necessary. They had reached the same conclusion. As though a decision had been agreed upon, they turned and walked slowly back to where they had left the old man, talking as they walked. Almost there, Rowe stopped for an instant. "God, Al, I hope we're doing right."

After that he quickened his pace. Sergeant Balleras passed them on his way down to the beach. Rowe called out to him, "Sergeant, call the men."

Mang Pedro had been waiting patiently, fully understanding the position of the two men. The two details came up from the beach and from out of the trees where they had hidden the few boxes which had washed ashore. The commander called out, "Gather round."

Quickly they assembled. "Men," he began, "we have just had an experience that, as you all know, might have been fatal to us and to MISSION ISRM. We are now in enemy-occupied territory—territory that is under frequent enemy patrol. We have lost our boats—a complete set of gear, and a good part of our personal weapons. There are enough left for every man to have something to defend himself. That does not mean that every one of you will have arms. Lieutenant Hernandez will attend to the re-distribution of weapons."

The men began loosening the leather belts which held their weapons. "Hold it, Men. We have no idea what lies ahead. You all know what we heard today of the enemy's treatment of prisoners—and of those who befriended them. All this bears out what we were taught at AIB. At great personal risk, Mang Pedro has helped us so far. Now he has offered to lead us to shelter. He assures us that friendly hands will be waiting to help us salvage what may float ashore."

He stopped for a moment. There was absolute silence. "Proceeding from this spot will constitute combat reconnaissance, which you all know calls for scouting formation. A patrol ever on the alert—with a front and rear guard—a right and a left guard. All right, Men, FALL IN! Lieutenant, take over."

A redistribution of weapons was made as quickly as possible. As they started the march, the wind was dying away. Mang Pedro, marching at the lieutenant's left, maintained the quick pace of the younger men, from the start. After a brisk march of almost a mile, they came to the banks of a wide river where the trees grew to the water's edge. The moon cast a pale light which was reflected by the smooth running stream. Here was the river—but no huts!

In a voice that had not the slightest resemblance to the usual warm, resonant tone, Rowe demanded, "Where are the huts?"

"Other side of the river and little way up stream, Sir," said Mang Pedro with complete assurance.

The tense moment was so charged with poignant doubt that it seemed to flash around the group like an electric current. Was this old man what he had seemed or—was he just another very smooth . . . ?

Before either Rowe or Hernandez could bring himself to speak, Mang Pedro whistled a low, trilling call like a drowsy, crooning bird in the night. The breathless silence that followed was broken by the soft splash of oars in the water. A man in a small *banca* emerged from the shadow and identified himself.

"Who is this man?" asked Rowe, his tongue dry and speech difficult.

"He is guide to help us find way up the river. Remember? Mang José say he have guides ready on this side," said Mang Pedro almost happily.

They did remember, but in the series of shocks and disappointments, they had forgotten.

"Why didn't you mention him sooner?" asked Rowe.

"I think, Sir, maybe you forget what Mang José say. You and your men have enough disappointment for one night. I think I wait and be sure he is here before I tell you."

Lieutenant Hernandez spoke to the man who, like so many others, spoke more Tagalog than English. After a few words Hernandez turned to the commander. "He says the people across the river have a place for us to sleep. They had been told we might need to rest before starting up the river. Until he heard Mang Pedro's signal, he thought we were an enemy patrol. He was expecting us to come in loaded boats."

"My GOD," said Rowe, almost in a whisper. "I didn't think of that," realizing how costly such an error could have been for the man. "And STILL they're willing to help."

9
» » ENEMY OCCUPIED TERRITORY

So worked the FIGHTERS FOR FREEDOM, a nebulous, elusive band whose loyal members might be university professors, plantation owners, doctors, teachers, students, political leaders—local or national, small farmers, coconut traders in their tiny *bancas,* or humble servants in a wealthy household. There were also courageous men who owned and drove their cargo trucks loaded with salt, rice, corn or coffee, and who gave transportation to the couriers. They too stood to lose their lives if the vital papers carried in the double bottom of the couriers' *buri* bags were discovered by a sentry.

At the hands of the patient people who waited for the men of MISSION ISRM at the river bank as they were rowed across in the small *banca*, they met a sincere welcome and hospitality as warming as the hot tea the women brewed from their scant supply, and the clean dry clothes they provided.

Only four could ride with the boatman each trip. Before the last load had finished the meal they made of the hot tea and the C-ration some of the men had still fastened to their belts when they came ashore, the plans for the next move were well under way. Most of the men from the first two loads were lost in deep, noisy sleep on the clean *buri* mats on the floor.

An inner and outer perimeter of defense around the area were set up by the native men, with two men from THE MISSION for each perimeter alternating on short watches so that each man might get a little rest. With the coming of the dawn, there would be much work to do.

By the dim light of a coconut oil lamp, Rowe and Hernandez made their plans and a duty roster to cover them for the morning. They would split the work into three details. Detail No. 1 would start on the salvage operation and Detail No. 2 would take a *batel* and go back to Pandan to bring Sergeant Berg and the others up to date on what had happened. Detail No. 3 would have to be a procurement detail, for now FOOD had become a very real problem. They would have to find and buy from local people quantities of those things which would be hard to find farther inland in the mountains. With the details arranged, the two men fell wearily upon the *buri* mats arranged for them on the bamboo floor.

Just before dawn two men were to take a detail of local boys back along the coast in the area where they had come ashore and some distance down the shore parallel to the current, to search for the floating cargo. One of the guides who had come to meet them, spoke to the lieutenant in Tagalog. "I will go now and come back soon with my sons. They LIVE in this water. They dive like fish and they know every foot of the coast line. The water is very clear and in most places along the shore, very shallow. We will get back what you have lost."

Another, not quite so confident, added, "If *Hapónés* (Japanese) do not see it first."

But the first man was not to be discouraged. "My boys will GET it first."

This was encouraging. True, there were enemy patrols during the daylight hours, but with an alert air guard, and the narrow beach between the water and the trees, they might accomplish it. They could hope!

In the light of the new day, the cold, wet, miserable hours of the night before seemed like a bad dream. In the bright, warm morning sun this spot beside the deep, lazy river became a tropical paradise. A million raindrops sparkled in the sunlight as they clung to the clean, washed leaves and the blades of lush, green grass in the small clearing surrounded by *nipa* huts. Bright colored birds chirped and sang or darted here and there out across the clearing. The fresh, sweet smell of moist earth and growing things was in the air. They washed the salt from their clothes and walked barefoot on the soft earth as they hung their clothes to dry. The more fortunate ones cleaned and oiled their automatics and tommyguns to prevent damage from the salt water. One man having lost everything else said very seriously, "I always say it's a good thing to know that you have a good, seaworthy watch."

The guide detail set out for Pandan in a harmless looking *batel* of the new NICHOLSON LINES. The salvage operation was working out beyond their wildest hopes. Many of the boxes had washed ashore and the diving boys had also retrieved a great many of the heavier ones from the clear water on the floor of the gently sloping shoreline. Like those which had washed ashore the previous morning, those inspected gave no evidence of the salt water having penetrated the inner wrappings of heavy, brown, oiled paper.

The procurement detail, No. 3, required more instruction. They gathered round to discuss with the local men, the matter of available food supplies. "There is still food to be had—if you know the right people AND if you can pay the price," they said.

Then, for the first time, the men of MISSION ISRM began to have some idea of what inflation could really mean in an enemy-occupied country. The commander asked about sugar.

"Very little sugar is being manufactured—so—the price is very high and it is hard to find," said one.

"What do you mean by 'very little' and 'very high'?" asked Rowe, not knowing what to expect. (Sugar stocks had been his business in Manila.)

"Oh—one half cup brown sugar—five pesos," said the man in the same detached tone he might have used if he had said, "Oh you can get a good cadillac for $20,000." Obviously he had given up sugar long since.

"Five pesos the HALF CUP?" burst out Rowe, "and it takes two full cups to make a pound—TWENTY PESOS. That's TEN AMERICAN DOLLARS for ONE POUND of sugar. Why those dirty sons-of-bitches." Springing to his feet he said, "My God, are food prices like this in Manila?"

"Some things higher in the city—some lower," said the man, "but everything is very high. Is easier to get collaborators that way, Senor."

Plunging his hands deep into his pockets, the commander began walking back and forth nervously. Not quite understanding the commander's tremendous concern over food prices, Hernandez covered his momentary silence by another question. "What about meat?"

"Meat just like sugar—is hard to find. *Hapónes* take most of the cattle long time ago. Sometimes can find small pig—for 100 pesos. *Carabao*, if you can find him, three pesos, fish four pesos pound. Sometimes few fresh eggs—one peso each."

"One peso for a dozen eggs?" said Hernandez incredulously.

"Oh NO, Senor," said the man, a little amazed at the newcomer's stupidity, "one egg, one peso."

Rice, the staple food in the Islands, a chief import even in peace time, was very scarce and proportionately overpriced. Coffee was $12.00 per pound and tea $15.00. Matches were forty cents for the small pocket size box and cigarettes, $3.50 per pack in American money.

"You see, Senor, if a man is not very wealthy—or will not collaborate—he pretty hungry these days."

Having regained his composure somewhat, the commander sat down where he was when he first heard of the fantastic prices being charged for the simplest foods. Realizing that something must have hit him very hard, Hernandez did the usual—came up with something to get his mind off the problem. "Well," he said, "it looks from here as though it's a good thing we found the cabbage."

"My God YES!" said Rowe. "It sure as hell is."

That had been a day—the day the "cabbage" was lost, on the *Nautilus*. Late one afternoon, after a day of solid classes in the ward room, Lieutenant Hernandez was enjoying a cup of coffee with one of the ship's officers and Sergeant Berg was in his quarters, reading. A voice on the intercom said, "Lieutenant Hernandez and Sergeant Berg, report to Commander Rowe's quarters. Lieutenant Hernandez and Sergeant Berg, Commander Rowe's quarters."

The two arrived simultaneously at the open door and the commander said, "Come on in, Fellows and sit down." As they did so, he continued, "Al, you remember we spoke earlier about getting the "new" look off the money so we wouldn't go around blazing a trail for the Japs to follow us." "Right," said Hernandez, and waited.

Dropping into a deep, serious tone, Rowe said, "Sergeant, I have observed that our men seem to be a little more than usually fond of poker."

"Yes, Sir," said Berg, for some reason, instantly on the defensive, but the thought that went through his mind was, "So what, you pompous bastard, you were doing all right the last time I saw you in a poker game." He looked around guiltily, wondering if he had said aloud what he was thinking. The sergeant's only concern with money in the Army had been handing out pay checks on the first of the month.

With a sly chuckle, Hernandez asked, "You aren't thinking of adding POKER to the curriculum, are you, George?" Then realizing that his thoughts had been his own, Berg recovered sufficiently to say, "Well your timing is about right. We're cutting the training hours in half, tomorrow."

"Fine," said Rowe. "It's an order. Every man will play poker not less than four hours daily until further orders." "When do we start, Sir?"

"Right now," chuckled Rowe. "Lieutenant, tell Sergeant Reyes to assemble the men in the wardroom and Jerry, you get the money and take it down there. I'll stroll in when you're ready. This should be a hell of a lot of fun."

Jerry turned to go and Hernandez said, "I'll come in from the other end of the room."

"Good," said Rowe, looking at his watch he called after the sergeant, "Make it ten minutes from now."

"Right, Sir," said Jerry, looking at his watch as he hurried away.

Sergeant Reyes quickly rounded up the men and waited. As Commander Rowe approached in the corridor, he called out, "Ten-SHUN!"

The commander stopped just outside the door to wait for Sergeant Berg to come in with the money. Checking the time, Hernandez sauntered in casually from the other entry and Sergeant Berg, striding in behind him, threw a signal to Rowe over Hernandez' shoulder which clearly meant "NO MONEY."

From the commander's expression, it was obvious that something had gone wrong. Hernandez walked on through to him and Sergeant Berg paused midway through the room to call out, "As you were," and hurried on through to the commander.

"What's wrong, Sergeant?" asked Rowe.

"The money—it's gone, Sir."

"Gone?" said Rowe blankly. Then "GONE! It couldn't be." "Now that I think about it, I don't remember seeing it aboard," said Berg.

"Neither do I," added Hernandez.

"Well I haven't SEEN it either," exploded Rowe, "but HELL, I wasn't LOOKING for it. It was Commander Parson's job to see that the gear got loaded. We got it together. That's what he was there for. My God, what'll we DO without money?"

Rowe didn't often take things so seriously—but then he didn't often have a problem as serious as this. Not knowing quite what to do, Hernandez chose to play it light. He said, "And we haven't even got a drum."

"A DRUM?" growled Rowe. "What the hell good would a drum do?"

"Well, when the SALVATION ARMY needs money -," Al began facetiously.

Rowe interrupted angrily, "OK—OK—but dammit this is serious."

Then realizing that Al was kidding only because it WAS serious, he said with a wry grin, "I'm sorry, Al. I guess getting excited about it isn't going to do any good."

Al spoke quietly, "It HAS to be aboard, George. You were charged with it, weren't you?"

"Hell YES, I was charged with it."

Turning to Sergeant Berg, he said, "Jerry are you sure you looked through all the gear?"

"Yes, Sir," Jerry replied, "unless there's some stashed away somewhere that I don't know anything about—and if there is—well, it's about time I found it out."

The first shock of the discovery over, George was thinking normally again. "The ship's crew must have handled it," he said.

"That's right," agreed Berg. "Our men weren't up to it. Some of them could hardly get aboard on their own power. Remember? Boarding a submarine after 24 hours at 14,000 feet."

"Yeah, it had to be the crew. We'll check with them before we say anything to our men," said Rowe.

"I hope it doesn't come to that," said Hernandez.

"How much are we looking for, Sir?" asked Berg.

"Five cans," answered Rowe.

"I mean—dollars, Sir."

"Oh," said Rowe grinning wickedly. He was himself again. "Half a million Jap pesos."

"JAP pesos?" repeated Berg in a voice that said clearly, 'this thing has REALLY thrown the old man'.

"That's what's being worn in the Philippines this year, Sergeant."

Berg reached down and passed his hand carefully over his leg, then stretched it as though to be sure it was all right.

Rowe and Hernandez both laughed. Hernandez said, "He's not pulling it, Sergeant. It's on the level."

"On the level, Sergeant, they're the best damned, authentic, counterfeit, Japanese pesos the Australian printers could turn out on the lousy paper the U. S. Treasury could spare," said Rowe. "But let's FIND it, not discuss it."

"What do you SUGGEST, Sir?" asked Berg. (What the hell did they think he'd been trying to do?)

"You take the engine room and the galley, Sergeant. Lieutenant, get Sergeant Reyes and you two check the crewmen in quarters. I'll check first with the captain."

As they started away he said, "You know of course, that it's not bags of money you're looking for. It's five gallon cans of cabbage."

Each one followed through on his detail but no one had seen the cabbage. Commander Rowe started checking over the cargo himself, thinking that Sergeant Berg might have missed it—knowing full well that Sergeant Berg didn't miss things he was looking for, but at the moment he needed action.

The engine men had been busy below when the cargo had come aboard One or two from the galley had helped but no one had seen any cabbage. Sergeant Berg started back to the commander's quarters, ready to give up, when he passed the shower. The water was running. He stuck his head in and shouted over the sound of the water, "Did you help square away the cargo we brought aboard at Darwin?" "Yes," shouted back a tall, lanky bather, "Why?"

"Did you see any cans marked cabbage'?"

"I don't remember," the bather called back.

"Well THINK!" demanded Berg.

"I can't with this damned water in my face," bellowed the bewildered man.

"Well turn off the goddam water and TRY," Berg shouted back, catching up the towel the man had brought with him and thrusting it into the shower.

The man turned off the water, took the towel and started drying himself. "OK, Sarge, now what the hell's all the gripe about the cabbage?"

His face white with anger at the man's attitude, Berg said in a tone as level as he would have used with a little child, "I said, did you see any metal cans marked 'cabbage' in the cargo that was taken aboard at Darwin?"

"Gosh, Sarge, I don't know. I came aboard there myself. We took on supplies too. I helped square them away. But—wait a minute—yeah—yeah I think I did."

"You think you did WHAT?" Berg's voice was coming up again.

"I think I saw the cans."

"Where—what did you do with them?" asked Berg, gripping the man's arm and almost dragging him into the passage.

"Hold it, Sarge, goddammit, HOLD IT," said the crewman, his teeth chattering violently. "Let me get some clothes on." Then, with Berg still gripping his arm, "Anyway what's so damned important about a few cans of cabbage? I hate the stinkin' stuff."

"I didn't ask you what you liked," barked Berg in exasperation. "I JUST want to know what you DID with it." "OK then—let go of my arm."

Berg shook his head in utter confusion. "I'm sorry—really I am. I didn't realize I had such a grip on you—but tell me where in the hell you put those cans."

"Well, when I came aboard," said the man trying to rub away the deep, white fingerprints on his arm, "there were a lot of perishables stacked on the deck, topside. They had to be stowed away to make room for the rest of your gear. A couple of us were sent down to square them away. Being cabbage, well I just naturally put it with the rest of the green stuff—in the refrigerator."

Lieutenant Hernandez and Sergeant Reyes had just reported their failure to the commander. He was pacing the deck when Berg walked in with the first can of money. "WHERE in the hell did you find it?" asked Rowe and crumpled into a chair.

The sergeant explained.

"All right," said Rowe, "any one of you that wants to—go down and tell the men they've GOT to play poker till they muss up five cans of nice, crisp, frozen cabbage. I need a DRINK. Join me, Lieutenant?"

Berg looked at Reyes and smiled. "I guess the job is ours, Sergeant. Pick up a few new decks of cards and meet me in the wardroom. I'll wait till you get there to break the awful news."

The two sergeants then started off what probably was the greatest poker game ever to become a part of the daily curriculum of an Army training unit. Counting out large and impressive sums of the commander's genuine, authentic, counterfeit, Japanese pesos to certain of the men, Sergeant Berg said, "Now remember, Men, I'm holding you responsible for this money. I want every goddam wrinkled peso back in that can when the game is over."

Turning to Reyes, he said, "Sergeant would you like to join me in a cup of good, STRONG, black coffee?"

Now that they were actually here in the Islands, and had lost a great part of the rations they had brought with them—at the prices they had just heard quoted for the barest necessities, they were going to need that cabbage—plenty of it—providing they were able to find the food they needed.

While they were discussing what plan might be best to follow in procurement, a local man motioned for silence at a signal from out of the jungle. A native boy acting as a runner between the details working at the beach and their temporary HQs in the *barrio* (small group of houses) by the river, came dashing in to say that a Jap patrol boat—not too large—was cruising slowly down the coast. They should be able to see it in about ten minutes as it passed the mouth of the river.

"If it passes?," said one of the older men, dully. "If is a little boat, they may come up—if they look for food. Is never good when they come—no matter what they look for. If they find you here, they kill all of us," he said in the same monotone. The dull hopelessness in his voice told more than any words, the despair of a people, crushed if not conquered.

"He is right," said one of the men who had been telling about the food prices. "And if it is a big boat, they may drop anchor and send up a small one—or a scouting party."

"Quick, Men," said Rowe, "get your clothes off the bushes and be ready to take off if they start up. God help all of us is they find those damned boats." He looked at his watch. "I wonder if they saw the men going to Pandan."

Just then another runner came in to say that they had found two of the boats and had taken them in under the trees. They had come up just before the patrol was spotted, so they had buried them under leaves against some large logs. A real search of the area of course would uncover them, but there had not been time to go farther.

It was a tense moment. If the men from Pandan were already under way—if these kindhearted people were caught helping an American Intelligence Mission—If . . . Where in the hell was that other goddam boat?

One of the men standing at the edge of the jungle with his half-dry clothing in his hand, looked at his watch. A little later he looked again—it must have stopped. It had to be more than two minutes. He held it up to his ear. Maybe the salt water had gotten in after all.

As they sat listening, several men they had not seen before came silently into the clearing. They were greeted solemnly by the others and sat down to wait. Seeing the uneasy glances which passed between Rowe and Hernandez, one of the native men walked over to them and said, "These are our men. You did not see them last night, for they were in the outer perimeter of defense. They heard the signal." "Why do they come out where they can be seen?" asked Rowe.

"They wait for next signal. If the boat is coming up the river, it mean 'battle stations'. If is 'all clear' they go back." "And if it is 'battle stations?" Rowe asked.

"We are enough if the boat is not too big—not too many men. We take care of it."

"You mean you would attack a boat right here in the river?" continued Rowe in amazement.

"We do what we have to do," the man answered simply. "The river is deep. Is easy to sink a boat and take care of it later. We have to be very careful that not one of the yellow devils gets away to tell about it."

Twenty-six tense, nerve-taxing minutes dragged by before the "all clear" came. Shortly after that a shaky but well-instructed procurement detail set out to search for food. The quantities required were large enough to attract attention if the purchasing were not carefully done. That one thing—rations—could slow them down for days.

It was another long two hours before a runner came in shouting happily, "They're coming. The boat from Pandan is coming."

By the time the *Doña Juana*'s crew had tossed a rope to the landing, the welcoming party had arrived on the spot. The men from Pandan of course had the better of the others. They knew what had been happening. Rowe was the first to start questioning. "Did that damn patrol boat give you any trouble?"

"Not really," said Berg, "but they sure WORRIED the hell out of me for a long time. They came up from the south and cruised all around the island. The men had just finished loading the boat and covering the load with coconuts. It was tied up at your pier, Mang Pedro, down at the cove. I was on my way down to inspect the camouflage when the lookout called out that a Jap boat was coming."

"What did you do?" asked Rowe eagerly.

"What COULD I do, Sir? They stopped about 200 yards out and looked it over from the deck. I guess they've seen too many boat loads of coconuts to get excited about them—anyway they took off without any further inspection. All I can say is, it was a damn good thing the boys had found that rubber boat."

"Which boat," asked Hernandez quickly. "The one we lost last night or the night before?"

"You know, Sir, I think you fellows ganged up on me last night. I haven't had time to look in the mirror this morning. I'll bet you my hair's white."

"Why what do you mean, Sergeant?" asked Hernandez. They could joke about it now that everyone was safe and the sergeant seemed to have nothing serious to report.

"Well, I didn't worry too much about the storm. You'd been in one the night before. Not being able to reach you on the walkie-talkie was understandable. You might be out of range, and when the boat that was coming back was four hours overdue, I ordered the gear off the beach. It was getting too near daylight. Then I decided to hit the sack for an hour, so what happens? A man comes tearing down on the double and says, 'Sergeant, something's happened to Commander Rowe and the lieutenant'. Well that was a hell of a way to wake up, but anyway I asked him what. He said he didn't know—but your boat had just washed ashore—bottom up."

"I get you," said Rowe, "but what about—"

But the sergeant hadn't finished. "Yes Sir, I only had from 0500 to 1100 to worry about it. Of course there was the consoling thought that even though you and the lieutenant might be gone—I still had THE MISSION. I'd never thought of that before."

"OK, Sergeant, OK," said Rowe smiling broadly. "I guess we gave you a bad time, but we weren't exactly on a picnic ourselves."

Suddenly serious, Sergeant Berg said, "I gathered that, Sir. My first thought was to get into one of the boats Mang Pedro's men had brought and come on here as fast as possible. Then I thought if a Jap patrol HAD caught you, they might wait to see if any more would show. The worst though was the thought—what if you didn't make it to shore."

"You know, Sergeant, that gave us a bad time for a little while too," said Rowe, eyeing what looked like boxes of rations on the Dorm Juana. "I wonder," he said half aloud—"if that stuff's what I think—I just wonder if we can't still get on the way this afternoon."

10
» » WRONG RIVER

Jerry Berg had taken advantage of the delay in getting away from Pandan on account of the patrol. He had ordered a quick check of the salvaged boxes against Sergeant Reyes' list of matériel. No more was to be seen afloat or below the surface on either side of the strait. Apparently the greatest loss had been in weather equipment. Rations came next. Radio gear had suffered relatively minor losses—and above all—NOT A MAN HAD BEEN INJURED OR LOST.

The next step was to set up outposts along the route to their main objective, which at that point was to establish a radio station at the summit of Mt. Bacó, with the transmitter beamed out to Australia.

With the rations and other supplies Sergeant Berg had brought over on the *Doña Juana,* there was no real necessity for the first contingent to wait for the procurement detail. With what they had now, they could take their chances of buying what ever else they needed from farmers along the way, and now they could follow through using only the native boats.

Looking over the stacks of matériel the radio men had checked, together with the absolute minimum of other equipment and supplies which would be required to set up a station, the commander said quietly to Hernandez, "Now we know, Al."

"Good," said Al. "What do we know?"

"We know WHY they said 'If we haven't heard from you in six weeks, we'll send a party to look for you'. Remember?"

"I remember," said Hernandez thoughtfully, "but how DO you suppose they expected us to move all this gear to the mountains? After we leave the river, the only transportation they KNOW is man's back and *carabao.*"

"You're damn right it is—and they sure as hell didn't send along any *carabaos*. When we shoved off from the *Nautilus,* we wiped out about 200 years of progress in transportation. We won't see any wheel tracks on the mountains of Mindoro," said Rowe, his temper rising by the moment.

George Rowe had not been picked to command this difficult and demanding mission for nothing. He had a reputation for getting things done. "Goddammit—they EXPECTED it to take us five or six weeks to haul all that gear up the river, chop our way through 15 or 20 miles of jungle and then CARRY it over the low range and on to the top of Mt. Bacó. We figured a minimum of forty miles inland."

"Well, thanks to Mang Pedro, we have help," said Hernandez.

"Thanks to Mang Pedro and his *cargadorés*," said Rowe, "and we're damn well going to use a LOT of his *cargadorés.*" We can't be all summer getting our gear up there."

"There's no doubt about it, we're going to lose a lot of valuable time doing it ourselves," said Hernandez seriously, "but—well we can't just ..."

"I know what you're thinking," interrupted Rowe, but let's just lay it on the line, Al. Right now the important thing is to get in there and get a transmitter in operation. Every day counts! And here we are—hamstrung with no transportation. Where would we be right now, if we hadn't had these people helping us?"

"We have a lot of equipment we wouldn't have had," agreed Hernandez.

"You're damn right. We wouldn't even have BOATS we could USE— and the risk of compromising THE MISSION would be increased 1000 per cent by making continuous trips with supplies over the same route for weeks. It just doesn't make sense."

At about 1500, Commander Rowe, Hernandez, Mang Pedro and several of the ISRM radio men set out for the interior in one large *banca* and one smaller one. They took four native boys recommended as excellent scouts, familiar with both the river and the mountain trails.

Every mile they could go by water meant that many less of hacking and slashing their way through what had become dense jungle thirty minutes from the start. Traveling by boat, those thick vines and *lianas* overhanging the river banks might furnish a natural camouflage from passing air patrols.

Half an hour up the river, they heard the drone of a low-flying Jap Dinah-type recon plane. Both boats were able to nose in quickly, hugging the bank as the pilot made a careful reconnaissance of the river area. Apparently satisfied, he flew on. Several others flying north passed over, obviously enroute to some definite destination. Later a formation flew over—again on their way somewhere. It was to be months later before they knew why those planes were all flying north in the interior.

Perhaps two or three miles farther up the river, once more they heard the drone of motors coming in. This time it was a Jake—a low-winged, cabin type plane capable of carrying several passengers—following the course of the river downstream. It was equipped with pontoons!

The lead *banca* was again in position to take cover under the trees along the bank, but as the plane appeared overhead, the larger boat was rounding a small island and was caught mid-stream in full view. Anxiously the others watched—BAR's ready to fire upon anyone giving them any trouble. The men in the open boat sat quietly resting on their oars as though mildly curious as to the low-flying craft.

The commander breathed a long, deep sigh as the pilot took off without attempting to land or to fire upon the boat.

"Thank God that bastard's gone. He really had me worried," he said.

"The fellows in the boat probably picked up a grey hair or two," said another, as they started to move out into the stream.

"LISTEN!" said one of the native guides. The oarsmen held their stroke. "He's coming back."

"I wonder if there's something showing in their cargo," said Rowe.

"I don't think so," said Hernandez confidently. "I checked every inch of that load. There CAN'T be anything showing."

That time the pilot flew even lower than before, but the men in the large *banca* rowed steadily upstream, while those waiting in the shadows had their weapons trained upon the plane. Once more he circled, banked in and took off—unaware that if a man down there in the shadows watching him with binoculars, had seen one move to indicate that he was going to fire on that boat, they would all have tried, at least, to make it his last.

They continued up the deep winding river and the flowers and trees along the banks seemed to become more beautiful as they went along. Delicate, orchid-like flowers of exquisite colors clung to the leafy boughs, and birds of brilliant plumage darted in and out among the trees, while weird-faced little brown monkeys chattered and scolded at this invasion of their privacy.

As the shadows began to lengthen they came upon a point where the river widened into deep curves on either side to make way, midstream, for a peaceful and incredibly beautiful island, probably three hundred yards wide and three times as long.

Unlike the dense jungle along the river banks, fully half of the island was like a small meadow, where lush, green grass rippled before the breeze from the river bank to a narrow fringe of tall, straight trees—eucalyptus, *bagtikan,* and clumps of white *lauan,* known commercially as Philippine mahogany.

At the upper end of the island, more heavily wooded, was a small *barrio* composed of several *nipa* huts occupied by families of friendly natives. One particularly thick clump of low-hanging trees formed a natural hideout, that under the supervision of Sergeant Pascua, soon became an efficient forward base of operations. With each detail assigned and following through, the equipment was soon unloaded and camouflaged.

Friendly visitors were a rarity to those isolated people in July 1944, and once more the hospitality of the island people was evident. They brought two small pigs and a basket of *camotes* (sweet potatoes) which were put to roasting in a primitive, stone fireplace used at fiesta time. Soon the tantalizing fragrance of the roasting meat and the wood smoke floated out into the open air as the men set up camp and Rowe and Hernandez tried to determine by checking their position on the map, how far they would be able to continue by boat. They realized now the tremendous task ahead in transporting tons of matériel through the jungle, over one low mountain range, through the intervening valley and to the summit of the second and higher range.

As the sunset faded and the evening shadows fell, the villagers old and young came to join them around the campfire and sing and dance to the music of sweet-toned guitars. One of those guitars Commander Rowe had bought from a crewman on the *Nautilus,* when he realized how much it added to the community sings they had employed in lieu of exercise during the hours of intensive training in the crowded quarters of the submarine. That instrument went with them for many months until the jungle insects and the ever present mildew of the tropics took their inevitable toll.

As the darkness deepened and the stars came out the boys and girls of the village brought their coconut shells and to the rhythmic clop clop clop, clop clop clop, of the shells and the guitars, they dance the coconut dance, the *Bao* and then, to the plaintive tones of the guitars alone, the dance of the Rice Planting. For a little while they could forget the wartorn world outside, only because every few hundred feet, men were keeping watch at their perimeter of defense.

Next morning at about 0430, a young man named Martin arrived in camp. He had been recommended by Mang José and the mayor as a very reliable courier, officially connected with the FFF. He had rowed all night, upstream in a *banca*, to catch up with them. After a few hours rest, Martin was off to establish contact with a few known channels of communication in Manila, recognized by G-2. There were several activities which had to be gotten under way before anyone from THE MISSION dared venture into the city. Among others, they wanted to find Willie Hernandez, a young cousin of ATs in Manila. Willie's wide social and business background and contacts Rowe and Hernandez thought would be invaluable in many phases of their coming Manila operations.

While the lieutenant interviewed Martin in his tent, and briefed him on his immediate mission, Sergeant Aguilar was barking out orders to his men, drilling in an open area close by which, though limited in size, was adequate as a parade ground for his platoon. The sergeant had no intention of allowing his men to let down nor of wasting such an opportunity to impress the native population—up early sitting on their tall steps, watching their visitors. He was justly proud of the snap and precision of that well-trained platoon.

On their way upstream, the commander and the lieutenant were discussing the fact that the island was not shown on the map. "That is not surprising," said one of the guides. "The rainfall here is very heavy—sometimes 200 inches in a year. Rivers often change their course and a new bed replaces the old one. Sometimes both beds remain active. Then we find islands like this one."

He explained that the fringe of trees along one side and the heavier wooded area at the upper end indicated that it probably had been cut off from the mainland. The lower part, covered by fine grass, very likely had been formed by river silt. Being of recent formation, no trees had taken hold.

In the next few miles, however, they noticed that numerous small streams emptied into the river and after that, the river itself rapidly became narrower and much more shallow. Both Rowe and Hernandez were concerned over this development. Finally Rowe said, "Al, I don't know what's wrong here—but according to this map—well there's a hell of a mistake somewhere. They must have thought at AIB that this river was navigable for more than ten or twelve miles." "Right," said Hernandez. "I remember that briefing word for word. 'You will go up the Asis River at least twenty miles toward Mt. Bacó'."

The startled native guides almost dropped their oars. Mang Pedro turned to the lieutenant with a look of utter panic. "But Sir, you did not say Mt. Bacó! You said 'to the mountains'."

"But there is only one river," said Rowe, pointing to the map.

The two native men said something to each other, then Zamora, the one who had come most highly recommended, said, "What is the date on the map, Sir?"

"June, 1924," said Rowe blankly.

"That was twenty years ago, Sir," said the man.

"Twenty years ago," echoed Mang Pedro. "That would be about right. Twenty years ago the Pandan only little Hog, not a big river to put on map."

"The Pandan River?" asked Rowe and Hernandez at once. "Yes, Sir," said Zamora. This is the Pandan. The Asis is up the coast—I'd say almost . . ."

"*Limang* (five) *kilometros* from the Pandan," supplied Mang Pedro. "I go often to the Asis before the war."

"And you are right, Sir. It is much longer and goes much closer to Mt. Bacó," added Zamora.

They realized then that this sort of thing was a part of the price they had to pay for not being able to take their volunteers completely into their confidence—and how dangerous half information could be. They knew they were traveling in the right general direction, but they did not know that twenty years of tropical rainfall, storms and erosion had formed not only an island, but a completely new river. Now they had traveled almost to its source before they discovered their error. These were the things their native helpers could supply—they would have to make sure of their helpers—and then they would have to trust them.

"OK, Men," said Rowe, "We've made a mistake—but it's not fatal. We know now that we should have told you exactly where we wanted to go. But let's not waste any more time. The sooner we stop the others, the better."

The oarsmen reversed their position and minutes later they were on their way back down the river which, by the guides and on the record, was called PANDAN, but which in the memories of George Rowe and Al Hernandez, will remain forever WRONG RIVER.

As an excursion the Wrong River trip would have been a pleasure, but from the point of view of time lost to an intelligence mission, it was costly—at least 24 hours lost by the time they would be back at the starting point.

As a reconnaissance trip it had been worth something. They had an idea of how the air patrols worked and that it would be suicide to attempt a quick move, even in native boats. They had learned also that the jungle near the coast was much less dense than that which lay farther inland.

Working through the many miles of jungle between the coast and the mountains, with the amount of matériel they had to move would take weeks. UNLESS—unless they went farther afield and found enough loyal, local men to help.

There was very little conversation as the return trip began—rushing along downstream over the deep, dark water. The green coloring, they discovered, was mainly reflection of the solid, canon-like walls of luxuriant foliage reaching skyward on either side of the stream.

After a while the commander said, "Al, you know those big *carabao* carts, don't you?"

"You mean the big baskets set on bamboo poles that hang from the *carabao's* shoulders?"

"Right."

"Sure. Everyone knows those," said Hernandez.

A moment later Zamora said to the lieutenant, "Sir, we will soon be at the fork in the river. We came up the south branch. If we take the north branch, it will bring us out only a short distance from the Asis River. I know men there who could ..."

"You are sure this branch will take us to the right place," interrupted Hernandez, a little dubiously.

"I am sure, Sir," replied the guide with only a flicker of a smile. He might as well have said, "I know where I'm going this time."

"These men you know there—who are they?" asked Rowe.

"They are Guerillas, Sir. The place I mentioned is a Guerilla hideout—a large plantation. There will be many *carabaos* there and the men will know which tenders it is safe to contact."

"What do you know about these Guerillas—what outfit are they from?" asked Rowe.

"Oh they are good men, Sir, and well trained. They are from Major Ruffy's command," answered Zamora confidently.

"My God! What a break!" was all Rowe could say.

Major Ruffy was Commander-in-Chief of Guerilla Forces in Mindoro, with the full blessing of GHQ. These men could go a long way in solving the problem ahead.

Arriving at the fork, Sergeant Pascua took his men in the smaller *banca* and went back down the river to meet any of the others who might have started upstream and to inform Sergeant Berg of the change in routes. The accomplishment of Sergeant Berg and his men during Pascua's absence was amazing. They had moved a tremendous amount of the matériel from Pandan during the night. (While we were eating roast pig and *camotes*, he thought.)

Upon learning of the new plans, the procurement detail with their native helpers of the Pandan area went through the countryside, rounding up some fifty *carabao* tenders and their animals to help with the move along the trail. Runners were sent out frequently to keep the CO and Hernandez informed of their progress and certain of the ISRM men were ordered to rest to be ready to start the trek north at dawn.

The men and animals assembled at dawn and were assigned to units, each one under the command of one of the sergeants of THE MISSION and briefed on the pending operation. The various units were dispatched a few hours apart, in accordance with their security schedule. The last detail to leave, started from a point three miles down the coast, where the floating cargo caught in the current had been retrieved by the salvage detail. With the enthusiastic support of their native helpers, Sergeant Pascua and his men accomplished what seemed to be the impossible, and arrived at the Guerilla retreat almost a day ahead of schedule.

Nature had neglected to furnish the tough, black hides of the ugly little *carabaos* with their own cooling systems, so half an hour out of every four on the trail, had to be spent at the wallows, if they were to keep going in that savage heat. In the lowlands near the coast the many natural water holes made this no problem, except for the time involved. Later, on the mountain trails it would be a different story.

In contrast to the piercing cold of a few nights before, the day was intensely hot. Much of the time they were in the shade of the jungle, but the simple effort of moving through the dense vegetation, unaccustomed to the torrid heat, constantly alert for enemy patrols, was enervating. A trail had to be cut wide enough for the *carabaos* with their heavy, bulky packs or the clumsy, sled-like carts. Slashing and chopping through vines, bushes, exposed roots, and fallen trees, up and down through deep ravines was rugged, exhausting work. Wet shirts clung to hot, sticky bodies and the mosquito netting veils secured under their helmets stuck to their dripping faces and curled into wet, soggy rolls under their collars. Most of the *carabao* tenders worked without shirts and in spite of the insect repellent brought out for them, there was an almost rhythmic slapping of shoulders, arms and faces as the men plodded along beside their animals.

Murky, humming clouds of mosquitoes rose from the damp, steamy earth as they passed. If the *"anas"* got in their deadly work, carrying the malaria germ from the bloodstream of one human to another, in time they could be as devastating as an enemy patrol.

Late that afternoon they found a spot to camp where men and animals could be dispersed for security. They had hardly more than stripped the heavy packs from the *carabaos* when a sudden wind, forerunner of an approaching tropical storm, put everyone but the outer guard to work at improvising a quick shelter. Boxes were piled high to form the corner posts and canvas was stretched over and around them to keep out the wind and driving rain. The shelters held for a while but about the time the men began playing catch with the flapping corners of the canvas, the rushing river which had risen under foot, went over the tops of their jungle boots. Certain of those among them still recommended it as a better place to ride out a storm than an open boat on the waters of Mindoro Strait.

Half an hour more of the howling wind and pouring rain went by before the hungry band could begin to prepare mess. Then, in the hush that followed the storm, there came a new sound in the forest—not the monotonous hum of the insects—they had already become accustomed to that. They stood silent, listening. Tension gripped every man. It was the sound of human voices and, whoever they were, they had gotten past the outer guard provided by the guerillas. As the intruders approached they heard the sentries call out the command to "HALT!"

The seconds between that challenge and the identification of the newcomers as friendly Guerillas seemed endless. Shouts filled the air as they welcomed the advance guard of another contingent of Major Ruffy's men. These rugged fellows, in true Guerilla tradition, had traveled day and night over almost impossible terrain in record time—all the way across Mindoro in response to the appeal of runners from the local Guerilla units who said, "The *americanos* are here. They need you." Others would follow.

The arrival of this trained Guerilla band was a tremendous morale builder. Not only were these men familiar with prevailing conditions locally, but some one among them was familiar with any given territory in the entire area. Also, unlike the civilian recruits, who had been more than willing to help, these men were trained, organized and strictly disciplined. They could be given an order of any kind and that was the end of it until they reported the detail completed. They were possessed of initiative, enthusiasm, and judgment. It was easy to understand that men such as these, bound together in a common cause, formed the backbone of resistance against enemy aggression.

Dawn saw the commander, the lieutenant, several of their own men and a party of picked scouts from the Guerilla band, on their way to the Asis River. They had left the equipment they carried other than that required for their immediate work, to be brought with the caravan. They sailed up the coast, making a thorough reconnaissance of the area leading to the mouth of the river. Soundings in the river bed indicated that the stream would be navigable for all the *bancas* and *batels* of the NICHOLSON LINES excepting the Flag Ship *Doña Juana*. That fine *curicannan* would be indispensable for deep sea trips back to Pandan where a platoon of Guerillas now stood guard over well-buried equipment and supplies, as well as for later trips into Manila.

There in the river delta they found a small, wooded island lying midway between the banks of the river, swept by a swift current on either side. This island, they decided, would make an excellent cache for reserve supplies and as such would serve a triple purpose. It would speed the penetration of Mindoro; supplies buried there would be more accessible for transportation to other areas later; and it should insure them against loss of supplies in the event that their proposed position should be compromised.

About three miles upstream they found a deserted *barrio* consisting of one large house with several rooms and a number of small *nipa* huts in orderly arrangement along the edges of a central clearing. The deserted village appeared to be a perfect spot for a forward base of operations for THE MISSION. It might even be suitable for the first of a series of outposts. If anyone wondered what had happened to the people who had once called this place "home", he kept that thought to himself. This was a deserted *barrio* and its value either as a temporary HQs, or an eventual outpost depended upon its remaining so, to all outward appearances. It was off-limits to anyone not actively engaged in staff operations in the houses.

The main body of the convoy camped out in the surrounding jungle. Immediately upon arrival the animals of the first contingent were driven away under the trees, and even before their packs were removed, the commander called an air raid practice. If the enemy should suspect their presence there, the first thing they could expect would be a bombing of the houses. After the alert, the men proceeded with the business of unpacking the tired little animals and camouflaging the supplies while the commander and the lieutenant went inside the new HQs to discuss the alert. Hardly had they sat down when the air alert sounded and an air guard came running in shouting, "Jap bombers coming."

The two men dashed out of the HQs shouting orders for the second alert. They could hear the roar of the motors as they came in fast and low—almost a sure sign of a bombing attack. Within a few seconds after the last man cleared the open space, they could see overhead a large number of Helen-type medium bombers in bombing formation.

To the amazement and relief of the men who stood waiting, the planes passed over with no indication of an attack, flying on out to sea. While they were still under the trees, hardly moving from astonishment at not being bombed, the roar came in again—and again the cry to "DIG IN". Every available hole and opening was occupied as the planes roared overhead a second time. They must have flown over to get their bearings—now they were coming in for the kill. But they passed on over without dropping a single bomb.

For a moment all felt relieved, when someone said, "We were lucky, but they can hardly miss the convoy on the trail."

Certainly there was that chance, with all those *carabaos* heavily packed or dragging the cumbersome, sledlike carts, some of them might easily be exposed in swamps or other difficult terrain. It would be impossible to keep them all under cover at all times.

Runners were sent back along the trail to see how the caravan had fared. Depending upon their position, the runners might be expected back in an hour to an hour and a half. Then as a perfect example of the esprit de corps characteristic of the expedition, they too had sent runners to see how the lead party had made out. The runners returned in about half the expected time. The alert signal of the Guerillas on the trail, three sharp, staccato notes on a high-pitched flute-like bamboo instrument, repeated in quick succession for several seconds, had come in time for every man and animal to be rushed out of sight under the sheltering trees.

11
» » ASIS OUTPOST

As the first pale grey rim of light appeared in the east, eight shadowy forms came out from the trees surrounding the clearing in the deserted *barrio*. They walked toward the river carrying two long, bulky objects unidentifiable in the half light. As the waters edge they stopped and seconds later, two large *bancas*, hidden in the jungle for the night, were slipped quietly into the stream.

Two details of men, one from MISSION ISRM, the other from Major Ruffy's Guerilla Fighters, took their places in the boats with Commander Rowe, Lieutenant Hernandez, Sergeant Berg, and Mang Pedro and shoved off, pushing hard toward Mt. Bacó.

Soon the rosy light of the morning sun falling on the river, the trees and the overhanging vines, painted a picture few men are ever privileged to see—and having seen—never forget. There are supposed to be some ten thousand flowering plants in the Philippines and there must be very few of them not found along the banks of the Asis River. Literally thousands of exotic blossoms of every imaginable color hung from the branches of the trees or clung to the tangled *lianas* swinging from tree to tree or branch to branch. Scattered among the deeper green of the leafy trees were *nipa* palms and the taller coconut palms, their smooth grey-green trunks curved by years of winds blowing in from the sea. Romping along the trunks were hundreds of the ubiquitous little monkeys, chattering noisily and blinking in the sun. The morning chorus of the trilling birds rose clear and beautiful over the humming sound of the insects, heard later when the birds had stopped their songs—and all through the night. The long, moss-covered air roots of the mangrove trees dipped deep into the dark green water and in its murky depths lurked crocodiles.

As they rounded a deep bend in the river, Mang Pedro said, "Behind those tall trees is the plantation of my good friend, Juan. I used to visit him here before the war."

"I know Mang Juan," said one of the guerilla boys. "He is a good man, and loyal too."

Commander Rowe had been looking appraisingly at the extended neck of land in the curve of the river, almost surrounded by water. "Slow it down, Men," he said. "This strikes me as a good spot for an outpost. What do you think, Mang Pedro?"

The old man was silent for a moment, then nodded his head and said, "I think you are right, Sir. Very good place." Turning to the native boy who had spoken earlier, he said, "You know the place, Julio. What do you think?"

"It is a natural for an outpost," said the alert young man quickly. "A good, deep river landing, hills back of water on three sides, difficult to approach except by the river, and easy to guard. Mang Juan raises much food for sale, too. Better he sell it to friends than take it to market and have the Japs get it on the way."

"I think we should stop and see your friend, Mang Pedro," said Rowe.

Mang Juan was not hard to find. He was sitting on a small platform at the boat landing, sad-eyed and dejected. As the boat came to a stop, some of the men called out a greeting in Tagalog. He replied with a solemn welcome and asked them to tie up the boat and come ashore.

Mang Pedro stepped ashore first and it was obvious from the tone of their voices and the firm handclasp that the two men were good friends. Mang Juan asked about a mutual acquaintance and Mang Pedro inquired first about the family and then asked about local conditions, enemy patrols, etc.

"No *Hapónés* long time now," said Mang Juan. "Three, maybe four months now. First they come to search for food and guns. They take everything ready for harvest. Then all the chickens they can catch, all the pigs they can see, all my cows that give milk—and now they kill my *cambing*." He broke off in anger and frustration. Mang Pedro then reached out and put a hand on his shoulder and said, "Is very hard, my friend, I know. I have seen many others lose a great deal, but I see my friends die too. You are alive, you have your wife and children. Many of our friends do not."

"What you say is true," said Mang Juan, "Just the same what I would give to see those *tina ma-an* ..." He was still too angry and hurt to go on, even to curse them.

"Ask him if he minds if we look at his place, Mang Pedro," said Rowe.

Hernandez listened carefully as the two men talked and in a few moments Mang Pedro said, "He does not mind, Sir. He says to walk up the path and see his gardens and his fruit trees."

The other man spoke again and Mang Pedro translated, "He says we are welcome to anything from the gardens or the groves."

"*Salamat Po,*" (Thank you very much), said Hernandez, and he and the commander turned and walked away from the pathetic scene to leave the two old friends alone for a little while.

As they walked away, Rowe said, "Al, what's a *cambing?*" Al laughed. "A milk goat," he said, feeling a little ashamed for laughing. "And I'm sure it's not funny to him." "Obviously," said Rowe, laughing too. "But how broken up can a fellow get over a damned old nanny goat?"

"It's probably not the goat. It's the milk supply he's worried about."

"What the hell do you suppose happened to his goat? He said there hadn't been any Japs here for four months."

"I don't know," said Al. "We'll ask him when we go back." The guerilla boy had been correct about the place. Growing in well cultivated plots were *camotes, pechay* (lettuce cabbage) tomatoes and other vegetables they did not know. Nearby were fine large bananas and mango trees heavy with rich, luscious fruit much like a peach but sweeter and more pronounced in flavor. Farther on was a field of sugar cane and to one side a rice paddy. Here and there an enterprising pullet advertised her wares and fat, white ducks waddled along the path ahead of them or took off for a swim in the *carabao* wallow where several of the plantation animals lay sleeping in the sun.

They walked back to the others and Hernandez complimented Mang Juan on his fine gardens and beautiful plantation. "I've been wondering, Mang Juan, perhaps I misunderstood you. I thought you said there had been no Jap patrols for a long time, but you say they killed your *cambing*. I don't understand."

Mang Juan shook his head solemnly. "No. No *Hapónes* long time. But *Hapónes*—crocodiles all the same." Seeing that his visitor still did not understand, he explained, "First, Sir, they come and take everything. They take my crops. They take my gun, my ammunition—whatever they can find. For a long time, every time a crop is ready for harvest, they come back. Now they not come any more. Maybe they forget about me. Maybe they dead. I hope so. But after they take my gun, the crocodiles they get worse and worse. Come with me. I show you."

They walked to the river bank and about seventy-five yards down around the point of land formed by the bend in the stream. On one side stretched a broad, graveled, beachlike shore. There they were, dozens of them. From this year's babies to a huge, weird-looking, wrinkled, old reptile, the grandmother of them all, slithering lazily in and out of the water or lying sleepily in the sun.

"There she is," he said, pointing accusingly at the old one. "Old Bertha."

It was Old Bertha, immense and horrible in her bulk and gruesomeness, who was directly responsible for his tragedy. But it was the Japs' fault that she was there. Then he told them. All her life the little *cambing* had gone down to the river for water. She had loved to romp in the sunshine along the shallow beach. "More than once I warned her," he said. "Stay away from her, little *cambing*, some day she will catch you in her big old jaws."

But the *cambing* still delighted in frolicking just out of her reach. Today she had played too close and Old Bertha had caught her—closed her jaws relentlessly—held her under the water until she drowned and then eaten her with gusto, stopping only to snap fiercely at any of the others who tried to steal a mouthful from her.

"But where do the Japs come in?" asked Rowe.

Mang Juan looked at him as though amazed at his stupidity then replied in broken Tagalog and English, "They took my gun!"

Suddenly seeing the .45 in Rowe's holster in a new role, his tone changed. "That is fine gun you have, Sir. Would you—Sir, will you kill her—*ah diablo* (the old devil) for me? It will no bring back my *cambing*—but I no have to look at her murderer."

Why shouldn't he shoot the old croc? Obviously it would give the poor fellow a good deal of satisfaction—almost as much as shooting a Jap. For the first time, Mang Juan smiled as he saw the commander reach for his .45 and fire two shots. Mang Juan's "old devil" had eaten her last meal, and because of that it was to be several hours before scouting party No. 1 would eat their next one.

Sergeant Berg and No. 2 party, following by the prescribed two hours in the second boat, with the heavier equipment, had reached a deep S-curve in the river when they heard two shots. Instantly they were alert. WHAT HAD HAPPENED?

"There's very little chance of it being a civilian gun around here," said one Guerilla. "The yellow bastards searched every house in the first two months of the war. They took every weapon and all ammunition and then made it a death penalty to have a gun in your possession."

"Then it IS bad," said Berg. "Our men would only have fired in self defense. That's the CO's orders."

"But those shots were close," he continued. "Our men should be a long way upstream from here."

"Unless they've been caught by an enemy patrol," said the guerilla fighter. He had passed by where those patrols had dealt with their victims. "If they recognized your leaders, those two shots might have—"

Suddenly Sergeant Berg sprang into action. "My God, Men, what're we sitting here for? Let's find out!"

As they pulled in toward the bank the guerilla leader said to two of his men, "You hide the boat and the gear, and DON'T let anything happen to that gear. I'm holding you responsible for it," and there was no doubt that he meant it. "Wait here."

As they touched the bank, Sergeant Berg, Sergeants Domingo Logan and Vidal Alvarez jumped from the boat and pulled themselves up the slippery bank. The guerila men were close behind as Berg said, "Let's go."

The men fanned out, in pairs, and worked their way steadily up stream just inside the jungle which was very dense at that point. They kept a sharp lookout in every direction, but could see no trace of their own party and no indication of an enemy patrol. After a while Berg said, "They couldn't have been this far away."

"Could they have been back of us?" said Sergeant Logan. "The shots came from this direction," said Berg.

"That's the way it sounded to me too—but where?"

Twenty-five yards farther they would have seen the second bend which, as the river runs, was probably a mile and a half from where they heard the shots; but as the crow flies—or a gunshot sounds, it was less than a quarter of a mile.

Meanwhile, back at the plantation it was agreed that this was a perfect spot for the first outpost. Knowing what might happen to Mang Juan and his family if anyone discovered that he had helped them, they offered to rent his place or buy it outright. He shook his head, "No, Sir, no money for helping my country. My place is yours as long as you need it. My boys catch pig now. We roast him with *camotes*. We have fine feast."

To the commander it was more important that the native people realize that they had not come to take what they could get. He said, "We appreciate your generosity, Mang Juan, but our food is coming soon." He looked at his watch. "They should have been here before now. I wonder what's keeping them."

An hour later, with no sign of No. 2 party, the guerilla leader with Rowe's group, sent two of his boys back downstream to look for them. Another two hours went by and they began to be very uneasy, not only for No. 2 party but for the searchers as well. Finally the men came back. They had gone all the way back to where they had last seen No. 2 party. There was no sign of them anywhere and no indication of their having beached their boat, but that didn't mean a thing. There shouldn't have been. Again there was the question, WHAT COULD HAVE HAPPENED? A party of that size, trained as those men were, didn't just disappear.

Having set up a perimeter of defense, there was little that No. 1 party could do, now that it was really dark, except to keep a sharp lookout on the river so the others would not pass by if they came upstream. They built a fire and sat down to wait. Mang Juan sent down a fine basket of fruit in lieu of the feast he had wanted to give them. When his boys had gone back and the fruit had disappeared like magic, one of the ISRM men said, "Don't we wish we hadn't been quite so noble about that feast now, Sir?"

"No we don't," said Rowe. "It's much more important that Mang Juan have a good taste in his mouth than that you have yours full of food. Anyway you'll get fat if you eat all the time. You'll be no good on the trail."

"We won't have enough strength to GET on the trail," groaned another as though in misery.

Someone else joined in with, "But wasn't that wonderful roast pig and *camotes* we had on Wrong River Island, Sir?" You guys should have been there. That was really great." "OK, you Fellows, I'm sure this hurts me worse than it does you," said Rowe laughing.

Suddenly there was a signal from the first line sentinel. The kidding was over. They sat listening, tense and silent.

For hours No. 2 party had waited for some word of the others. There was no point in waiting longer. They decided upon action. They would start a second reconnaissance. If their men had been taken prisoner, and they must have been or someone would have made it back to warn them, perhaps they could find the enemy camp. There would be no reason for an enemy camp to be dark. They were in possession here.

Agreeing on their plan of action, they started upstream again. When they had passed a little beyond the point they had reached the first time, the guerilla beside Sergeant Berg said, "Listen. Do you hear the difference in the sound of the animals? They're disturbed about something."

A moment later they saw the dim light of a campfire. About the same time, the outer guards detected something moving in the bushes and sounded an alert—one familiar to all. Then they knew. Someone in each group recognized someone in the other. There were shouts of recognition—questions—recriminations.

"You idiots, you stupid bastards, where have you been all day? Why didn't you come on with the chow?"

"Where have WE been? We've been looking for YOU, expecting to find you dead or tied to a tree somewhere with the ants eating you."

"What do you mean looking for us? We've been right here all day, waiting for you."

"Well where IS the chow? My belly thinks my throat's cut."

"You should be bitching about chow," said Berg. "We've been crawling this whole damn area on our bellies for eight hours looking for you—thinking you'd been shot. Why didn't you send a runner back?"

"Runner, hell!" said one of the guerilla searchers. "I rowed up and down that goddam river for twenty miles looking for you."

"And what do you mean SHOT?" said Rowe. "We didn't hear any shots."

NO ONE in No. 2 party was buying that one. With his teeth very close together, but with the discipline of 18 years of soldiering behind him, Sergeant Berg said, very calmly, "Maybe you didn't hear them, Sir. But I know a gunshot when I hear one—and I did."

Then someone in No. 1 party remembered and cried out, "Commander, YOU fired the shots, Sir."

A roar of laughter followed and No. 2 party heard about Old Bertha. The tension was broken and the commander said sheepishly, "I'm sorry, Men. But for hours we've—well all right—we've been worried as hell about what had happened to you. The men went miles back down the river looking for you and well, I'm just sorry. That's all I can say except—" He grinned that funny, onesided grin that often came when he was about to pull something on someone or was a little bit embarrassed. "Except that now you see what can come of disobeying orders—EVEN YOUR OWN."

Early next morning temporary HQs were established at the plantation house where the men who would be permanent party were quartered. Runners were sent back to call up a guerilla unit to help with the activation of the post and set up a perimeter of defense. Big, handsome Sergeant Logan was placed in command of the activation of Asis Outpost.

12
»» TO THE RIM OF THE WORLD

A pink glow was beginning to show above the tops of the tall trees at the plantation outpost when a cleancut, stalwart, young German trader (it said in his travel papers) stood beside a large native *banca*, ready to shove off. He was surrounded by a healthy looking crew of young *cargadorés*. His crewmen were smart boys—as good as the radio and intelligence schools at AIB could turn out, together with some of Major Ruffy's best trained Guerilla Fighters. Their travel papers indicated that they were accompanying the trader to attend to business interests in the north of Mindoro and were now enroute via the coast.

These men had a dual purpose in the North, not stated in their papers. GHQ wanted photographic coverage of the big gun locations on Verde Islands and other installations in strategic Verde Passage, the natural sea lane from the Pacific to the Orient—a vital east-west link between San Bernardino Strait and the South China Sea, the gateway to Manila.

There was no doubt in Jerry Berg's mind that he was just the boy to get it for them, and there was little reason for anyone to argue the point. Photography had been his hobby for years and anything he might have lacked before, either in know-how or equipment had been amply supplied at AIB.

The first step toward the eventual radio network they would establish surrounding the HQs of the enemy high command in Manila, would be to establish Coast Watcher and Mobile Radio Stations along the north Mindoro coast. Hidden under a false bottom in the *banca*, with a layer of fruit and vegetables for camouflage, along with the photographic equipment was the radio gear to accomplish that phase of their mission.

Rowe, Hernandez and Berg agreed that having lost a full day on the

Wrong River expedition and now another halfday at the outpost, there was not time for the sergeant to go on the Mt. Bacó reconnaissance. He would take his men in one *banca* and start at once for the North, while the others continued upstream.

As the men picked up the oars, the trader called out to a blond "German trader" stepping into the second *banca*, "III bet you the first photo taken of the Jap's big guns on Verde Islands, that you won't be ready to report on what we bring back."

"I'll take that bet," said the blond man heartily. "That lüger of mine that's buried at Pandan says we will."

"It's a deal," shouted the first man. Already his boat was out in the swift current heading downstream.

In addition to the actual work required, their mission involved a 90-mile march through the jungle along the coast, and return, probably by the same route. The commander was willing to part with the lüger to see the sergeant back, his mission accomplished, by the time they were ready to report to GHQ, for he anticipated making contact with KAZ-Darwin in a very few days.

Minutes after Sergeant Berg's party was on the way, Rowe's men dipped their oars into the water and started toward Mt. Bacó. In this party were several of the guerillas, Zamora, Mang Pedro and two of the Wrong River scouts. They followed the river as far as possible and then took off on foot across a clearing and several open fields. Suddenly they were engulfed in deep jungle, inhabited by thousands of the inevitable little brown monkeys.

About noon they came out into a relatively sparsely wooded area and a cool, clear running stream. The day was very hot and they had almost emptied their canteens. Hot, tired, and thirsty from trying to conserve their water until they knew they had more, they filled their canteens and treated the water for drinking. Then they took off their clothes and went for a swim in the clear, cool stream. After a meal of the water and some D-ration, they went on their way refreshed.

Once more they were in deep jungle, with low-lying creeping vines and as always, the noisy, scolding monkeys. There, the guides told them, sudden, violent tropical storms often made a roaring river of the area within a few minutes. Obviously, anyone trying to traverse the area with a heavy load would be in difficulty. On the next trip they would be transporting not only heavy, but valuable and irreplaceable equipment. Also, later, their agents would require a quick, all-weather route to the main HQs. They gave up the route at once and started back to where the lowlands had begun, in search of a higher, safer route. Almost as they turned, just such a downpour as the guides had described came down upon them. Even from the point to which they had backtracked, they had difficulty struggling through the water and twisted runners (from which the natives cure their jungle twine), now lifted off the jungle floor by the swift, swirling water. Steadily it rose—knee deep—hip deep—WAIST DEEP as they staggered to safety. A few more minutes making up their minds and MISSION ISRM might have been without a CO or an exec. Water, for which men on Bataan had died, seemed to haunt their every major move.

Just prior to the storm the two local guides had become involved in a heated argument over alternate routes. One of the guerillas decided they had gone far enough with it and, in a dialect he had no idea either of the *americanos* had ever heard, said, "Listen you goddam dopes, if you're going to lead this party, you'd better shut up and do it before the *americanos* get mad and hire one of these monkeys to replace you."

Wretched with fatigue, their shoes and clothing heavy with water, they struck out in another direction toward higher ground. They followed a shallow ledge to the foot of the first low mountain range, where they took refuge for the night in a solitary *nipa* hut. With the information given them at AIB and the combined knowledge of the guides and the guerillas, they felt that they had found a passable route over the first low range and up to the higher range beyond. There they hoped to find a place suitable for their main radio transmitter.

From the hut they sent back runners to Asis Outpost to summon a radio group forward, with instructions to try for contact with KAZ-Darwin, from the top of the first range. The chances were not good—but it was worth a try.

Early in the morning they started on up from the hut, the last indication of human habitation in that wild, mountain area. At the top of the first range, they glimpsed something of the grandeur that awaited them from the top of the higher one. On the last few miles they were resting fifteen minutes out of every hour, and blessing the rugged training they had cursed while they were getting it.

On they went to the top of the highest peak. Suddenly they were no longer tired! They stood enthralled at the magnificent panorama—purple mountains, deep verdant, shaded valleys, blue sky and bluer sea. The tiny island of Pandan lay like a fragment of jade on the blue water, silhouetted against the pink haze which sometimes obscured it from view even with their high-powered lenses.

Mt. Bacó was probably another twenty miles inland, another twenty miles of rugged, jungle-covered mountains from their projected activities. There was no need to go farther. Here, at the rim of the world they would build it—THE TOWER OF ISRM.

13
» » THE TOWER OF ISRM

Probably the feature that made Commander Rowe and Lieutenant Hernandez first realize the value of the TOWER OF ISRM was its full circle of vision. What a spot for observation of His Majesty's Imperial Fleet and Air Force—the top of the world!

A topographic model of the TOWER OF ISRM and the surrounding area looked like a huge *sombrero*. The tower mountain rose sharply out of the encircling valley, making the crown of the hat, with the lower, surrounding ridge forming the wide, rolling brim. A break toward the south, the dip in the brim, provided the channel through which ISRM radio subsequently was beamed out to Australia.

The TOWER, built at the top of the peak under a natural camouflage of trees, rocks, and vines, consisted of a complete Detachment HQs. An Orderly Room, Operations Office, and the Mac Arthur Room stood along a single level with hidden windows. An adjustable antenna on the radio tower, high among the tall tree tops, slipped up and down, in and out of the trees and the sight of enemy air patrols.

Clustered about the Detachment HQs, one level below, stood four sentinel guard stations, quarters for officers and men, and farther down at the bottom of the mountain in the rolling brim, were four villages of Guerilla Fighters and the 'little men," tiny, pygmy tribesmen of the wild mountain regions of Mindoro.

The sweep from the bottom of the crown to the roll of the brim of this hat-like terrain was covered on the east, south and west by swampland, and deep jungle stretched away to the north. The dip on the south ended in a sheer cliff, dropping several hundred feet into swampland, covered with rank *cogón* grass, eight to ten feet tall, razor-sharp and swarming with mosquitoes. In the event of a surprise attack by the enemy, which seemed unlikely with the four guerilla villages below, the swamp would serve as a disposal area for certain devices which must not fall into the hands of the enemy.

In the Orderly Room a sergeant did round-the-clock duty. As their activities progressed, the watches of the night often surpassed the daylight hours in action and excitement. Once the channels of communication were established between their HQs and the Batangas and Luzon areas, there was an almost constant stream of men bringing information or departing with orders for new activities.

The Conference Room, used for personnel meetings and instruction, was a busy spot from the beginning, and later, as the undercover forces throughout the islands increased in number and activity, was never empty.

General MacArthur and the Joint Chiefs-of-Staff had planned their campaign in the Pacific around coordinated land, sea, and air forces. The combined forces which would stage the reinvasion of the Philippines would require Naval data, including enemy shipping lanes, harbor defenses, and ship repair facilities. They would require information on air fields, activities and facilities. Particularly important was target information of every kind. An excerpt from a message received from GHQ in mid-August, 1944, indicated the promptness with which such information had to be handled.

. . . RE: AIR WARNING—REPORTS WILL BE PASSED ON YOUR NORMAL FREQUENCY AND MUST REACH THIS HQS WITHIN TEN MINUTES OF TIME OF DETECTION TO BE OF OPERATIONAL VALUE.

Rowe and Hernandez had been put through intensive indoctrination in Army Intelligence (G-2) to familiarize them with the basic requirements and specific techniques employed in obtaining and transmitting such information in time for effective action against the enemy. In classes in the Conference Room at ISRM they passed on that training to new recruits in undercover work, trained them in the requirements and techniques and drilled them until they were ready to go into the field as efficient secret agents. Radio operators, for example, were in short supply. Many of them had to be trained rapidly as the network grew.

Training men to make observations of military operations and installations and then translate those observations into maps, drawn to scale of sufficient accuracy to guide air attack, strafing or bombing was an exacting task. One single feature omitted, even the hour of observation, could render the finest piece of work, and perhaps a week's time, useless.

Without the hundreds of such maps prepared by the agents who took their places in the channels of communication, MISSION ISRM could not have been accomplished.

Planning of missions and briefing of personnel before departure was done in Operations. Leading from there down to the Radio Room and Officers Quarters, was a camouflaged outside stairway. At the intersection of the stairway and an underground corridor, street markers pointed the way to Tokyo and to Broadway. At another passage, a bulletin board held Orders of the Day, Duty Rosters, and the latest news bulletins. There the men first saw such headlines as MUSSOLINI IS SLAIN—HITLER A SUICIDE—TOJO A SUICIDE—GERMANY FALLS.

The Photo Lab under the supervision of Sergeant Berg, housed the photographic equipment and operating area for processing photographic records for the expedition. In that rude darkroom where they had only to WAIT for the darkness—and sometimes hurry to finish while it lasted, they developed and printed probably the nearest to a complete ensemble of photographs in existence of Southern Luzon,

Verde Island Passage, Northern Mindoro, and Manila Bay. The clear water from a nearby mountain stream was so clean and chemically pure that it met the exacting requirements of the photo lab without filtering.

Just around the corner from the Photo Lab was the entrance to "Savellana & Delfin's Underground Warehouse," a dugout in the mountainside on the same level with the Sentinel Guard Station.

If ever there had been trails upon these mountains before that July day in 1944, when Commander Rowe and Lieutenant Hernandez led the recon party to the site chosen for THE TOWER, they had long since been obliterated by Nature's busy hands. Probably no human beings other than the little Mangyan people, tiny remnants of pre-historic man, had ever inhabited the area. So for the gratifying speed in transporting the tons of equipment and supplies through difficult bogs and swamps, over rugged mountain terrain, under frequent enemy air patrol, they were indebted to the skillful *carabao* tenders whose patient little animals, being lowlanders by nature, often suffered for the lack of cooling waterholes.

First to reach THE TOWER after the original reconnaissance had been the *carabao* caravan and the technical men of THE MISSION. The radio men began at once to unpack, inspect, and assemble the equipment that had met with so many hazards on the 4000-mile trip from Brisbane. This was their first opportunity to evaluate the losses and possible damage to the equipment.

By the time the first contingent was ready to leave Asis Outpost for the tower site, volunteers from the guerilla units and from the Mangyans had begun to arrive at the outpost. The coming of the Mangyans was a result of the commander's knowledge of the work of the Director of Non-Christian Tribes on Mindoro Island. Getting word to the director was one of the first duties on his agenda after leaving Pandan. Four of the little men came first, bringing gifts of welcome, and to make certain that they were wanted. Satisfied that they were not only welcome, but needed, they came in companies to help.

There are perhaps 11,000 of these tiny, tribal people indigenous to the island of Mindoro, identified by ethnologists as "a primitive pygmy people, unassimilated descendants of prehistoric immigrants from other Pacific and Indian Ocean islands and the mainland of Asia." The tallest to come to ISRM was not quite four feet. Back at AIB, when the matter of native assistance was under discussion, there arose the inevitable resistance against a possible recurrence of the betrayal of the Philipps party. Commander Rowe was of the opinion that these little people, completely oblivious to the value of money, would not be bought off easily by the enemy. It made little difference to them who was in power, since their normal existence began and ended in their tribal villages far from civilization, but even they resented the Japanese as enemy invaders.

These strange, little, frizzy-headed, black fellows had an amazing capacity for detecting the approcah of a distant airplane. They worked at the job in teams of four. At the first awareness of an approaching plane, which they never were able to explain to anyone else, two of them would fall to the ground, pressing their ears hard against the earth. The other two would scramble up the tallest tree and in complete silence, hold fast to the topmost part of the trunk. Soon a few signals would pass between the two pairs and they would come up pointing, invariably in the direction of the approaching plane. In the long move from Asis Outpost to THE TOWER, their warnings came in every instance in time to disperse the *carabao* convoy before the fast, enemy recon planes could spot it.

As the caravoy (*carabao* convoy) approached the site, a heavy rain soaked the clay of the mountainside to a slick, gummy mass. The commander was climbing up the trail with a guerila aide, some distance ahead of the heavily loaded animals. The thick, inflexible soles of his heavy boots began to slip in the miry clay. He went down to his knees, still skidding backward, clutching at rocks and bushes, anything to stop the slide. Getting back to his feet, he looked down at his clothes and hands covered with the sticky mud. His only comment to his waiting companion whose mountain climbing experience had been both extensive and recent, was, "Goddammit—all this had better pay off."

A few days later when the commander's quarters had been finished on the second level of the Detachment HQs, he looked out one morning and saw several of the little men cutting and shaping steps in the mountainside with great precision, from his quarters to the HQs, probably fifty steps up the hill. Realizing the time it would take to do the job as they were doing it, he spoke to Captain Bill Dodson, who had come from Major Ruffy's unit with a large guerilla force, to do the excavation for the HQs construction. "Did you tell the little guys to make the steps, Captain?" he asked.

"No, Sir," said the captain. "It was their own idea. They wanted to do it for you. They were out there almost an hour before reveille."

"Well, can't you—don't misunderstand me, Captain, I think it's swell, but could you get it across to them not to build a botanical garden, just cut some steps?"

The captain smiled. "You understand, Sir, it's because—well they're doing it for YOU and besides, they're really artists at heart."

Amused and a little embarrassed at the sentiment, Rowe said, "Well, tell them not to do it with their hearts, just use their hands."

What could you do when people were like that? Later, when the food supply dwindled far below requirements, the

Mangyan detail almost always found some kind of food to keep them from actual hunger When the guerilla outfit was there in full strength and an Intelligence class was in training, three hundred men often answered roll call. That called for food! Whatever the Mangyans had, they wrought from the jungle. Their methods were ingenious. Trapping a flock of birds sometimes netted a meal. The hearty fruits of certain trees or vegetables growing wild on the valley floor could be mixed with the rice, which often was scarce. Sometimes they brought a deer, sometimes a wild boar. Rarely did they return to camp empty handed.

One night the commander and the lieutenant had kept the men in a large, intensive Intelligence class hours beyond the usual break time, to keep their minds off the fact that there probably would be no evening mess. Captain Dodson had returned with his men from a long march to the northeast, where they had cleaned out an enemy platoon which had been causing trouble. They had arrived at about the usual time for evening mess. Mang Pedro, who had long since taken over the responsibility of the kitchen, had been weighing the problem of what he could feed the men. He had a choice—Parsons or one of his trained MP's. Parsons was his old pet goat that Sergeant Berg had brought up on a trip to Pandan. Mang Pedro had been worried at that point that Parsons might find his way to the Jap mess kettles. The MP's were little brown monkeys he had caught and trained to keep the other monkeys away from the food in the kitchen. Capturing them had been simple, for the monkey is an easy prey. Once he closes his little black fist on food, he will not let go of it. A small round hole cut in a coconut so that the round piece will fall back into the shell, will get his hand inside; but nothing will get it out.

A few coconuts chained down would have supplied plenty of meat; but so many of the men had trained them for mascots and to keep guard over things they wanted watched. "I don't know, Sergeant. I just don't think the men could relish it," said Mang Pedro as one of the little beasts came up and sat on his shoulder, chattering away in his squeaky little voice. "They're so damn human, it would be like eating a child."

But the Mangyans saved him the painful choice by hurrying in as fast as they could, with the load they carried, a choice young deer.

Obviously, all volunteers who reached Asis Outpost had to be thoroughly screened. Many were not permitted to come on to THE TOWER. The never-to-be-forgotten Captain Dodson had been among the earlier arrivals whose credentials were unquestionable. Bill was a handsome, fierce-fighting mestizo and one of Major Ruffy's outstanding officers. His American father had found both fortune and romance in his profession of mining engineer in the islands and had remained there to enjoy the life he found so much to his liking.

"El Capitan," with his square shoulders, curly, black hair, eyes almost as black, his deep cleft chin and flashing smile would have met even Hollywood's requirements for the role. He too was a graduate mining engineer and, typical of many of the men found leading the guerilla groups, he possessed rare ability, courage and finesse—everything required to command a rugged guerilla unit or to meet high-level military personnel on their own ground.

Island-born, Bill had no language problem. No time-honored custom ever upset his plans. Invariably he was a step ahead of the things which might have thrown a man with a lesser knowledge of the people, their customs and superstitions, or without his sympathy and affection for them.

As though all that were not enough, Bill brought with him his orderly, Pablo, a flat-footed, powerful-legged little dwarf, whose unusual capacities and equally unusual duties would have distinguished him in any company of men. Pablo strummed a haunting, sweet-toned guitar to accompany his plaintive island love songs beside the campfire on the trail or in moments of stolen pleasure at retreats along the way, which may have served the purpose of his fellows better than his own.

But it was nothing so ordinary as music that distinguished Pablo. He was a very fast, very excellent swimmer, faster even than the crocodiles. Often the captain's men would have to cross a river. Likely as not, no boats were available. Like the Asis River, most of the others were infested with crocs. Often there was no indication that they were there; but that did not mean that they were not. At Dodson's "All right, Pablo. Get ready," Pablo would strip off his scanty little garments. He could have no interference in his work. Dodson would pick up a small stone and skip it along the surface or toss it into what appeared to be a deep hole. This usually brought the crocs to the surface in seconds. If none appeared, Dodson would say, "All right, Pablo. You try it now."

Once Pablo tilted his head to look up at the captain and said, very seriously, "That was very small stone, Sir. Maybe it didn't wake up the crocs. Maybe you could try bigger one."

"It was big enough. Into the water now," said Dodson, smiling down at the little fellow who knew without doubt, that his "capitan" would be watching every move.

Once when the crocs were hiding in the deeper water, Pablo came literally leaping back to the bank with a croc close behind. As usual, the captain was there, with outstretched hands, to pull him safely up the bank. Maybe it was because he knew he could—or because his captain expected it—or because never for a moment did either of them become careless. Whatever it was, Pablo always won.

Captain Dodson arrived at THE TOWER the first time, just as they were ready to start construction of the permanent HQs of Station ISRM. Under the natural camouflage of trees, the whole mountain became a seething mass of *carabaos* and men. On the trail they moved like a huge company of giant ants, up the mountain and back down again to the valley.

With the technical direction of the radio men and the guerilla interpreters who spoke the Mangyan language, the little black men shinnied up the towering trees to set up the sliding antenna, which moved up for use and down for hiding from enemy patrols.

A prerequisite for radio is, of course, electrical power and theirs had to be powerful enough to carry their beam two thousand miles to Darwin. No high tension lines marred the landscape of the mountains of Mindoro. Their power had to be generated on the spot, with a simple, bicycle-like device and a pair of strong legs. Fortunately there were plenty of strong legs and until they had established contact with KAZ—Darwin, most of them weren't going anywhere.

On the afternoon of 17 July (they had landed at Pandan on the ninth), a temporary Radio Room was opened up in a tent. A generator was set up and the pumping began. While the men were still busy with the Mangyan men setting up the antenna, Corporal Barcenas and Corporal Felix Reyes settled down to taking turns at some serious pumping. While they pumped, Sergeant Carillo and the talented "Doc" Pascau, who doubled as dentist, radio man, medic and in any other capacity requiring skill and ingenuity, along with Corporal Bugarin, inspected and checked the radio gear as it was unpacked.

After about an hour, the hands on the indicator on the foot-powered generator began to climb slowly upward—1—2—3—4—5. They could open up! They tuned in a receiving set. Broadcasts from Chungking, Tokyo, Hong Kong, Singapore, Manila, practically any city in the Orient and in almost any language.

At AIB they had been assigned a frequency and a time to communicate with KAZ. At that time on the first day, with the indicator barely below the recommended "5," they made the first attempt. For the eight days since their landing, there was plenty to report. Sergeant Berg's party was off to the north, Asis Outpost had been activated, the crew of an enemy plane had been captured, along with their maps and weapons, after their plane had crashed almost at the door of the outpost office, and the TOWER OF ISRM was well under way.

All were eager to see if the first call of "ISRM calling KAZ" would get through to GHQ. The hour passed with no contact. Failure to make the first contact, with the power at the minimum level, was disappointing, but nothing to worry about.

On the second day with the indicator well above the mark, they waited eagerly for the hour to arrive. Once more the radio men seated themselves at the long bamboo tables made for their use. "ISRM calling KAZ. ISRM calling KAZ," over and over again until the hour passed. It was discouraging; but when they left Australia, AIB had said, "We won't expect to hear from you in less than a month." Maybe they were on the air too soon. KAZ might not be listening yet. Maybe tomorrow—

Every one was busy. There was no time to sit and worry about not contacting KAZ, but there was no doubt but that it was on everyone's mind. The radio men had taken a vow to have no haircuts until they had sent a message to KAZ and received one in return. Now the others began to kid them about joining the House of David.

On the third day, with plenty of power generated and the equipment thoroughly re-checked, they tried again. When the third call had gone unanswered they sent a message through—but still only impenetrable silence from KAZ.

After the second failure to make contact, the men who had checked the gear on arrival, asked another team to go over it with them. They made an almost microscopic examination of every piece, every connection and every part of the antenna, and now they had failed again.

That night the commander talked to the radio men. "Are you satisfied that the equipment is OK?" he asked.

"Sir," said Sergeant Carillo, who had helped inspect the equipment both times, "I'd stake my life on it."

"OK," said Rowe. "At first I thought the trouble might be here. Now I wonder. It could be storms between here and Australia. I want you to stay on the air from now on until we find out. Set up a weather chart. Get out your standard wind charts and check whatever weather reports you can pick up, against them. See if you can come up with anything." The weather check proved nothing. No storms were reported, but in that great distance there might be any number of unreported storms.

Maybe it was the location. Maybe it wasn't so good after all. Rowe and Hernandez talked it over and before they were through, could almost see the whole camp being moved on to Mt. Bacó. "Dammit, Al, do you suppose they knew something at AIB that they didn't tell us, something that caused them to pick Mt. Bacó?"

"My God, George, I don't know. I hadn't thought of that. Let's ask Dodson. He's a mining man. He'd know of any mineral deposits that could cause the trouble."

Rowe got directly to the point when Dodson came in. "Bill, what do you know about these mountains?"

"Well, I know a good deal about them, Commander. What specifically, did you want to know?"

"I want to know if there are mineral deposits here that might be grounding our radio—keeping us from getting out. We can get all those stations in. Why can't we get out?"

"I'm no radio expert, Sir. There's a hell of a lot I don't know about it; but I do know these mountains. There are no mineral deposits here, or anywhere south of here on this island, which should interfere with radio transmission."

"You're sure of that, Captain?"

"I'm sure, Sir," said Dodson looking the commander straight in the eye.

As time went by, George Rowe was to learn that if Bill Dodson said "I'm sure of it," he could be sure of it also.

"We're narrowing it down, Al," said Rowe. "The men say the equipment is in perfect condition. Bill says it can't be mineral deposits. With the gear we have, we've GOT to get through. That's all there is to it."

But they didn't get through the next day—nor the next. By that time the permanent Radio Room was finished. They had the best equipment that science and industry had produced. There were four ATR's, two 88's for short range intercommunication in the ISRM network, the powerful NEI's, and three BC's for traffic to Darwin.

On the seventh day, the commander and the lieutenant went down to the Radio Room at broadcast time. They waited silently while the operators tuned in and started calling KAZ, hoping, maybe praying a little, that this time there would be an answer.

Walking slowly back to their quarters at the end of the hour, they heard a man say to another, "I'll bet you 10 to 1 my name will be the first one up, to go back to Australia for more equipment."

"One of us is wrong," said Hernandez, half aloud.

"Are you all right?" asked Rowe.

"I'm fine," said Hernandez. "Why?"

"Well what the hell did you mean, 'one of us is wrong'?" "Oh that," said Hernandez. "Well I had just made that bet with myself a few minutes ago. So, one of us is wrong." Rowe grinned and shook his head hopelessly. "Sometimes I don't know about you, Fellow. Sometimes I just don't know." They began seriously discussing the possibilities. They had been there perhaps ten minutes when Rowe said, "We'll keep on trying here for a few days. Then if—"

Someone came running wildly up the path that had just been cleared to the new quarters. Villalon stuck his head inside and shouted excitedly, "It's Australia, Sir. KAZ is coming in!"

Back he dashed to the Radio Room directly in front of the commander and the lieutenant, military regulations completely forgotten in the excitement.

They were halted just inside the door by the tense silence as the operator strained every nerve to pick up the message coming in. Sergeant Carillo finished copying the message, jerked off his head set, shouting with joy, "It's KAZ all right. They picked us up that first day. They got our message too."

So it hadn't been their equipment. It had been right, from the start!

The first message to penetrate the air waves from ISRM to GHQ—SWPA was dated 19 July 1944, and (decoded) read:

GREETINGS: ISRM RESUMES VICINITY POINT PLANNED. PARTY

SENT NORTH TO PICK SITES CW STATIONS. ALSO PARTY NORTH PHOTOING LUBANG VERDE ETC. INTELL PARTY ALREADY MANILA ARRANGING NET. HEAVY SEAS COLLAPSED RUBBER BOATS. NECESSARY JETTISON MANY RATIONS AMMO ETC. TO SAVE TECHNICAL EQUIPMENT.

Signed/NICHOLSON

It was not until 1700 on 23 July that they received that shot in the arm from KAZ. Instantly they were like wild, happy kids, shouting for joy—pounding each other on the back, calling for the others to hear the news. It was the real McCoy—a message from KAZ to Commander Rowe which read:

ADVICE OF ESTABLISHMENT OF YOUR POSITION HAS BEEN RECEIVED BY ME WITH SATISFACTION. AYE COMMEND YOU AND YOUR OFFICERS AND MEN UPON THE SUCCESSFUL COMPLETION OF THIS PHASE OF YOUR IMPORTANT MISSION.

Signed/DOUGLAS MAC ARTHUR

14
» » UNDERCURRENTS

In August 1944, a survivor of the Major Philipps Expedition found his way to MISSION ISRM. Master Sergeant Alfredo A. Alberto came in via the FFF. He had served 16 months with the expedition and had spent six months as an unattached American soldier, living in the jungle, foraging for food, stealing it from the enemy when there was none to be had elsewhere. He had come in contact with several guerilla outfits and was familiar with their activities as well as local conditions generally. He had also learned a good deal about the enemy, his tactics and some of his weaknesses.

Eventually, however, Sergeant Alberto's greatest contribution to THE MISSION came through his knowledge of electronics engineering. Later as the re-invasion became imminent, their equipment became more worn as well as spread thinner throughout the area network. There were times when only the enginering know-how and the bulldog persistence of Sergeant Alberto kept ISRM on the air—at a time when uninterrupted communication with GHQ was imperative.

A few weeks later, 1st Sergeant Benjamin Harder, another escaped member of that party, following a similar route, reported for duty at THE TOWER. Finally T/Sergeant Vicente Pinuelo, the last surviving enlisted man of the party, reported for duty with THE MISSION. He was soon back on the road to the northern Mindoro area, equipped with a mobile transmitter to cover the territory he knew well from the undercover side.

The Philipps Expedition, unlike MISSION ISRM, had been strictly Army. However, the executive officer, Lieutenant Ruben Songco had received his commission at Annapolis, reporting for duty with the Philippine Army upon news of the Manila attack. He was reported to have escaped the night the station HQs was ambushed, the Major slain and the station captured. Later he was reported to have been wounded and hiding in the wilds of North Mindoro; but all efforts to contact him had failed.

Until mid-summer 1944, radio transmitters not in enemy hands were a scarce commodity in the Philippines. The USAFFE contact had been snuffed out simultaneously with the fall of Corregidor. The capture of the Philipps station left Colonel Wendell W. Fertig in Mindanao and Colonel Kangleon in Leyte, able to make direct contact with GHQ. However, in June 1944, about a month before the landing of MISSION ISRM, Colonel Bernard L. Anderson had received a small set from GHQ in Australia, via submarine, which enabled him to reach a relay station on the Bondoc Peninsula on Southern Luzon, and to report through them to KAZ—Darwin.

Colonel Anderson, like many other outstanding guerilla leaders, was an escaped American officer from Bataan. He had an unusual capacity for selecting and training men for difficult and demanding assignments. His own executive officer, "Bimbo" Manzano, enlisted as a recruit under his command, and earned one promotion after another until at 22, he had risen to the rank of Major.

The name "Anderson" had become a legend in North Luzon. His code name *"Tatang"* was the Pampagna equivalent to "father" and he was held almost in awe by his men.

By the summer of 1944, there were probably 25 recognized guerilla outfits in operation. One of the first to be organized was that of Walter Cushing, later Major Cushing, then a civilian mine operator. Taking his men out of the mine the morning after the attack on Manila, he led them through the province of Abra, where they picked up volunteers, supplying them with arms and equipment from the Philippine Constabulary. On 5 January 1942, the day after the actual fall of Manila, his men began ambushing Japanese trucks and convoys along the coast highway from Lingayen to Manila.

Major Russel Volckmann, a West Point graduate, Regimental Comander (G-2) in the 11th Division, Philippine Army on Bataan, also escaped and became a leader of a considerable guerilla force on Luzon. Volckmann became Lieutenant Colonel and broke his command into seven units, of which Major Lapham led the 6th Division in the northern area of Nueva Ecija, Tarlac, Pangasinan, and Nueva Viscaya.

Captain Peralta, a Philippine Army officer, who by August 1943, had risen to rank of colonel, had assisted in organizing guerilla outfits in Panay, Masbate, Romblon and Palawan Islands, sending supplies and officers to various groups. The supplies were financed in part by the free government on the island of Panay, headed by Tomas Confesor, a popular political leader and educator, called the "Stormy Petrel of the Philippines."

Other well-known operating bands of Guerilla Fighters were those of Bowler, Sinarez, Marking, Valera, The Hunters (formed from the Manila ROTC under Miguel Ver), Abcede-Villamor (Major Villamor having been sent from SWPA in Australia for that purpose).

Two other American Army officers, Smith and Hamner, decided to take their chances in a sailboat to Australia when Corregidor fell. Later both men were returned via submarine to carry on guerilla warfare and Smith eventually became the commanding officer in the island province of Samar.

Another officer named Parsons evacuated to Australia on the *Gripsholm,* returned later and made many subsequent trips back to that country. He became a potent force in the resistance picture.

An outstanding and colorful character was Colonel Wendell W. Fertig, a U. S. Army Reserve officer, who had come to the Philippines as a mining engineer in 1936. Called to active duty in June 1941, with the Corps of Engineers, he had built air fields on Luzon, in Bataan and on Mindanao, finally assuming command of the forward echelon of Engineer Troops in the battles of Bataan. In the last few hours before Bataan fell, Colonel Fertig took a special detachment of Engineers to Corregidor to extend Malinta Tunnel and keep open the heavily bombed road network on the island.

He had been sent to Mindanao to survey airfield construction progress there and was scheduled to proceed to Australia when Corregidor fell. Continuing as Assistant USAFFE Engineer, he soon began assembling an army of guerillas made up of American and Filipino troops who had in one way or another avoided surrender. Fertig's Guerillas began active operations against the Japanese in September 1942, and by early 1944, had regained posession of 90% of the island of Mindanao.

In June 1944, an Intelligence officer, Rosenquist, came by submarine from Australia to join Colonel Fertig's command and another, a U. S. Naval officer, Simmons, came to handle a double assignment of Intelligence and Weather.

Not only had the American and Philippine flags flown over Fertig's HQs throughout the entire occupation, but his troops were dressed in the remnants of official uniforms and fought as uniformed troops, overrun in the Japanese conquest, but NEVER forced to capitulate or recognize the loss of the island of Mindanao by their troops.

At the height of activities at the TOWER OF ISRM, they received much assistance from Colonel Anderson's men, Major Edward Ramsey's outfit, and the Hunters, whose commander, Miguel Ver, gave his life to save his men, holding off an entire enemy platoon with his own fire to cover the retreat of his men. A piece of note paper from his organization, received later at THE TOWER, bore evidence of his character. Printed at the bottom of the sheet were the words,

ONLY THOSE WHO ARE NOT AFRAID TO DIE ARE FIT TO LIVE.

Major Ruffy, commander of the guerilla force which had become a part of MISSION ISRM and which had gained full battle strength, had worked directly with Major Philipps. Many of this group were sent at once to ISRM Intelligence and Radio schools to be trained for specific phases of intelligence in the field.

The women of the Philippines also had their part in the Resistance effort. Facing worse than death if they were caught, they carried food and medicine to the sick and starving survivors of the Bataan Death March. They smuggled whatever they could into the open-air torture chambers of Camp O'Donnel at Tarlac and at Cabanatuan Prison. There, starving men, ill with malaria and other diseases were herded into barracks, two where there should have been one, on bunks of bare bamboo. The only covering they had was their filth-encrusted clothing, with no water to wash either the garments or the raw, infected sores it rubbed.

Most of the time there was not enough water to drink. NEVER was there enough for sanitation. Men were shot for going into the jungle in search of edible roots or small animals to cook with their hopelessly inedequate supply of rice and bayoneted to death for desperate attempts to quench their maddening thirst.

Into such places the Filipina women, dressed as men, took whatever they could to ease the suffering of their own and American POW's. Others managed to get food and money to prisoners on Corregidor, making daring trips at night in small rowboats to where the American POW's were loading scrap metals retrieved from the ruins for shipment to the war industries in Tokyo.

As the enemy bore down upon the cities of the Philippines, nurses fled to the wild, jungle-covered hills from the hospitals and joined the guerilla armies, formed by the escaped American and Philippine Army groups. Establishing crude hospitals under *nipa* shelters, they worked with almost no medical supplies and pitifully inadequate equipment to care for the wounded and the sick.

The guerilla Nurse Corps which came to MISSION ISRM with the first contingent of Major Ruffy's men, in the very early days of THE

TOWER OF ISRM, were splendid examples of the courage and loyalty of these young women. This group of eleven volunteer nurses had been organized and trained by a very capable woman, Mrs. Collado, head nurse in a Manila hospital at the beginning of the war. She was assisted later by two other RN's, from other hospitals, Nurse Vallaruel and Nurse Garcia, who later went on with other similar outfits in need of their services.

With the number of guerilla fighters attached to ISRM HQs by late August 1944, there were always large numbers of men suffering from illness. Malaria and dysentery were the worst offenders. The small hospital was usually overflowing. Seldom were there enough beds and it was not unusual to walk down past the building at sick call and see the ground covered with men who had come for help, but could not sit up while they waited for whatever treatment was available for them.

The only complaint ever heard from the nurses, who often worked round the clock without rest, was against the regulation that every available nurse was to join the men working at confining duties such as map making, etc., in the HQs offices, for a half-hour march each morning. There was little time for recreation, but both officers felt that getting away from the scene of their work for a little while, looking away over the peaks and valleys to the distant sea, talking and laughing with the others for a half-hour period each day was the least that could be done to help keep them and their taut nerves from the breaking point.

There were also women in strategic places in business and in society who became channels of communication for THE MISSION. As time passed, there was scarcely an enemy activity in the Manila, Cavite, Batangas and North Mindoro areas which escaped the watchful eyes of some one of the 3000 men and women drawn from all strata of life and trained for such observation.

It has been said on military authority that no small part of the Allied success in the Pacific was due to the efforts of Coast Watchers. Particularly on the Australian mainland, CW's trained by that country's Naval Intelligence, are credited with having saved the country from air attack and perhaps invasion, reporting with their portable shortwave transmitters, the approach of the enemy sometimes minutes, sometimes hours before they arrived.

In line with the policy of OSRD (Office of Scientific Research and Development) relative to field testing of new scientific devices, MISSION ISRM was given the responsibility of field testing the Radar Detector Unit for operational reconnaissance, not yet released to the Armed Forces. On 1 August 1944, Sergeant Berg reported from their first outlying radio station, J-MAC in the extreme northwestern tip of Mindoro, that they were functioning as Weather Station, Radar Detector Station, Photographic Center, and Radio Transmitter—with two Mobile Units in operation on Luzon.

The loss of so much of their weather equipment in the landing operation was to hamper them all the way. The instruments by which they were making weather observations were ingenious devices improvised by trial and error method, employing what parts they had, some Navy know-how, some knowledge of jungle lore, a hand anemometer, bamboo wind vanes and velocity devices, and a thermometer from a photo kit. Results were surprisingly accurate.

When weather became an Important factor, a thorough check was made of the matériel buried at the Asia River Delta island and a detail sent to unearth and search all supplies on Pandan; but eventually they had no alternative but to radio GHQ this message:

WEATHER KITS MISSING. HOWEVER CAN ACCURATELY IMPROVISE EVERYTHING EXCEPT BAROMETER. TO IMPROVISE PETCOCK WHOSE WEIGHT DETERMINES FREE LIFT OF BALLOONS PLEASE SIGNAL EXACT WEIGHT IN NUMBER UNDISCHARGED CALIBRE TWENTY TWO REPEAT TWENTY TWO BULLETS EQUAL THIS WEIGHT. IF NECESSARY FOR EXACTNESS USE DISCHARGED BULLETS. STILL CHECKING FOR EQUIPMENT.

A few days later this reply came through:

REFER YOUR NUMBER SIXTEEN: NUMBER UNDISCHARGED CALIBRE TWENTY TWO LONG RIFLE CARTRIDGES EQUIVALENT TO WEIGHT OF PETCOCK IS FORTY REPEAT FORTY CARTRIDGES.

Weather info being of such tremendous importance since the air activity was about to begin in the Manila area, GHQ made a special effort to furnish additional equipment. Submarines were still running the blockade, but trips were not frequent from GHQ and the time involved made quick supply impossible. Shortly after the cartridge incident another message came through from KAZ:

THREE UNITS WITH ADEQUATE EQUIPMENT TO INSTALL SIX STATIONS WERE DISCHARGED YOUR AREA. IT IS HOPED THAT ENOUGH WILL BE LOCATED YOUR AREA TO PERMIT THE ESTABLISHMENT OF ONE COMPLETE OBSERVATORY. FAILING THIS, SIX ADDITIONAL UNITS WILL BE DISCHARGED WITH NEXT DELIVERY. SUPPLY YOUR AREA WILL BE IMPOSSIBLE FOR SOME TIME.

GHQ was making urgent requests daily for reports on the contents of Manila Bay, air bases and activities, anti-aircraft, troop, and supply data.

Soon the few men available at ISRM for operation in and around Manila were feeding the vital information to them. From other parts of Mindoro they began to receive messages and runners came from Bongabong, Calapan and Naujan on the east coast and as far south as San José as well as from offshore islands.

As a warning to agents preparing to go to Manila, a message came saying:

> WOMEN SPIES USING LIFE REPEAT LIFE MAGAZINE TO LURE INTEREST AND COMMENT. DICTAPHONES IN ALL LARGE RESTAURANTS IN MANILA.

Rowe and Hernandez had begun very early to establish their Intelligence school, where they started training the more promising of the guerilla volunteers. Now with the reinvasion in the offing, the two men had been busy every day and far into the night with the plans for building up the many new channels of communication which would be required to operate at maximum efficiency. They had only a few weeks now to build and train that force of secret agents.

From the beginning, the commander's orders had been to "STAY OUT OF MANILA," so it rested with the lieutenant to secure volunteers in and around Manila to carry out the plans.

With all operations at THE TOWER progressing according to plan, Lieutenant Hernandez and Sergeant Berg prepared to make a joint Mission-to-Manila. They knew now that the trip consisted of a six-day trek through the jungle on foot to the north coast of Mindoro, then a 36-hour trip by sailboat if the wind and weather were favorable, and another four-day march through the provinces of Batangas, Cavite, and Rizal. There were Jap sentry posts every few miles, from the south coast of Luzon all the way into the city.

They planned to penetrate the Manila area via Verde Island Passage from Abra de Ilog, a coastal town of North Mindoro. The two parties were scheduled to leave eight hours apart. A very efficient communication and warning system between the two groups was the result of a well trained and organized corps of runners and a chain of carefully selected and verified undercover retreats.

On the evening before the take-off, Hernandez prepared a roster naming the men he wanted to go with him. The list included four of the AIB-trained technical experts, his guerilla Aide, Captain Garcia, his very excellent bodyguard, Zamora, and his faithful friend, Mang Pedro. In addition to these he asked for the four high-point men from the first Intelligence School grads at ISRM, and "a squad of well-trained, dependable Guerilla Fighters." Now that everything was ready for his first Mission-to-Manila, he knew that this had been his keen ambition from the minute he became aware of the full significance of his assignment to MISSION ISRM.

Those were difficult and trying times for the native leaders. Differences of opinion, even personal disagreements sometimes brought about trouble between guerilla groups. Such an incident, in which a squad of very young Guerilla Fighters had been condemned to death by firing squad, had come to the attention of the lieutenant shortly after activation of THE TOWER OF ISRM. These "men" (the oldest one was eighteen) had been charged with a multitude of crimes, ranging from pilfering to murder. Their leader had been killed shortly after they were organized. Driven by hunger and fear, they probably had been guilty of many of the charges. However, a number of features of the case made the lieutenant want to know more about them.

He ordered them brought to him individually for questioning and after hearing their story, decided that the death penalty had not been justified. He ordered them brought back to stand in formation in front of his tent. Stepping out to where they stood at attention, he walked up and down the line, looking squarely at each one. Back in position he said,

"Men, I have read the crimes with which you are charged and the sentence imposed. I have also heard your story. I give you one more chance—to live."

That was a decision Al Hernandez was never to regret. With them, his "Cut Throat Squad," he could—and would have gone anywhere.

Commander Rowe and the lieutenant saw Sergeant Berg and "Baker" party off down the mountainside just as the dawn broke through the shadows of the night. Eight hours later the lieutenant and "How" party would follow down the trail.

As they walked back toward their quarters the commander took out a cigarette, fumbled it nervously, finally lit it and took a long drag. He inhaled deeply, held it for a moment and blew the smoke out hard with a sound like a long deep sigh.

There was something on his mind. Hernandez waited for him to speak. He would when he was ready. Finally he said, "Al, I haven't slept much all night. I've been . . . Could we walk over to the point for a few minutes?"

They cut off from the main path and turned toward a point where they often went when they had something really private to discuss. Arriving there, Rowe began again. "I've been trying to make up my mind if I should talk to you now—or if I should wait a little longer—maybe until you make another mission to the city."

"If there's something I should know, George, there's not much point in . ."

"Oh, it's nothing about THE MISSION. I mean it has to do—what I'm trying to say is, it's a very personal thing." "I'm sorry, George. I thought it had to do with—maybe you'd rather NOT talk about it."

"No," said Rowe, "I've made my decision. I know you'll understand that I don't want you to jeopardize your own safety or THE MISSION."

"Naturally," said Hernandez.

Rowe continued, "We've never talked about how we came to be in this outfit." He hesitated again.

"That's true," said Hernandez.

"Forgive me if I seem a little—if I don't express myself very well. When you've kept something inside so long, it's hard to get started." He looked at Hernandez. "We both know that my orders are to 'stay out of Manila'."

"Right," said Hernandez, wondering what was so difficult for him.

"I kept kidding myself that somehow I'd find a way, but when Sergeant Berg came back with his reports, I knew I didn't have a ghost of a chance."

"No one expects you to try to make it, George. You're too important to THE MISSION."

"Oh it's not that, Al," interrupted Rowe, "I've got some very special reasons for wanting to get there. Manila is my HOME, Al."

"Your HOME?" stammered Hernandez in amazement. "I wasn't there when the city fell. I was in California on business; but my wife was there and my boy." For a moment he couldn't continue, then, "He was four then. He'll be seven now—if he's alive. I don't know. I've never heard a word, but whatever it is, Al, I've GOT to know."

"My God, George," said Al, almost in a whisper. "I had no idea. I'll do anything I can, you KNOW that."

"I know you will, Al," said Rowe, speaking more easily now that it was out. "But you and I both know the rules of this game are plenty rough, so be careful. Don't try to see them yourself, but when you find the right opportunity, try to get word through to them."

"Don't worry," said Hernandez, "I'll play it safe."

"Here's a list of people who might have contact with them," said Rowe, handing him a paper. "Memorize the list and destroy it before you leave the outpost. Of all you do, make sure you don't carry it past there."

Some of the most influential names in the Islands were on that list, on down to the gardener and the stable man. "Tell her that Marlanda's master is well and not too far away—that he will soon be coming back to her. Tell her . . ." His voice broke and his eyes were suspiciously bright. "Tell her she is always in my thoughts, and to hold fast until I come."

His story finished, without another word, Rowe—not Commander Rowe, USN—not the commanding officer of a secret intelligence mission, but George Rowe, husband and father, turned and walked back to his quarters. She would know the message was from him, if they could find her, for Marlanda was his riding horse.

It was about mid-morning when a sergeant reported to Hernandez that the guerilla squad assigned to him for his Mission-to-Manila, had reported for inspection. As he stepped out of the light of his quarters into the bright morning sunlight, it was he who snapped to attention, mentally at least, for six of the ten men who stood before him rigid and expressionless, at attention, eyes straight ahead, had stood before him in the early morning sunlight once before—and he had said to them, "I give you one more chance—to live." Because those men had lived, he was to come back from this mission—and keep on coming back until MISSION ISRM was accomplished.

He looked in a few hours later to say goodbye. The commander lay on his cot sleeping. He looked very tired. Hernandez left without disturbing him.

15
» » MISSION TO MANILA

The first day on the trail they made excellent time in spite of mud and high water on the river trails at the foot of the tower mountain. Leaving Asis Outpost behind, they were constantly on the alert for enemy patrols, which were always on the lookout for guerilla hideouts and signs of their activities.

About noon of the second day, after hours of walking under a blistering sun, they came again into the jungle. The lieutenant called out to "take ten for a rest" and dropped down under a tree. Mang Pedro and Zamora chose a tree nearby. Two runners came back from Sergeant Berg's party, with a warning to keep to the left trail through the area. They had spotted an enemy patrol on the right trail, heading in the same direction as How party, almost paralleling their route.

The lieutenant had just fallen asleep when a large snake given to climbing trees, began lowering his mottled body perpendicularly from an overhanging branch. Looking exactly like another tree, reaching to the ground, the snake suddenly let go and fell upon the lieutenant, coiling around his neck. Hernandez sprang to his feet from a sound sleep and shouted, "Good God! What was that?"

The snake, probably as frightened as the man, slithered down the front of him and away into the jungle.

Instantly, Hernandez was surrounded by the native men. It was a good omen, they said. "Nothing could be better, Sir. That is the best luck of all. The man THAT snake falls on can do anything."

"He can go anywhere, and can win great fame," supplied another.

"But don't forget he has to do something himself," said a third.

"So what do I do?" said Hernandez, going along with the idea, for the moment.

"You must go to the nearest stream and bathe in its waters. And there's the stream right there."

"But I can't go bathing in the water. We have to get under way."

"But you wouldn't DARE not to, Sir," said one of the native men, horrified at the thought.

"Come now, Men," said Hernandez, laughing, "This is a military expedition, not a place for superstition and old wives' tales. We stopped for a ten-minute rest. It's been twenty now. Fall in. Let's go."

"Oh, *Teniente*," wailed one of the guerilla squad. "You cannot do that. We will all be lost."

Another said, "If you do, Sir, we can walk straight into Manila unharmed. We could leave our guns, everything behind."

Another, trying to back up the first ones, said, "No one can harm anyone who is with you, Sir. Isn't that worth something?"

"If you don't, Sir, we may all be killed on the way," pleaded another.

"Listen, you men, you know you don't believe that old superstition," said Hernandez. "If something happens to us, it's not going to be because of that damned snake, or because we didn't take half an hour and go swimming." But he thought to himself, "If something did happen to some of them, the others would never forgive me."

The lieutenant gave no sign of weakening, so one of the more quiet ones, whose college days had come to a roaring, screaming halt as a Jap bomb crashed through the library roof while he was studying, came up with a solution which though it was not original, certainly was apropos as he presented it, and had to do with a compromise. "Maybe there is something to what they say, Sir. Supposing you WERE wrong—what then?"

Hernandez shook his head. "Not you too! I was counting on you."

But the student said, "Once there was a very wise man, Sir, a philosopher who had been taught that there was a Supreme Being. Many people believed in this Being, but the philosopher did not. His good friend, el Padre, KNEW that this Being existed and that those who did not believe were in for a bad few million years after the Great Day. 'So my friend, what will you do when the day comes and suddenly he is there, and you see him, and you know you have been wrong?'

"For many days the philosopher pondered the question and at last came up with a compromise. If in the end it came out that el Padre was right, he would suffer throughout eternity. If he, himself, were right his only satisfaction would be that of being smarter than his friend. If on the other hand, this Being did exist, and he HAD believed, it would not have hurt him and he would even have saved the time spent arguing about it. So (according to the quiet one), even though the philosopher did not believe, if he made himself believe that he believed—you see it could get quite complicated, Sir—BUT WHAT DID HE HAVE TO LOSE?"

A joint Army-Navy expedition, flanked by technical experts, would not be considered a likely place for superstition. However, sitting under a jungle tree, with a dozen or so native boys convinced that great misfortune would surely follow the one who refused to perform a simple rite (and you were the one refusing it), could have a very disquieting effect.

"OK," said the lieutenant, "You know I don't believe that silly superstition, and I don't think you do either. I think you just want a good swim. Be ready to leave here in twenty minutes."

He said to himself, "Maybe a swim will make me feel more like walking. I certainly don't feel like it now."

As the day wore on and Hernandez had to call a rest stop after a much shorter march, Zamora and Mang Pedro shared a feeling of anxiety. Always before, he had set the pace. No one could walk farther and faster than *"Teniente."* They said nothing to him but walked close beside him and watched carefully. By late afternoon they knew they were right. In spite of all the mosquito nets, insect repellents, atabrin pills, and other precautions, he was well into a malaria attack. By doubling the next rest period he was able to proceed. Later, the chills began and he too faced it squarely—HE HAD MALARIA.

Runners came back again to warn them that a party of Japs was searching for someone who had been reported in the area. They could not find out whether it was a group or an individual. "How" Party was covered by a right and left guard a little ahead of the main group, and neither guard saw any indication of the searchers, but suddenly the main party came face to face with a detachment of the Jap Constabulary. Either they were not the search party or they did not want to get involved with such a large group of natives whom they probably guessed were guerillas. In any event, they marched straight ahead falling into single file on their own side of the trail. Not a word passed between the two lines of men.

Shortly after that Lieutenant Hernandez stumbled and went down to his knees. He had to admit that he could walk no farther. A blanket and two bamboo poles were made into a stretcher and the men carried him until a *carabao* could be found. Plodding along with their unconscious leader strapped to the back of a *carabao*, their exhilaration vanished. "Looks like the snake didn't do so much for HIM," said one of the squad.

"Maybe you have to really believe in it yourself. I don't think he did," said another.

About mid-morning of the next day, the lieutenant opened his eyes and looked about, wondering where he was and what he was doing on the back of a *carabao*. Mang Pedro and Zamora were walking beside him. Zamora saw his eyes open and said, "How do you feel, Sir?"

"AWFUL," said Hernandez. "How long have I been out?" "Since the sunset, Sir," said Mang Pedro. "Do you remember—you say you can walk no farther?"

"No. I remember I was freezing, then I was burning up. Where are we? How much time have we lost?"

"About half way, Sir," said Zamora. "We traveled through the night, with one two-hour rest stop. I have some broth I made for you then."

"Where did you get anything in this wilderness to make broth?" asked Hernandez.

"Was very easy, Sir," chuckled Mang Pedro happily. "He just find chicken and cook the broth." He was delighted to see his young friend conscious again.

Three days later they arrived at the north coast of Mindoro. They had lost very little time because of the malaria attack. The party had moved fast, probably keeping to the trail even longer hours than he would have required of them.

At the town of Abra de Ilog, runners from Baker party were waiting to guide them to an undercover retreat a few miles along the coast. On his first mission to the north, Sergeant Berg had found this beautiful seaside *hacienda* on the shore of a peaceful little cove, almost surrounded by high mountains and commanding a perfect view of Verde Island Passage.

The wide front windows of the *nipa* house and the full width bamboo porch made the most of the sea exposure, but from even a short distance, the house itself was lost in the blend of the grey-green roof and the natural camouflage of ever-changing light and shadow, dense tropical foliage, palm trees and giant ferns which almost touched the thick *nipa* roof overhanging the porch.

Along the shell-lined walks stood a dozen or more large banana trees. One night Hernandez found himself sitting up suddenly, out of a sound sleep, trying to remember where he was. He lay back on his pillow with a nostalgic smile. It was not the sustained applause of an audience from backstage he was hearing, but the lush, broad leaves of the banana trees slapping in the breeze blowing in from the sea.

The hundreds of coconut trees which completed nature's camouflage, had grown straight and tall in the shelter of the towering mountains protecting them from the strong monsoon winds which blew in, in season. Every ship passing through Verde Passage could be seen by a lookout with high-powered lenses, stationed in a crow's nest in the top of one of those tall coconut palms.

This tropical paradise eventually was to become a valuable and highly important base of operations for the duration of THE MISSION. At the top of the high mountains in the background, they would place the successor to Station ISRM, when that position would be compromised, and Rowe's Landing would be built later, where the deep, swift river flowed into the sea, to give port service to guerilla fighters and secret agents reporting from stations throughout the island network and the landing party of a general from the first invasion forces, in a PT boat.

"How" Party arrived at the *hacienda* during a violent storm which had begun with a torrential downpour and had grown in intensity as the howling wind blew in. Coconuts and palm fronds ripped from the trees and zoomed through the air. Three dark, storm-bound days gave the lieutenant time for much-needed rest and recuperation before starting on to the city. The malaria bug was to hound him for the remainder of THE MISSION.

During the wait for sailing weather, "Jig," their recently established CW, stationed a few miles down the coast, relayed a message to them from ISRM, which read:

IF HERNANDEZ STILL YOUR VICINITY ADVISE HIM HURRY REPEAT HURRY TO POSITION CONTEMPLATED AS DAILY REPORTS CONTENTS MANILA BAY URGENTLY NEEDED. ADVISE IF THIS MESSAGE DELIVERED TO HERNANDEZ.

Just before Baker Party was ready to shove off, a runner came from Jig, with another message:

ADVISE BERG TO COMPLETE MISSION OUTLINED AND RETURN HERE BY SEPTEMBER NINE REPEAT NINE. URGENT REPEAT URGENT THAT WE HAVE ALL RESULTS BY THAT DATE INCLUDING THOSE OF LONG *BANCA* RIDE. THIS IS URGENT REPEAT URGENT.

The "long *banca* ride" was of course, the trip across Verde Passage. With the passing of the storm came the time for the dash—if a 36-hour trip in a sluggish little sailboat can be called a dash—to the Batangas shore. Out there, they would have no place to hide. If they were challenged, it would be up to their wits and good luck to get out of it. This time Baker Party, now inter-island traders in copra, coconuts and cattle, set out several hours ahead of How Party in three small sailboats.

Due to Sergeant Berg's long service in the Regular Army in the Manila area, they thought it wise to guard against his being recognized as they neared the Batangas coast where they intended to land. As they approached the landing place, the sergeant slid into a place beside a mobile radio unit and a set of long-range photographic equipment, under a false bottom in his boat. The top part of the load was a blanket of rough, brown coconuts.

In a description of the landing, later, one of the men said, "The sergeant really didn't need to worry about looking like a young man with a military mission. He looked a good deal more like an OLD man with rheumatism."

Messages sent to ISRM by Jig, during the time they were en route, gave those at THE TOWER OF ISRM an idea of the enemy traffic they were dodging. They were:

(1) ONE PARTY ON RECON TO CALAVITE FOR SECOND TIME EYE WITNESS ONE SHIP BEACHED TOTALLY DAMAGED. SEVEN JAP SHIPS SUNK BY SUBMARINE NEAR AMBIL ISLAND.

(2) AT ONE SIX THREE FIVE CONVOY SHIPS SIGHTED BETWEEN COLO ISLAND MARICABAN ISLAND GOING SOUTH TWENTY SHIPS . . . (Descriptions followed in code.)

(3) HERNANDEZ LEFT ONE TWO ZERO ZERO TODAY. SIGHTED FOUR FREIGHTERS AT ONE FOUR ZERO ZERO. SMALL PATROL BOAT AHEAD.

Fourteen other vessels were sighted by How Party going through the Passage. Passing Verde Islands, a strong enemy fortification, on which one of the first guerilla agents had reported 75-mm guns and their positions, they were alert for any signs of being spotted as they sailed by in their small *batels*. Pulses quickened as lights appeared, and slowly dropped back to normal as the lights died away in the distance or changed their course. They were heading directly toward Balayan Bay. There they would be past the danger of the enemy guns on Verde Islands.

Throughout the entire crossing probably not more than an hour passed without some enemy vessel large or small, steaming alongside putting them on the alert. Sometimes it was a lone cruiser, sometimes a convoy of several warships. Most often it was a single cargo vessel, but luck was with them. Sometimes the crews only looked at them, sometimes they waved, but not once did any kind of craft stop them for identification or questioning.

A few hundred yards off the southern coast of Luzon, with a rim of pale light showing in the east, out of the half-haze, half-darkness came the unmistakable sound of a motor boat. No one they wanted to see would be coming in a motor boat in those waters. Quickly they changed course and headed for a small fishing village where the guerillas thought they knew who was friendly and who was not.

16
» » 'HOW' PARTY PERILED BY INFORMERS

In the foggy, half-light they could not tell if the motor boat had gone or the motor turned off.

"Holy Mother of GOD, that was close!" said one of the men.

"You're not kiddin'," said one of the Cut Throat Squad. "We make a hundred mile trek through the lousy jungle—dodge Nip ships for 36 hours through the Passage—sneak by the big guns on Verde and then, a hundred yards from shore just miss gettin' fouled up by a goddam half-ass motor boat."

"I just hope we didn't change course so fast they knew we were running away," said Captain Garcia.

"We only HEARD them. We couldn't see them, so how the hell could they see us?"

"Well, we'll have to put in to shore now. If we wait another twenty minutes, it will be daylight and ANYONE can see us."

"Then let's get to gettin'," said one of the men. "My legs are so cramped now I don't know if I can stand up."

"What's the matter, you going soft?" queried the man next to him, stretching his own aching legs and rubbing his knees.

"Going soft or not, 36 hours is a hell of a long time in a *batel*," answered the first.

"How about that poor bastard without a country? He had to stay afloat the rest of his life," kidded another.

"Well, give me a bigger boat or a short life," said the first.

"OK, Fellows," said Captain Garcia, "I don't know about a bigger boat, but if we stay here much longer we can probably take care of the short life."

The captain knew this area and the fact that this village on the Luzon coast was a particularly hot spot. It was the end of the line for anyone attempting to flee the island and a point of penetration for anyone trying to reach Manila and enemy HQs.

They headed in to the beach and the shore party disembarked and slipped in under the trees, perhaps half a mile from the village of Baha, unaware that two dusky figures lurking under the trees had moved quickly into the dark shadows a short distance from where they came ashore. The men they had not seen moved fast toward the next village to the west, where How Party had intended to go ashore on the west shore of Batangas Province to start the last lap of the Mission-to-Manila. The other two boats followed in close and leaving the shore party, took off across Balayan Bay to hide out until dark, when runners would be sent back to give them further instructions. Any kind of local craft operating in these waters was almost certain to run into some kind of enemy interference, Coast Guard, Coast Watchers, or Shore Patrol. They could not take the chance of remaining there during the daylight hours.

Thirty-six hours in the small boats, constantly alert, in the wind and sun, had left all of them tired and taut. They needed rest. Thanks to Colonel Volckmann's careful planning, rest stops for undercover foot travelers on Luzon had been spaced about six hours apart.

Captain Garcia and two other guerillas familiar with the area hurried off to a family they had contacted before and found to be friendly to the guerilla fighters. They wanted to find out if there were enemy troops stationed there and to make arrangements for the party to rest for a few hours and secure food supplies. After about an hour they returned and reported that no troops were in the village, but the rest stop was not where they had expected. The first family contacted, always considered loyal citizens, had closed the door on them. From the next contact they learned that only a short while before, the family had become suspect.

"Could they be afraid?" asked Hernandez.

"I don't think so," said Garcia. "It might have been fear in the beginning, but I felt it was outright unfriendliness." "That's about it, Sir," said one of the guerillas who had gone with the captain. "I knew them before. If you ask me, they've sold out to the enemy."

"Then we're really taking chances staying here at all," said Hernandez.

"That's right, Sir," said the man who had seen the people, "but no more than being on the trail anywhere in the area near here. Maybe not as much. They may think we'll be afraid to stop and get a patrol out looking for us right away." The entire party was too tired to start out on the trail and they had to have food to start on that long march. The second family contacted lived farther on at the opposite end of the village. Keeping well back in the jungle growth they skirted the main part of the town and came up to the rendezvous a few at a time.

Later in the day two men from the village came to say that they had heard of the landing party and that they were in need of supplies. Obviously then, they had been watched as they came to the rest stop and the information about their needing supplies must have been passed on by the first family.

Representing himself to be the leader of the party, Captain Garcia went out to meet the visitors, one of whom represented himself to be a guerilla major, and offered the necessary food supplies. By staying close to the window of the *nipa* house where Hernandez was listening, Garcia managed to keep the conversation so he could hear. He agreed to take the supplies if the alleged major could make delivery.

The major said he was taking a great chance in supplying them with food and for security reasons said the delivery must be made well out in Balayan Bay—at midnight!

Neither Hernandez nor Garcia was sold on the man's story. "I don't know why," said Hernandez, "it's nothing you could put your finger on. I just don't trust him."

"Nor I, Sir," said his aide, 'Taut we do have to feed the men. We have a long, hard march ahead, with very little chance of picking up supplies in the mountain country."

This was true. The travel restrictions of which they had already been warned by agents at ISRM, would keep them off the main highways and out of the towns.

"This middle of the bay delivery at midnight is a perfect set-up for a double cross," Garcia continued, "but I figured I could take enough men in two of the boats to take care of any ordinary patrol they would send out. We can shoot it out if we have to, and you and the rest of your party can get away while we're at it."

During the afternoon a friendly villager came to pass the word that a Jap Army truck was roaming the highway. He had recognized Captain Garcia in the early morning and believed that others who knew him had reported the landing. The truck was probably looking for them. They were in a bad spot. Undoubtedly the Japs knew where they were. They could not hope to get away without being seen and even if they wanted to try, they would have no boats until after dark.

The men had become accustomed to sleeping only a few hours at a time. By noon most of them were up with time on their hands. Naturally a poker game got under way. Among this group was a technical sergeant from AIB who, in all the play aboard ship, breaking in the pesos, had never won a poker game—not even in counterfeit money that he couldn't keep. As a runner came in to say that the two trucks were headed that way, the men threw in their hands in the scramble to get under cover—all but the sergeant. Half an hour later, coming out of hiding, he pulled his hand out of his shirt pocket. He held four aces.

Although the Army trucks passed without stopping, the family who was hiding them said there was far more than the usual activity. Making sure that their gear was well hidden, they crawled, two at a time, to the top of a nearby hill. From there they could see the various approaches and would have a chance of getting away if they actually were being hunted by an enemy patrol. However none came and no more was seen of the trucks. After nightfall they returned to the beach where the hotels had come to pick them up. They too had escaped any real difficulty during the day.

While their original plan was to go on to the west and land on the Batangas shore, there was still the doubtful rendezvous with the major. They still had no supplies. The family where they had stayed had offered to try to procure some things for them, but with all the activity and so many people aware that such a party was in the area, it would have been dangerous for the family as well as the party for them to be looking for supplies in any quantity.

Captain Garcia took one *batel* with a squad of guerillas to go to meet the major. They arrived on schedule and the other *batels* moved about, passing at intervals. Hours passed and no major. At 0200, just as they had started to move off, he came zooming up—in a fast little motor boat—but with no supplies. He said he had been warned that the Japs suspected him and were following him very closely. They discussed the possibility of his bringing supplies to them at Lemery, a village of some size on the eastern bay shore. He thought he could. He would try, but not until morning.

A second meeting was arranged and off he went in his fast little motor boat, and off they went too, in the direction opposite from Lemery.

While the captain talked with him, the men had sized up his boat and decided that he was not radio-equipped. He would have to make actual contact with the Japs to report what had happened. With the speed of his take-off and the cover of darkness, it was simple to sail away to the west, toward Baha and the other villages along the coast.

Loading and unloading their gear, the trip to the top of the hill, the constant look-out for enemy trucks and patrols and finally, sailing about for hours waiting for the major, following so closely upon the long channel trip with only a few hours between, all added up to a very long and tiring day. The dawn of the second day found them still between Baha and the next village.

Again Captain Garcia and his two men went in search of shelter. This time they had to find their own. The lieutenant was still weak from the malaria attack. Even the men who were well and literally lived on the trail were tired. They agreed to stop at a deserted hut for four hours and take the chance of losing any possible pursuers in the mountain region that lay ahead, between them and their destination. Right now, they had to have rest!

Leaving the boats near Baha, they started out after the rest stop, along the edge of the jungle, passing a long chain of villages nestled between the mountains and the sea, from San Pedrino Point, past Talibayog, Sampiro, Balayan, Tuy, and others, they came out at Zobel's Land. Situated high on a plateau, this mountain area reached across the peninsula, almost to the shore of the South China Sea.

They took refuge in a sheltered spot under a rocky ledge from which they could keep a lookout and Captain Garcia took a few men and went out to make a short reconnaissance.

They learned that in this mountain settlement there were 89 men who had sworn to fight to the last man, if it came to that, to withstand the enemy. The terrain was such that a few men could hold off a great many for a long time. With this great natural advantage, they had not the fear of the invaders which many of their countrymen felt.

These people were hospitable and willing to aid the expedition in any way, giving them food and shelter immediately and offering to give them the supplies they needed for the trip. Shortly after they arrived there, runners came from the coast to warn them that Sergeant Berg's party had heard that such a party had been seen landing, and to be on guard. Runners from a guerilla station in Balayan brought that news, which had already been relayed to ISRM.

Heading back toward THE TOWER, in compliance with the commander's radioed orders, Sergeant Berg's men had learned of the unfriendly watchers who had reported the landing and sent this message:

RELAYED FOR BERG: RETURNED TO ABRA. ARRIVED CAMP X PM. HOW PARTY LANDING AREA BAHA WAS REPORTED TO NIPS BY SYMPATHIZERS CALATAGAN. NIPS BEATING BUSH THAT AREA. HOW PARTY BELIEVED SAFE. TRAVELED FAST AS THEY LEFT BALAYAN. TRUCK DRIVER REPORTED TO MAYOR OF TUY NIPS HAVE TAKEN COMMUNITY AND ARE AFTER ONE HUNDRED

AMERICAN SYMPATHIZERS THERE.

Captain Garcia again took a platoon of guerillas and went out in search of information. They had to know just what had happened back on the coast and whether it was likely that the Japs actually were hunting them. Runners were to return at intervals to keep them informed. The recon party backtracked and found that patrols had been searching the area, but their information was not definite. They sent runners later to say that they were going farther, to the Lake Taal area, southeast of Manila to see what conditions were there and if possible to find out if the party had been recognized.

While they were gone, on the evening of the second day, one of the local residents had reason to make a trip to Manila.

There was a standing order to confiscate all civilian trucks or cars of any kind, but this man had succeeded so far in making trips in and out of the city by using a narrow mountain trail just wide enough for his Ford truck. This little-used, poorly kept road was one of the two trails leading in and out of this highly inaccessible area, and led almost to the bay shore, in the outskirts of the city.

After the urgent message from ISRM instructing him to "hurry to position contemplated," Lieutenant Hernandez was furious at being delayed in this out-of-the-way place where he could accomplish nothing. The man who was going to the city was glad to take as many of the party as possible. He usually had to make the trip alone. Hernandez seized upon the opportunity to take radio and photographic equipment to set up the transmitter and lookout station they needed on Manila Bay, to meet GHQ's urgent requests for daily reports on the contents of the bay. However, they had to leave immediately if they were to go.

Realizing that it might be days before they could go any other way, without waiting for the reconnaissance party, Hernandez took the technical men he needed to leave in the city, together with Mang Pedro, Zamora, two other trained guerillas and as many of his Cut Throat Squad as could crowd into the truck. Quickly they loaded the equipment, covered it over and set out over the lonely mountain road, wearing the faded garments of the poor traders who had come across Verde Passage. In the blackness of the moonless night, their clothes presented no problem; but on arrival at the house of the members of the Resistance Movement in Manila, their activity was really curtailed by that error. Agents were called, however, who were able to handle the necessary details and in a few hours, a camera-equipped look-out was established high up on the fifth floor of an office building overlooking Manila Bay, and a short distance from that office, a transmitter was installed to report daily to ISRM.

It seemed impossible after the long trips they had made on foot for so many weeks, that in so few hours, bumping along at what seemed a tremendous pace in the little truck, so much had been accomplished. Before they had cleared the city limits, the first message to THE TOWER OF ISRM for rebroadcast to GHQ was already going out over the air.

17

» » HERNANDEZ ESCAPES

Everything had come off without a hitch. Now that they had disposed of the radio and photographic equipment, the return trip should be simple, and the driver had taken care of his business and escaped from the city once more with his truck.

Dashing along the country road, it suddenly occurred to Hernandez that the cedula he carried said he was a coconut trader with residence in Mindoro and that he was dressed for the part. The travel pass which had been prepared for him to get out of Manila, as originally planned, stated that he was employed by the Inspection Division of the Imperial Government, under orders and traveling at Government expense, to make surveys of the rice problem, and the coming harvest in Batangas and Mindoro. He was NOT dressed for that! Changing either his papers or his clothes was impossible. One thing might help. He was going OUT of the city. Also, on that lonely road, so far from the main highway, there might not be sentry posts. They had seen none the night before—but it had been dark then, and very late.

They rolled through Rizal Province and into Cavite, unchallenged, and Hernandez heard himself humming, "One More River to Cross." Approaching the Cavite-Batangas border, they stopped for a huddle over the best way to proceed from there. He had to tell the others his predicament. This was serious—not only for him but for anyone suspected of being with him.

The truck driver also had his worries. Many a good truck had been picked up at this border. Having decided upon their strategy, they went on to about a mile outside the border village. Mang Pedro, Zamora, the lieutenant and three of the Cut Throat Squad got out and walked through the town. The driver and the others were to go on through and wait for them on the other side. Carrying only the meagerest supplies of food and water, they walked along briskly, making excellent time. Mang Pedro, Zamora, and Hernandez went first and the three other men followed, close enough to see anything that might happen to them. Soon they were through the village and into the outskirts with only scattered houses and gardens.

They were gratified to notice that there was no sign of the truck having been confiscated. Obviously the others had passed through without difficulty. What a break this had been! The station had been established days ahead of their most optimistic plans. It MUST HAVE BEEN the snake!

Rounding a sharp bend in the road, where nothing but open country had been visible the previous night, they walked straight into a Jap sentry post and heard the sickening command to HALT!

Knowing that Zamora's papers were in order and that his were not, Hernandez whispered, "Show him your papers first."

Zamora handed over his papers with a great show of confidence. "This says you are a coconut trader," said the MP in an oddly Anglicized Japanese. "How do you take coconuts to the city—on your back?"

"Oh no." said Zamora. "I take coconuts to city in fine *batel*. I make him myself—take me long time. New government need my *batel*. I glad to help. They pay me good pesos so now I go back home and build new one."

"OK. You go," said the MP, turning to Hernandez, "but you, Stupid One, what are you fumbling with and why are your hands shaking?"

He might have asked more if he had noticed the one thing the Stupid One could not control. His shirt front was throbbing with the pounding of his heart, for in his right hand he held the nondescript cloth bag he used for a briefcase. In it were the money they had brought for the trip, the data he had acquired in the city, and the Rice Inspector's Travel Pass. He could have discarded the travel pass earlier, but it was a definite part of the strategy for the next few days and might be impossible to replace. He fumbled awkwardly, apparently trying to extract his cedula from a tattered wallet.

Already cleared and dismissed, Zamora turned to him and said, "Here, let me hold that for you."

Hernandez held out the bag to him and said nothing, continuing to struggle with the wallet. The MP was thoroughly angry and disgusted with his clumsiness. Then as though expecting his companion to follow momentarily, Zamora strolled on casually. With the travel pass and the other papers safely past the MP, Hernandez pulled the cedula out of the wallet and handed it to a second sentry who had put out his hand for it.

"What you are tlying to get away with?" asked the second MP angrily. "This is no traver pass—is onry cedura. You cannot go one plovince to o'er one with this."

"I don't think he's so dumb," said the first MP To Hernandez he said, "You think you are very smart, but you do not fool me. You will learn. Maybe you learn faster in jail while we find out why you carry no travel pass."

"How long you keep in jail?" asked the Stupid One. "Maybe few days—maybe few weeks. What difference it makes?"

Then remembering Zamora, the first MP looked around but he had disappeared in the jungle which grew almost to the roadside. He smiled broadly. "That was a slick one. He got away with the Stupid One's bag."

To Mang Pedro who had stood patiently while the others were being processed, the first MP said, "All right, Old Man, let's see your papers. Is this man a friend of yours?"

"Friend?" parried Mang Pedro. "Maybe. I never see him before yesterday. He go same way I go. We walk together." Looking at Mang Pedro's travel pass, the guard said, "Where are you going, Old One?"

"It tell you there, Sir," said Mang Pedro respectfully. "I go back to my village. I am old man and sick. No can do work in city any more. New gov'ment say go back to my village and leave food in city for workers. So, I go."

"All right. You go. But this one, why is he going?"

"I not know, Sir. I no ask—he no tell me." Then he added confidentially to the MP, "But I think you right, he plenty stupid."

Mang Pedro was sent on his way and in a few moments Al Hernandez found himself being roughly pushed through the door of a cell in the village jail. A simple, but strong, bar-type lock pushed into place by a Japanese jailer, assured his remaining there.

Sitting in a dark, dirt-floored, mildewy cell, its one window high above his head, he had nothing to do but think. After a while he began wondering if it were his imagination or if there really were bugs crawling on the back of his neck—on his arms—and finally all over his body.

With his bag safely away, there was nothing left to identify him with THE MISSION. His heart sank—not even chlorine tablets to purify any water his captors might eventually bring to him.

"My Cut Throat Squad will manage it some way," he said to himself, then (not very enthusiastically), "If they don't, it will only be MY life. THE

MISSION will not be jeopardized." With that very scant comfort, he thought encouragingly of the uncanny ability of the guerillas to keep in touch even at great distances and to effect rescues under seemingly impossible circumstances.

After a while two young Japanese officers came to question him. They spoke in Japanese and broken English. Hernandez appeared to understand only a little of their English and attempted to make himself understood in Tagalog, with a scattering of English words here and there. Their private conversation in Japanese, however, left no doubt. They were convinced that he was not the ignorant native trader he pretended to be. He stuck doggedly to his story and with the possibilities facing him at that moment, it was no trouble to keep a solemn face.

After an hour or more, getting nowhere with their questioning, the officers left. Shortly after that he heard the notes of the bamboo flute, a signal of guerillas on the trail. Thank God that hadn't come while the officers were there! In that moment of realization that his men were out there, waiting for the darkness to cover their rescue activities, he might have betrayed himself.

About an hour later another pair of interrogators came. Their questions were in good, University of California English; but they too failed to establish that he was any other than an especially dim-witted character who had picked up a canteen where some American soldiers had camped. The second pair went on their way.

A sudden shaft of light from the setting sun came through the small rectangle cut in the wall above his head. Traveling slowly along the wall, it faded into darkness. With the coming of the night, a native oil lamp was lit in an outer room and its yellow glow came dimly through the barred door, casting long, weird shadows across the gloomy cell.

The high staccato signal had brought the group together out there in the jungle, where they had climbed trees to keep out of sight and to have a better view of the jail. With the deepening of the darkness they could no longer see what went on around the jail. Stealthily, noiselessly, they moved closer in, finally pushing the Ford truck in close to hasten their escape when the time came.

Insofar as Lieutenant Hernandez knew, no one had even looked in at him after the second pair of interrogators left. This did not fit into the pattern they had been told to expect in an enemy prison. Of course, they had brought no food or water. Maybe that was the way they would do it—with no effort on the part of the captors. He drank slowly, a swallow or two at a time, from the water left in his canteen. It might be hours before the guerilla fighters would stage the rescue. But not for a moment did he doubt that they would attempt it. At least three of those men out there were alive because he had saved them from their death house. If they were left alive to do it, they would not let a Batangas jail become his—that he KNEW.

He sat in the darkness, listening, waiting. An MP carrying a small table and a native oil lamp led in two more interrogators. This time it was a captain and a major. As the officers came through the cell door, the MP shouted at the prisoner, "STAND UP!" In a moment he went out and came back with two chairs.

These men also spoke good, stateside English. However at the beginning, they simply sat and looked at him, flashing a strong light on and off in his face as he stood with his back against the wall. The major smiled constantly, but the smile held no hint of friendliness. Very quickly he sensed that these men knew more than the others had. One of them carried a briefcase which he placed on the table. Several times he appeared about to open it. Then he would wait, with that smirking smile. At last he opened the case and removed a thick file of papers, photographs, and newspaper clippings, which he examined with great interest as though he had never seen them before. It was then that Hernandez realized that these men knew who he was. He wondered if they knew why he was there.

In a tone of exaggerated friendliness, the major said, "Don Alfredo Eufronio Guillermo Omez de Hernandez—what a shame you took so much trouble to deceive us. You should have known you could not do it—and with your connections too. We could have been very good friends. Too bad—now we cannot trust you."

If they knew that much, they probably knew everything. He stuck to the role of the simple coconut trader and made no reply.

"All right, Hernandez," said the major. "You may as well tell us what you are doing here—where you have been and where you were going when we caught you. We know all about you—and your mother! She is getting to be an old lady. You could have made it very easy for her, but you leave us very little choice."

"No und'stan," said the prisoner, shaking his head in bewilderment. "Me have no mother. Long time no mother." "Don't lie to us, Hernandez," warned the captain, holding the light steadily in his eyes. "You won't get away with it and you must know we have ways of dealing with people who try."

The major went on turning page after page of his report. "Whatever happened to the Studio of the Dance—the little white house between San

Marcelino and Taft on Isaac Peral . . . and where is Mr. Westmorland?"

They knew who he was all right. How much more did they know? One thing he was reasonably sure they did NOT know—where his mother was. That was one of the first things he had taken care of after establishing the connection between Captain Dodson and Major Ruffy's command. He knew that his mother was safely hidden away in a mountain retreat where no Japanese was likely ever to find her. He wished the Manila newspapers hadn't been so kind—and so generous with their comments back in 1937, '38, and '39 when he had been having such a good time. He remained silent. Anything he would say now would be the wrong thing.

"Come, come Alfredo de Hernandez. Don't be shy. It is nothing to be ashamed of. You must have had some of the loveliest ladies of your country—AND OURS. You were in Tokyo in—(he referred to the report), 1938. Right?"

Hernandez made no reply and the major continued. "Who is the beautiful Miss Guia Balmori, the Queen who was judging the floats with you? Was she your dancing partner? What a delightful profession!"

Suddenly his tone changed to one of cold, cruel, almost personal hatred. "What are you doing here, Mr. Al Hernandez of Hollywood and Chicago and where were you going when the Kempi stopped you?"

Still playing dumb, Hernandez said, "No und'stan Hollywood, Chicago."

"You understand all right. Your lectures at the University of the Philippines were in English, or have you forgotten?" Hernandez shrugged his shoulders, looked blank, and said nothing. The captain picked up from there with, "Not being able to understand might make it difficult for you here, Mr. Al Hernandez, when the guards ask you if you are hungry. Maybe you do not know how to say you want water." "Speaking of water," cut in the major, "Where is the canteen you brought here with you?"

The captain flashed the light around the dark corners of the cell. As it fell on the canteen, the major got up slowly and picked it up. He opened it. A horrible sinking feeling went over Hernandez as the man put the canteen to his lips and tasted the water.

"So! You found the canteen where the Americans had camped," he said mockingly, then sprang at him and fairly hurled the words at him, "Did you FIND the chlorine tablets you used in this water?"

Holding the canteen in the beam of the captain's flashlight, the major began to pour the water slowly into the dirt floor. "It may be a long time— and you may get very thirsty—and hungry too, if you cannot understand what we say. Do you want to talk while there is some water left?"

Hernandez only shrugged dully. He would take his chances on waiting for the guerillas.

Draining the last few drops from the canteen, the major handed it to the captain saying, "We will take it with us. An American Army canteen will be a nice souvenir of the late, famous Mr. Al Hernandez of Manila, Hollywood, and Chicago. Maybe his wife will like to have it to remember him by. Take good care of it, Captain. Perhaps it will be our pleasure to take it to her in California—the last thing to touch his lips."

Turning again to Hernandez, he said, "Maybe you could remember how to talk if we find some of your friends from the Philippine Exposition. You must have had many of them. Maybe they come now and help you remember what you are doing here."

Suddenly there came a weird, inhuman cry, somewhere between a scream and the sound of the breath being knocked out of a man, then the sound of running feet. One of the guerilla party had accidentally violated a basic law of jungle warfare. He had allowed a cry to escape from his victim as he crumpled to the earth.

The two enemy MP's playing cards in the jail office pushed back their stools, reached for their automatics and rushed for the door, their guns blazing. Their fire was returned from out of the blackness of the tropic night and the two MP's fell, their smoking guns silenced.

The guard who had been standing facing Lieutenant Hernandez' cell rushed to release the interrogating officers. As they pushed through the door, the guard with a powerful thrust threw the prisoner across the cell against the opposite wall and dashed out through the open door. He dropped the bar into place and ran. Two more shots put out the lights in the outer room as the two Jap officers and their rescuer rushed from the cell row.

Out of the darkness came the thud of hard fists falling on human flesh—men falling—rising—falling again in the melee that followed. Grunts, gasps, scuffling feet; but scarcely a word was spoken as the men fought it out hand to hand with the enemy. These men had learned—the hard way—that voices can be recognized.

A guerilla fighter dashed down toward the pale rectangle of light from the small oil lamp the interrogators had left in the cell (the only light left in the jail). There stood the lieutenant, gripping the bars of the cell door, trying to see what was going on outside. Quickly the bar was lifted from the lock and he stepped out—a FREE man! They hurried out to the darkened outer room full of struggling men. The two interrogators were quickly and expertly bound, gagged and tossed into a comer. A shot from the last of the oncoming guerillas had taken care of the guard who had tried to rescue them.

The struggle over, the guerillas hastily gathered up their wounded. Sickened by the odor of human blood—and the thought of how much of it was from their own men, they carried three wounded men to the truck which stood outside. The sound of those shots would bring any other troops or MP's in the village on the double.

They hurried away over the rough back road and the narrow, rocky mountain trail to their highland hideout. There they carefully lifted the wounded men from the truck to take them into the house for further treatment. They had given only the simplest first aid. Those who reached for the third man realized that he was past all help and drew the cover over his face.

Lieutenant Hernandez had gone in with the wounded men to do what he could for them. When the last one—the youngest of his Cut Throat Squad—was not brought in, he walked back outside. He drew the blanket aside and looked sadly at the young face. His hands passed over the smooth, pale cheeks, brushed back the thick wavy hair, and gently touched the brow. Tears rolled down his cheeks as he covered the boy once more—the boy who had given his own life to save his. He turned and walked into a wooded area back of the house. He had to be alone for a little while.

Captain Garcia and his reconnaissance party had returned from their mission to the east, ahead of the lieutenant's Manila party. Garcia had been anxiously (and angrily) striding back and forth on the trail, pausing now and then, straining his eyes to see far down the trail. Upon their arrival he had gone in with the others to give assistance to the wounded men. A little later he went in search of the lieutenant. Things were serious! Their landing had been reported, and now, the enemy knew Hernandez' identity and probably his mission. He would be a hunted man from that hour forward.

In a tone in no way resembling that of a military aide addressing his superior officer, Garcia said, "There we were out there like a bunch of boy scouts, seeing if it was safe for our leader to walk along a country road or a lonely river trail—and what does he do? He doesn't walk. He doesn't run. NO. He gets into a forbidden motor car and rides as fast as he can—straight into enemy HQs. What do you think Commander Nicholson will say when he hears this?"

With the faintest flicker of a smile in his eyes, but with a very solemn face, the lieutenant looked at him and said evenly, "Anyone who's thinking of telling him had better be a lot more worried about what I would do IF he ever heard about it."

Garcia stopped pacing. He laughed and the tension was gone. "Just the same," he said, "You keep on taking chances like this and we won't have to worry about what the commander or anyone else would say about YOU. We'll have to keep constantly on the move now—and ALWAYS under cover."

There was so much to be done in Manila—so many agents had to be recruited—and this took time. The contacts could not be direct. Also there was the message relayed to them just before the crossing to Luzon, with instructions to forward reports by the next Australian-bound submarine.

They HAD to get back into Manila and they could not lose any more time!

18
» » A SECOND TRY

Back at the hideout in Zobel's Land, runners were dispatched on two missions. One was to make contact with the boats standing by in any one of a number of places, depending upon the circumstances. They would be somewhere along the shores of Batangas Bay. The second was to procure suitable clothing for the party moving into Manila. After the trouble on the inner mountain road, they would have to cut back to the main highway, change their identities and travel the highway through the Lake Taal area.

Before they were ready to leave the hideout, the second of the Cut Throat Squad died of his wounds. Twin crosses were left to mark their graves in that wild, high, clean mountain country.

Between the hideout and the city there would be many sentries. They could not afford to have any further discrepancies between travel papers, reasons for travel or clothing. The official ban on civilian use of trains left two alternatives. They could walk or use horse-drawn *caratelas*, available for public use in the towns. In this area there were no roads—to say nothing of *caratelas*. So once more they started off down the narrow trail. At the lower level they picked up a still-narrower trail, well camouflaged where it turned off from the other one, and probably known only to the guerillas. It led to the official FFF post where food, shelter, and a change of clothing would be waiting for them.

They neared the village of the undercover retreat at midday, and splitting into two groups, proceeded with extreme caution. Runners were sent to make last minute reconnaissance. One group passed an enemy patrol which they learned at the retreat had been in search of Hernandez. The runners came hurrying back to tell them that the undercover retreat was under surveillance. Another rendezvous had been arranged not far from the village theatre, which stood at the edge of town.

It was fiesta time and a large company of dancers billed at the theatre had attracted an enthusiastic holiday crowd. Hernandez and his men mixed casually with the townspeople celebrating the fiesta. They had caught sight of Garcia and his men coming in from another direction when suddenly a military truck appeared with much blowing of the horn and dropped MP's back of them at two intersections and moved forward with more men to patrol the theatre entrance and approaching streets. Some of the party mingled with the crowd, listening for information that might accidentally be dropped or intentionally passed on by other undercover men. One checked the situation at the rear of the theatre. The guard apparently had not been posted for the specific purpose of looking for them, but rather as a precautionary measure.

Word was passed to both Hernandez and Garcia that a wall at the rear would cut off escape in that direction. Leaving the crowd and going another way would be impossible with the MP's at the end of the block. Neither man dared to risk passing the MP's at the ticket window; but they could not stand outside when the crowd went in for the next performance. Then one of the men came back to say that there were rear doors on both sides of the theatre. This might be it—if they were careful—and LUCKY.

Captain Garcia had also been a professional dancer in civilian life. He was a native of Madrid and was appearing at a Manila theatre with a Spanish company at the time of the invasion. He had soon cast his lot with the guerilla forces and had been in active service with them from the beginning.

Now the only possible chance for escape lay in passing through the theatre to a group of trees, gardens and small houses on the other side. They went along with the crowd well toward the rear while one of the men purchased tickets for them. Then working their way through the crowd, they disappeared down the dark aisle to the wings, where, to their horror they discovered THERE WAS NO PASSAGE BACKSTAGE!

The dance on stage had opened in full swing. With the large cast, there had not been enough dressing rooms and tables had been placed along the walls for props and costumes. On one table lay a number of large, elaborate Spanish shawls. Both men being excellent dancers, caught up shawls, threw them about their shoulders and danced out onto the stage. Joining the lively dance going on, they clowned their way through the number, dancing fast and furiously as the tempo increased. They were on the other side of the stage when the music stopped and the performers took their bows. Amid cries for an encore, the two unscheduled entertainers dashed out, tossing their shawls behind them, and cleared the back door. They slipped through a thick hedge of bamboo surrounding a garden and lost themselves in the trees and bushes of the back-yard gardens, while the MP's scanned the crowds entering and leaving the theatre. They might have been looking for a man who answered the description of the prisoner who had escaped the Batangas jail.

As they stepped out to the main highway a few hours later to board a *caratela* bound for Manila, there was little to connect the two excellently groomed young cattle men in white sharkskin suits, white shoes and Panama hats with the small scale coconut traders on Balayan Bay a few days before—or the fumbling dim-wit at the jail. Their dress and conduct marked them as men of means. Zamora made an effort to keep near them without giving the impression of being with them. Insofar as they knew, Garcia and Hernandez were the only ones known by sight and identifiable as being together. Mang Pedro boarded the *caratela* and took a seat well toward the back where he could keep an eye on what went on back of them.

Zamora made an effort to sit in the seat with Garcia and Hernandez but dropped back and sat in the seat behind when a Japanese pushed in brusquely and sat down between the two.

Most of the Japanese aboard had little to say but the Filipinos carried on a normal conversation. The two cattle men talked to them about business conditions in the area, asking about cattle for sale, making no secret of their purported business.

Before leaving the undercover retreat they had talked about whether they should leave their automatics with Sergeant Pascua, who was there when they arrived, but decided against going out unarmed. Sitting there, three in a seat, with his automatic under his arm, Hernandez found it difficult to feel that it was in any way inconspicuous. One wrong move and the man beside him would feel the hard steel—and he would probably find himself back in the hands of the Kempi Tai at the next stop.

It was not until the intruder left the *caratela* and they had cleared the village where he got off, that the lieutenant breathed easily. An hour later they reached the next FFF station in the outskirts of the city.

The rule was to let lesser known agents in the city and unknown guerillas take care of public activities and make daylight observations. The one exception they made to this rule on the Mission-to-Manila had serious repercussions. A prominent young society matron and long-time acquaintance of the lieutenant arranged a dinner party to give him an opportunity to meet and talk with women in position to act as agents for

MISSION ISRM. Among them were former students of his at the university and his Holly-York studio in Manila.

The hostess included in the guest list a popular newspaper woman who was Hernandez' publicity agent for the Philippine Exposition, and whom she believed to be a loyal member of the Fighters for Freedom. After dancing with his former business associate, and making no effort to ascertain her political sympathies, Hernandez saw her in a whispered conversation with a man whom the hostess could not identify and whom she certainly had not invited. Then the file of photographs, newspaper clippings and other data in the Japanese major's briefcase at the Batangas jail were no longer a mystery. She was still doing publicity on Hernandez but not FOR him. He made no more personal appearances.

There was so much to be done that Hernandez found it difficult to confine himself to the secret HQs during the daylight hours. GHQ wanted specific data on so many areas and installations which required close personal inspections. However, so many new channels of communication were needed that the time was taken up in meeting new people, starting many of them on their training, and receiving reports from agents already established. A strict time schedule had to be observed throughout the entire activity for one very important thing was to keep the identity of the various agents a secret insofar as possible. A strong determining factor in securing dependable agents for THE MISSION with such speed was the fact that they were an Intelligence mission operating in enemy OCCUPIED territory—not in ENEMY TERRITORY.

It was their good fortune to enlist some of the most brilliant professional and military minds in the Islands to aid them. At the outbreak of the war, Dr. Renatto Guerrero, Dean of Medicine at the University of the Philippines, had seen his class rooms become warehouses and his laboratories ammunition factories. When the day came that he could help to avenge that wrong, no assignment was too dangerous—no day or night too long. Working beside the doctor was his young wife Joey. Almost every day Joey managed to get into the prison at Santo Tomas, smuggling in whatever she could of food, clothing and medicine to ease the suffering of American soldiers and interned American and Filipino POW's. At last the doctor was to see on her hands the withering whiteness of Hansen's disease, for which she later came to Carville, Louisiana, for treatment. As she walked down the gangplank at San Francisco, she was met by the Fifth Army Band, playing the Philippine and American national anthems, General Mark Clark, with a great armful of red roses and a special welcoming committee from the City of San Francisco. Joey went home with her body cured, and wearing a decoration from the U. S. Government for her services to her country and ours.

Dr. A. Legarda, also an eminent physician and surgeon of Manila, headed another channel of communication, making whatever sacrifice was required of him, not the least of which was to ever remember his Hippocratic oath, his obligation to suffering humanity—whether his patient were invader or countryman. But this gave many opportunities to learn the secrets of the enemy and to hurry those secrets on their way to help in defeating the enemy and prepare for a successful re-invasion.

Another influential, though highly controversial character in the Resistance Movement, was that of Brigadier General Manuel A. Roxas, of the Philippine Army, later to become president of the postwar Republic of the Philippines. Early in the war he was held prisoner on the island of Mindanao, later released and brought to Manila to become a member of the Jap-sponsored Philippine Cabinet. As Commander Rowe often said, there was one thing the Japs could not control (thank God), their inclination to brag. They bragged to General Roxas about what they were going to do to the Americans—and how they were going to do it. That was when Manuel Roxas, at first really very ill, then later, pretending not to recover, began receiving visits from agents of ISRM at his bedside. Time after time he supplied invaluable information that was hurried to one of the network's stations and on to ISRM within the hour.

An incident that took place on the island of Lubang is an example of the work of small bands of guerillas who made it impossible for General Yamashita and his men in the field to keep their secrets. On the island of Lubang, off the coast of southwest Luzon, was an enemy airfield. Near the field an important fuel storage point served the Imperial Air Force as a fueling station. At one time there were approximately 15,000 drums of gasoline stored there. Out in the jungle, where they could check on what was happening at the field, was a small band of guerillas, a part of the FFF. They were led by a young lad who worked with ISRM with a miniature radio set. He was referred to only as "Skippy." He made his contact with ISRM and the Japs began to have trouble with their gasoline. The enemy no longer had full control of the skies by that time and, supplied with the exact location of the gas drums by Skippy, American planes came in and bombed the location. After a night bombing, the major in command decided to move to a new hiding place—but he had not enough men to do the job. Casually dropping by next morning to see what damage the bombing and fire had done, Skippy learned of the major's problem. He couldn't leave the poor fellow in a spot like that, so he offered to find help for him. He was not going to lose track of that gasoline. One by one the guerillas wandered out of camp and appeared before the perplexed major.

"Me José Sanchez," said one. "Me live on farm—have no work for long time—no money—no food. You have any work to do, Senor?"

Soon another boy passing by saw José. He too came to the officer in charge. "My friend, Jos6, he is working for you. I like work for you too. You need more help?"

Did he need help? The major began to smile broadly. "What is your name?" he asked, beginning to see a way out. "My name Ramirez," said the new boy.

"Listen, Ramirez," said the major. "Have you any more friends who like to make some money?"

"Oh YES, Senor, I have Pedro, Carlos, Manuel, Emilio, Miguel..."

" Fine, fine!" said the major. "You go back—bring your friends. I have work for all of you. I pay you good."

The friends of Ramirez came and moved the gasoline to the cemetery. Skippy promptly reported the move and the bombers came again that night and there were more explosions.

The guerillas heard the explosions and saw the fire in the night. Next morning they came back to see if the major had any more work for them. That time they moved what was left of the gasoline to a point near the town of Tilic. That night Skippy's little radio crackled and the same thing happened all over again. The planes came and the gasoline went. This time there was no more work to do. There was no more gasoline. In desperation the Jap major cried out, "I think we have someone with us who cannot keep secret. Wherever I hide the gasoline—American bomber come." In the five long, busy, guarded days of the Mission-to-Manila, a tremendous amount of vital work was accomplished. Agents were contacted, tested, and accepted. New channels were established, but one thing remained before they were ready to return to ISRM. GHQ had asked for an up-to-date city map with current information on all public utilities and military installations.

Room service at the Manila Hotel had become second to none in the Orient. There the enemy high command was served by the best trained men and women U. S. Intelligence had to offer. So, it was a Room Service man who located such a map, through a friend who worked at the city hall—for the puppet government. By day the map hung in the office of a young major. At night it was stored in a metal cabinet in his office. The young officer trusted the key to that cabinet to no one. He carried it on his person at all times, in the watch pocket of his uniform.

Hernandez had to get that map—but HOW? Always obliging, Room

Service set about finding a way. The RS man whose duty it was to serve the young officer, began by telling him of the Latin dances so popular with the young people around the city. The officer soon became interested. Seeing that he was on the right track, the man said to the major, "You know, Major, when you see those pretty girls doing the dances you are going to want to dance with them too."

"I have never danced," confessed the young man. "I wish I could, but I don't know how."

"Why don't you surprise your friends—learn to do some of the dances before you go?"

"Where could I ream?" he asked eagerly.

"There is a new waiter in the big dining room downstairs. He is very good. I think he would teach you if I asked him." Thoroughly intrigued with the idea, the major said, "Go get him—now. I have tord the others I have to work tonight so I cannot go out with them."

"I will go and see if he can come now," said the Room Service man, hurrying off to get Hernandez and see that Sergeant Pascua and his *calesa* were standing by in the event that quick transportation became a factor.

In a few moments the RS man returned with the dancing waiter. Bowing humbly—all smiles—the waiter said to the major, "Never do I think I have the honor to teach Japanese officer to dance, Sir."

Almost as though imitating the teacher, the officer said, "Neveh do I think I have the opportunity to ream Ratin dances."

"We start now, Sir. OK? Maybe I have to go back to dining room, but we start anyway."

Hernandez, now a dancing waiter, described the dance as the young officer listened carefully. "Now—you tell me just what I tell you," he said when he had finished.

The major repeated his instructions word for word. "Wonderful!" said the waiter. "You learn very fast. You very smart man. Is why you are officer in Japanese Army?" "Japanese Army officer habe to ream fast," he smiled. "You teach me now, I ream fast Ratin dances."

"Yes, Sir," said the waiter, smiling. He was thinking how the Japs sounded when they said, "Japanese rob Firipino," meaning of course, "Japanese love Filipino."

"Now," said the waiter, "I take your hand—so. When you dance with *magandang dalago* (beautiful lady), you take her hand—so. Now we count for the rhumba—1 - 2 - 3 - 4, 1 - 2 - 3 - 4, 1 - 2 - 3 - 4."

Timing his own steps so the officer would have to bump into him, the waiter made the first try for the key. "Dammit," he thought, "They should have included pick-pocket techniques in our training." He HAD to get that key.

After much counting and several bumps—on the third try—with his pupil laughing nervously, and very apologetic because he could not follow the simple instructions, the waiter's fingers closed over the key. He stopped dancing and said sympathetically, "Sir, I think it is my fault. I am maybe good dancer, but not very good teacher. I think you do better to practice by yourself. Here—I show you."

Taking a piece of chalk from his pocket, Hernandez drew a square on the polished floor, with cross lines for the major's guidance in practicing the rhumba step. He stepped into the square, placed his hands on his hips and began dancing, counting as he did so, "1 - 2 - 3 - 4, 1 - 2 - 3 - 4, 1 - 2 - 3 - 4." You make it rook bery simpre," said the major, "Maybe I ream now."

"Oh you will learn, Major. You will learn. Just keep practicing. You will be doing hot rhumba before I come back. You wait and see," said the waiter, encouragingly.

Hernandez watched the major for a moment as he concentrated on the dance, oblivious to his loss and the price he was paying for a dancing lesson. Closing the door behind him, Hernandez hurried down the back stairs, handed his waiter's coat to the Room Service man who had called him and walked nonchalantly outside. Sergeant Pascua's *calesa* (one-horse taxi) was waiting to carry him swiftly away to an undercover worker who would make the attempt to get the map from the city hall.

Covering his steps at every turn, the undercover man soon had the vital map and was off to deliver it to Sergeant Pascua, who happened to be driving in the area, innocently looking for a fare.

Room Service had another call. The major wanted his teacher back. He thought he had mastered the step now. But the waiter was not there. "He is gone, Sir—skipped out. The head waiter caught him stealing from the pantry. But was OK. He was not very good waiter anyway. We find plenty better ones."

"But not one that can teach me the rhumba," said the major. "Too bad—he was good dancer. Better dancer than thief," he said, laughing heartily at what, at the moment, he thought to be a very good joke.

19
» » RETURN FROM THE CITY

The lieutenant's first Mission to Manila had been a real success. Now a rendezvous with several guerilla leaders from Major Edward Ramsey's command in southeastern Luzon had been set up for a point en route to the south coast, where How Party would shove off across the Passage on the return trip. Several of the guerilla leaders were to return to THE TOWER with them for further Intelligence training.

Hernandez was still very sad over the loss of his two boys. The only other disappointment on the mission had been his failure to contact Willie Hernandez. He had felt that if he were in the city himself, he could find Willie. He had had agents hunting for him for two months now and he began to fear that something really serious had happened to his cousin. It seemed hardly possible that a popular young man, son of a one-time general of the Army and later governor of his own province, could disappear and leave no trace among either relatives or friends.

A graduate of LaSalle University, associated first with a local banking firm and later with an American company, importers and exporters of heavy gear, and having lived in the city since childhood, Willie could mingle with almost any group without exciting comment. Such a man would be invaluable to THE MISSION. They would have to keep trying.

Late at night, after a final inspection of certain important installations marked on the map from the city hall, How Party left the city. Their scheduled stop for the second night was with a well-to-do family far to the south of Manila and east of their previous mountain hideout in Batangas. Directly back of the large house which was surrounded by a wide, high-walled yard, was a church and convent. In front of the house and across the street, was the enemy-controlled police station. This large home with its spacious grounds was so close to the police station that it had never fallen under surveillance.

On the morning of their scheduled departure for THE TOWER, Lieutenant Hernandez woke up with another attack of malaria. Among the guerilla leaders who had arrived there to meet them was Captain Johnny Ysmael. It was in a large building owned by his family that they had established the lookout and photographic center to report on the contents of Manila Bay. Like Willie Hernandez, Captain Ysmael's family connections and business contacts were such that his association with many persons in various positions was a natural, everyday occurrence.

Information furnished by several of the early arrivals served to bring the map virtually up to the minute. Although burning with fever by that time, Hernandez worked desperately to get all the entries made while the men who could pass the information to him were available—and before he became too ill or lost consciousness entirely as he had on the trip to the city.

The group was assembled in the long, central room of the house with the huge wall map spread on the floor. The lieutenant was kneeling on the map, making entries as they were given to him. His hands shook as he tried to finish the job.

A guard lounged lazily on the front porch, apparently napping and reading a newspaper, intermittently. Turning several sheets of the paper at one time meant one thing to the man stationed just inside the window. Folding it or dropping it meant another. Only in an emergency was the guard to speak to anyone on the inside. The men were deep in their task when the guard rattled the paper noisily. A Japanese officer and two enlisted men had come out of the police station and stood looking directly across the street to where he sat.

With the sound of the rattling paper, every man was on his feet, with the exception of Hernandez, who stopped as though transfixed—one hand in mid-air, as the guard spoke.

"An officer and two EM's from the police station are crossing the street," he said in a low voice.

A guerilla officer who had been helping with the map stooped to pick it up. "No," said Hernandez. "Leave it where they can see it. That will bring them into the house."

"They're coming toward the house," said the guard. "They're on the sidewalk in front of the gate."

"All right, Men, if it's their lives or ours, remember—it has to be quick, and quiet. No shots—no outcries. TAKE COVER!"

As the others disappeared behind doors, large cabinets, and tall screens, he too stepped behind a tall *sawalit* (woven, split bamboo) screen and waited. A moment later the guard said, "All clear. They've gone on down the street."

A few days later, a cartographer back at THE TOWER copying portions of the city map, remarked that some of the entries looked a little wobbly. "Probably so," said Hernandez. He could be casual then. "I was going into a malaria attack when I made those entries."

Consistent with the narrow-margin timing of the entire trip, just as they were filing out of the house under the benevolent shadow of the convent, a runner came asking that they wait. Willie Hernandez was on his way there! After all those weeks of searching, they would wait!

It would be several hours before Willie's party could reach there and, after such a long march, they could not start on at once. They would have to have food and at least a short rest.

But what of the men down on the south coast? They had brought the *Doña Juana* up from the Pandan area to hasten the return trip. They had orders to pick up How Party within certain time limits and they would be there. The size and lines of the *curicannan* would have stood out anywhere and it was no secret that the enemy was becoming hard pressed for shipping to handle troops and supplies. U. S. Navy ships and aircraft had already strewn the ocean floor with enemy ships from Cape Engano on northeast Luzon to San Bernardino Strait. A 90-ton *curicannan* would not he there long without being confiscated.

"I don't like to have them waiting for us there. It's too dangerous," said Hernandez.

"True," said Garcia, "but those men have learned how to get out of tight spots."

"But they were told to meet us at a certain time and barring, well barring damn near anything, they'll be there," Hernandez argued. "I've already had to change their orders once."

"They'll handle it, Sir. They ALWAYS do what has to be done," said Garcia, "and you should . . ."

"And who should know that better than I?" finished Hernandez.

Finding transportation for twenty men was not going to be easy, and they could not afford the time to walk all the way to the coast. In addition to the men waiting there with the boat, there was also the need to get a great deal of material they had, back to ISRM in time for the report going to GHQ by the next submarine. *Caratelas* would be their only chance and there was no hope of spacing departures. Their number would have to become a part of the strategy, but not until they had left the local police station a few miles behind. Until then they would have to walk.

In the next town they secured three *caratelas* and after considerable maneuvering, appeared to arrive by chance at a wide river bridge at about the same time. All vehicles crossing the bridge had to be inspected at the toll gate. The guerilla officers from Manila, being accustomed to outwitting the Japs, offered to run interference for the lieutenant. He was carrying a great number of compromising papers, including the city map of Manila and a number of hand drawn maps of target areas with special installations. In addition, the entire party was armed.

It was agreed that Willie and the lieutenant, Captain Garcia, Zamora and Mang Pedro should follow the guerillas in the second rig. The remaining men from ISRM, including the several survivors of the Cut Throat Squad, should take the third. This time all travel papers were in order.

The first *caratela* went through without difficulty. They were not checked for arms. Only their travel papers were examined. Many of the enemy soldiers, now realizing their unpopularity, were content to keep the native population under control with as little effort as possible. As the second driver stopped for inspection, the men in the third rig set up a great clamor about having to wait so long. They were going to a dance. If they had to wait there all night, the dance would be over. They demanded that the guards take them ahead of No. 2 *caratela*.

To keep them quiet, the guards apologized to the occupants of the No. 2 rig and took No. 3 first. Then the men in No. 2 rig put on an act of being outraged at having to wait while a rig full of rowdies on their way to a dance were taken before them. The driver agreed with them at first and they demanded that he go on without waiting for inspection. He hesitated but they only became angrier and after a few threats relative to his personal safety, he took off. A mile or two down the road, he stopped and said they had to get out. He should not have passed the bridge without his fares being inspected. That was enough to make him lose his license, he said, and the fare was not worth it.

A few hand grenades Willie had stashed away within easy reach, convinced him that it WAS worthwhile to take them to the next village— the one at which the *Doña Juana* was to meet them. As a special concession, they did let him drop them at the outskirts of the town, where they could thin out on the way down to the waterfront.

The men in No. 3 rig, however, defeated their purpose in their loud clamoring, for their driver was adamant. They had no choice. They could just get out and walk. He owned his rig and he didn't intend to lose it and probably his license also. He was not being persuaded. The next hour was an uneasy one for the party trying to keep out of sight in the shadows of the trees and small buildings near the beach, and for the men on the boat who had stalled a patrol through two rounds on their detail. They pretended to be making a repair on the boat, which if the MP's knew anything about boats, they could have told by looking was a phony excuse.

When at last the late comers hurried in on foot, they took a look around and all made a run for the boat. Darkness and a brisk breeze kept them sailing along full speed over the black water without interference. Throughout the rest of the night and the early morning hours ships passed going one way or another. Lights appeared and ships came close. Sometimes the *Doña Juana* would have to tack to the right or left to avoid close contact. But one by one, they sailed away and disappeared in the distance.

A squadron of planes roared overhead in the darkness toward Luzon on their mission of destruction. The men in the big sailboat did not know it then, but the softening had begun. Those were carrier-based, American planes. It was more than gratifying to find a message on file at THE TOWER OF ISRM, which read:

> DMAC REPORTS APPROXIMATELY ONE HUNDRED PLANES SIGHTED OVER CUENCA REPEAT CUENCA NEAR LIPA AT ZERO TWO ZERO ZERO AND WERE INTERCEPTED BY TWENTY FIVE JAP PLANES. JAPS ORDERED COMPLETE BLACKOUT ALL TOWNS BATANGAS. ALL DISTRICTS WITHIN FIVE KILOMETERS MANILA BAY EVACUATED BY CIVILIANS SEVEN SEPTEMBER. MANILA ENTIRELY CLOSED TO INCOMING CIVILIANS FOR FIFTEEN DAYS.

It had been one of Sergeant Berg's Mobile Units which had reported the planes. "Mobile Radio" at that time meant a man moving from one place to another with his portable transmitter on his back. The other recognized type was a motorized unit. With the increased area now being covered, only motorized units would be adequate for the job. In things of this kind, local men such as Captain Ysmael could be of great value. He knew dealers who owned cars which had not been sold at the time of the invasion and which they had been able to keep under cover, avoiding confiscation by the enemy. When the need for such a vehicle was established, the captain arranged for delivery of a truck for the transmitter and a sedan for a getaway car. Continued trips to a spot where they could make contact with ISRM, would be hazardous, but the need was urgent. With a fast car under cover, the radio men had a much better chance of escape if some night an enemy patrol caught up with their mobile transmitter.

The time out to paint a transfer company sign on the truck and subsequent delivery to an isolated spot probably saved the truck from being taken over by the enemy. The fresh, new sedan was grabbed from the hands of the driver making delivery, before it reached the point where it was to be put into service. Later, however, another sedan operated for months as a taxi between Manila and Taal Lake. The drivers managed to pick up reports over a large area, striking out late at night for the high ground near the lake where they could relay their reports to ISRM.

A "mobile radio" not found in the books was Sergeant Pascua's *calesa*, with sound and camera equipment attached. His efficient taxi service was in steady demand between Manila hotels housing enemy officers personnel. So he went about serving—and photographing—individuals and military installations, sometimes recording conversations, all of which were sent to ISRM. A few days in the taxi business and the sergeant became expert at getting his horse and rig into any position necessary to photograph anything or anyone with a potential military value.

A great deal of first-hand information and knowledge of current and prewar conditions by which it might be evaluated, in relation to re-invasion operations, came with the men who had joined How Party on the return trip to THE TOWER.

Landing under cover of darkness at Abra de Ilog, they sent the reports which could be relayed to ISRM and rested for the night. Good weather, dry trails, and no incidents added up to a record trip for a large party—less than six days on the trail!

Approaching THE TOWER from the western edge of the perimeter of defense, they reached the West Guerilla Village first. Commander Rowe and all the men who could leave their posts had come to welcome them. The leaders from the North were introduced but it was obvious that the commander and Captain Ysmael needed no introduction. Their hearty handshake and smiling enthusiastic greeting told that they had known each other in better and happier days. "Well I certainly didn't expect Commander Nicholson, U. S. Navy, to be George Rowe, but it's damn good to see you, Commander, even if you are a long way from your ship."

Laughing heartily, still shaking the captain's hand, George replied, "And it's mighty damn good to see you. You're the first person from home I've talked to for dam near three goddam LONG years."

"We've often wondered what happened to you. I've talked to a lot of fellows, but no one seemed to know anything about you—where you'd gone or anything."

"Oh, I'm a son-of-a-gun when it comes to writing letters," said Rowe laughing again to cover his eagerness to get away long enough to find out what Hernandez had to tell him about his family.

They were getting too close to things Rowe did not want to talk about. Hernandez casually changed the subject with, "It was in one of the captain's office buildings that we set up the lookout station on Manila Bay."

"So THAT'S how you got the job done in such good time," commented Rowe, while a quick look and a half smile passed between Captain Garcia and the lieutenant—but there was no danger that the commander was going to hear about it.

Nothing, however, could hide the hunger in George Rowe's eyes as he contrived to get away from the others for a few moments. All the questions that would not wait came tumbling out. "Did you find her, Al? Is she all right? And my boy, how is he?"

"She's fine, George. They both are. Things haven't been easy. You knew they wouldn't be. But they're both well. I think she would have come back with us if we could have brought her."

"Where is she and how did she manage?"

"Naturally, there was no time to do anything when the attack began. She was afraid she would be taken into custody because you were an American Naval officer—and they were picking people up everywhere, herding them into prisons."

"Yes, yes," said George, "But what did she do?"

"She tried to think where they would be least likely to look for her. She decided that it would be with the old couple you had on the list."

"That was good thinking. She's a smart lad," said Rowe, his eyes glowing with pride and happiness.

"Naturally there was no chance of getting into a bank or anything of the kind. She decided to try to escape with the boy and leave everything else."

Rowe nodded approvingly. "Yeah, she'd look after him, no matter what."

"She didn't dare take a taxi and she was afraid to try to drive her own car, so she packed what the boy had to have and a few things for herself—what she could carry in a handbag—and they starting walking to the home of the old people."

"My GOD, Al, that's miles!"

"Right. And she and the little fellow got pretty tired, but it was dark, except for the light from the burning buildings. When they couldn't go any farther they'd sit down somewhere in the shadows and rest. Then they'd get up and go on. They made it all the way without any kind of interference."

"Poor kid, how did she manage?" said Rowe, shaking his head, picturing their agonizing flight from their home with roaring tanks and battle-mad enemy troops overrunning the city, while enemy bombers rained destruction from above.

"Her biggest real problem was that she had to cut herself off from all resources because she didn't dare identify herself. That and leaving the house and everything in it unprotected."

"What happened to our home, do you know?"

"Yes," said Hernandez, "but you aren't going to like it." "I suppose they bombed it or deliberately burned it down."

"No. It's serving as quarters for a Jap general and his staff. He rides back and forth in your Cadillac every day to his Manila Hotel headquarters."

Rowe's hand clinched into a tight, hard fist. The knuckles stood out sharp and white. "Those dirty goddam sonsa-bitches," he said, grinding his teeth together. "My wife has to leave everything she has—get along with nothing—go hungry. I live out here in a goddam jungle hut, walk hundreds of miles all over this goddam island, and those bastards living like kings ON MY DOUGH. Do you know what that house alone cost me? Damn near a hundred thousand pesos. If I ever get my hands on one of those . . ." He stopped, too angry to pursue the thought. "How did you find her, Al?" "I sent two good men. One spoke English, the other Japanese, so they wouldn't have trouble wherever they had to go. But she didn't know you or anything about you—never heard of you, in fact, until one of the men said he came from Marlanda's master."

"God, I'm glad I thought of that," said Rowe almost reverently.

"When she knew the message really came from you, she couldn't hold the tears back any longer."

Virginia Rowe was certain that only George would have thought of using his horse's name as a clue. By that she knew that it was he who was near and would be coming home to her.

It might have been relief that came into George Rowe's eyes when he knew that his wife and son were safe; but somehow Al Hernandez had a strong feeling that it was a greater determination than ever to get to Manila and personally set them free.

The guerilla boys and Mangyans had gone all out to celebrate their safe return. They had built a long, low dining table of bamboo and jungle twine. The little men had searched the jungle for exotic blossoms, beautiful orchids, rare plants and leaves. Beautiful and fragrant tropical fruits which at the St. Francis Hotel in San Francisco or New York's

Waldorf, would have cost a good sized roll of "cool, crisp cabbage," completed the table decorations.

With the introductions and Rowe's and Hernandez' conference over, the men proudly uncovered their masterpiece. From heaven only knew where, they had assembled the makings for a wonderful, spiced barbecue of chicken and pork called *adobo*, a feast dish in the Islands, reserved for very special occasions. There was also brown rice, a succulent salad from the delicate bud of a jungle plant, and at last a delicious dessert of thin sliced coconut packed in tart fruit juice and brown sugar and left in long sections of bamboo until ready to serve.

Judged by any standards, the food was excellent, and after the scant rations the Manila party had been able to carry on the trail, every delicious mouthful was superb.

Lieutenant Hernandez was deeply touched by the demonstration and Commander Rowe, overjoyed by the news from his family, which of course he could not talk about. As his contribution to the celebration he decided to announce something which he had been considering for several days.

For some time the matter of rank in the Guerilla Army being so superior to that in the U. S. Army-Navy Expedition, had created something of a problem. It had been downright embarrassing for all concerned, when a Tech Sergeant found himself having to say to a guerilla colonel, "Sir, that's an order."

After a quick huddle with Hernandez and Berg, the commander announced that he had orders promoting both Lieutenant Hernandez and Sergeant Berg to the rank of Captain and the Tech Sergeants to the rank of Lieutenant. Everyone was happy over the promotions which they all thought well deserved. Certainly it was going to simplify the situation for the principals involved, even if Rowe had been explaining, in the huddle, that HE HAD WRITTEN THE ORDERS HIMSELF.

An hour earlier, when Al Hernandez had entered the enclosure around West Guerilla Village, with a successful mission behind him, the one thing he could think of was getting out of his clothes, under a warm shower, and falling into his jungle hammock and to sleep. But a moment after the commander sat down, several guitars appeared and the men began to sing the plaintive folk songs of the Islands and to harmonize in popular old American ballads.

Once more the commander rose and said, "Captain Hernandez, I know you are very tired after your long and strenuous mission, but it wouldn't seem right to end this celebration without at least one dance."

Hernandez stood up amid enthusiastic applause. The weariness seemed to have left his face, still gaunt from the ravages of malaria. "Since surprises are the order of the day, I too have a surprise for you. For several weeks some of the men have been rehearsing when and where they could, and I am proud and happy to introduce to you, Captain Dodson's Dancing *Troubadorés.*"

Music from the native guitars provided accompaniment for the dancers in several beautiful, old folk dances in which their graceful bodies swing and sway to the tapped-out rhythm of the hard, dry coconut shells. Then came a hilarious comic dance a caricature of the *bao* with a little jitterbug thrown in, and finally the bamboo dance, in which two men, seated, hold parallel two long bamboo poles, about 18 inches apart. The beauty of the dance is the precision with which the dancers step in and out to the music as the poles are struck together, with a click, click, click—click, click, click, to the tempo of the music.

That night probably stood out from all others for that oddly assorted group—business men, scientists, students, entertainers, reserves and regulars assembled at THE TOWER OF ISRM, on the return from the Mission to Manila.

20
» » LIFE AT ISRM

Life was strangely incongruous at THE TOWER OF ISRM under the rigid requirements of an Intelligence mission and uncompromising military discipline, deep in an area for centuries the solitary abode of Pygmy tribesmen, whose only garment was a loin cloth and whose medium of exchange was common salt. At rough, bamboo tables, in a *nipa* covered communications center, they worked with ultramodern precision instruments and tested special electronics devices that were the last word—still spoken in a whisper—while their transportation was as old as civilized man.

There was no hurry-to-wait routine there. When a man was ready for his assignment, and frequently he worked day and night to get ready for it, he hurried off on foot, to active duty—often thrilling, hair-raising duty.

With an Intelligence class in full swing, it was not unusual to look into the map room at 2200 and see perhaps fifty young men at drawing tables, working with the utmost precision, by the dim light of a native, coconut-oil lamp, to acquire the skill required in expert cartography. They were learning to draw to scale the maps which later they would send back to ISRM, to keep GHQ informed of the location of every anti-aircraft gun, ammo dump, camouflaged airplane runway, fuel dump, plane dugout, food stockpile, searchlight, shelter, lookout-post, ship-repair shop, dock and loading facility—every potential target in and around the City of Manila.

Captain Hernandez made his first inspection of the day at 0400, to see what had taken place during the night and to observe the enemy dawn patrol, to check for any unusual activity as they passed over or near THE TOWER.

The point where the two men had gone when George had told Al about his family, was their private conference room. There at the top of the world they stood, sometimes at sunrise, sometimes at sunset just before evening mess—thrilled almost to sadness by the beauty, the immensity, the vast loneliness stretched before them. In the evening, deep purple shadows softened the rugged outline of the lower range of mountains surrounding the TOWER, as a coral sun slipped into the deep blue water of the distant South China Sea.

Standing there one day scanning the sky and sea, observing a formation of enemy planes heading in toward Luzon, George pressed his lips together and began nodding his head slowly but emphatically. He had just reached a very definite conclusion. "Al," he said, "I'll bet you that Caddie I won from you last night in the poker game, that those goddam. . ." Suddenly he was excited "Yessir, that's it. That's it—sure, by God, as hell."

"Fine, fine," said Hernandez completely in the dark. "I agree. You're absolutely correct—a thousand per cent. But how about finishing just one sentence so I'll know what the hell it is you're so sure of."

"Those planes. I've been trying for weeks to figure out some pattern to what they do. Now I've got it. They come in from all directions to some place south of here, probably San José. There they funnel-in, and fly straight into Manila and the surrounding airfields."

"So? You're the flier in this outfit. What then?"

"That IDENTIFIES THEM. The Nips know automatically that a plane coming in from any other direction isn't theirs. Of course our observation would be too limited to make a definite statement. We'll put out the word to the other islands and see what comes out. But I'm pretty damned sure what it'll be."

That keen, clear reasoning revealed one of the enemy's best laid plans and incidentally became a strong factor in the choice of action when they faced immediate evacuation when THE TOWER OF ISRM was compromised.

Rowe and Hernandez often worked far into the night preparing instructions for agents going on special missions, preparing reports to be dispatched to Australia by the next submarine, or doing any one of the thousand things that came up to keep them long after the others were in the sack. Of course there were always the guerillas standing watch far below and the lone sentinel in the crow's nest, watching through the night.

One night when roll call was near the peak and the food supply exhausted, they were working alone—tired, long since out of cigarettes, and very hungry. The outraged intestines of one of them gave out with a lusty growl. They looked at each other accusingly, and with a wicked grin, Rowe said, "I hear you're on a diet, Captain."

To which Hernandez replied, "Yep. Have to watch the waistline with all this food and no exercise."

"I guess we should be glad the Nescafe floated that night when all the rest of the rations went to the bottom," said Rowe philosophically.

"My God, YES," said Hernandez. "How would we ever have made it?" Putting his pencil down, he got up and walked down to his quarters and dragged out a duffle bag and dug down until his fingers closed around a small, hard, rectangular package. Back in the office, he stood for a moment with his hand behind him. Rowe looked up, a little puzzled, and said, "What have you got there?"

Something I'll trade you half of, for the Caddie you won from me on the 'air funnel to Manila' deal."

"Oh NO you don't," said Rowe. "I didn't WIN the Caddie on the air funnel. I just KEPT it. Anyway, what've you got in your hand?"

Hernandez held it out for him to see—a small tin of bouillon cubes in a red and gold foil wrapper. "Read the note," he said. "She had it stuck on with a piece of a band-aid."

George reached for the note and read it aloud. " 'Darling: Some day you may need this. Save it till then. Carmelita.' Well, we'll never need it any worse—I HOPE!" he said.

Taking themselves off down to the mess kitchen where Mang Pedro's MP's (Monkey Police) scolded noisily, they found a pan, far too large for the purpose, but it would have to do. "How much do you think we should use?" said Hernandez.

"Not that we'll ever need it again—the Mangyans are sure to find something tomorrow, but let's just use half of it."

"OK," said Hernandez, counting the cubes as he dropped them into the pan. They stood drooling as they waited for the water to heat, and Hernandez stirred it gently. Carrying the pan of hot broth back up to where they had been working, they pushed back the papers and sat drinking it slowly, savoring every warm, delicious sip. There in the stillness of the night, in a rude, *nipa* covered shelter on a lonely mountain top, two young men bound by a common purpose, had shared for all time something more than a pot of bouillon.

Another unforgettable experience at ISRM was to sit high up on the mountain and listen to the voices of probably two hundred guerillas around the evening campfire, far below, as they sang and strummed their guitars. Their pleasures were simple and moments devoted exclusively to relaxation were few. It would be impossible to imagine how full the hours could be so far away from GHQ—the enemy—and the rest of the world. By now they were well on the way to the full complement of 3000 active agents, in many parts of the Islands. As a liaison instrument, THE TOWER OF ISRM stood like an hour glass whose sands flowing through the narrow passage were as steady as the stream of communications between the Islands and GHQ.

21
» » THE TOWER POSITION IS COMPROMISED

By mid-September 1944, U. S. carrier-based task forces had reduced the enemy air force by almost 2000 planes in four weeks. Then they took on the job of cleaning up Manila Harbor, setting off a few ammo dumps and testing the antiaircraft strength in the city. Simultaneously, Commander Rowe took a party on an important mission to the North. He wanted to make an inspection of certain areas and to investigate reports that a large number of boats were hiding in the coastal waters southeast of Luzon.

The Air Warning System of THE MISSION also required strengthening there and he wanted to meet personally with Colonel Anderson and Major Ramsey, also escaped from Bataan and now commanding a large and very active guerilla band. Major Ramsey's only request for help had been for radio equipment, when his envoy met with Captain Hernandez at the big house near the convent. The commander had ordered the gear sent to him at once and now they were working with Rowe's men in the constant quest for information on enemy activities, often going where an Intelligence Unit cannot go—into combat with enemy troops.

On the return trip, Rowe had stopped at Asis Outpost. Under command of Lieutenant Logan, the post had become a model of efficiency and strict military discipline. "We should call him Logan von Rundstedt," said Rowe. "He has that place running like a Wehrmacht post and it looks like a full-fledged Intelligence station. From Reveille to Retreat, they're training, drilling, training in jungle tactics, Intelligence classes. He's improved all the buildings and extended the landing into a long loading pier."

"I told you if the Japs ever came up the river, looking for us they'd probably never go any farther," said Hernandez.

"Well you're right," said Rowe. "You'd never take that for an outpost." He laughed, and said, "And those phony maps they've got all over the place. He's made a hell of a lot more than a stopping place or a listening post out of it."

"How do you like that security setup?" queried Hernandez.

"Isn't that something? He may keep out some that should get here, but he'll sure as hell never let any through that shouldn't. If he'd been set up like he is now that son-of-a-bitch Ortega would never have gotten through. Of course it was lucky that he did, but the odds against something like that happening again are about a thousand to one."

"Ortega" was the name they had given to a prisoner they held, charged with responsibility for the betrayal of the Major Philipps Party. He came to ISRM claiming to have been sent to bring them important information relative to enemy activities in the northeastern Mindoro area. However, one of Dodson's Guerilla Fighters had been active in the North at the time of the ambush and slaying of the major and the torture death of at least a part of his men. It still was not known whether all of them had been slain. Ortega stoutly denied the charge, disclaiming any knowledge of the affair and they were unable to break down his story. The Guerilla Fighter was known to be a loyal and honorable man and there was no reason for him to bring a false charge against the suspect. The evidence was too strong to allow him to return to wherever he came from, so "Ortega" was held prisoner under guard to await trial by the proper authorities when that time came.

Shortly before the enforced evacuation of THE TOWER Sergeant Benjamin Harder, a survivor of the Philipps Party and possibly the one man alive who actually knew their betrayer, found his way to ISRM and reported for duty with THE MISSION. When told of the prisoner, Sergeant Harder said, "I saw the face of the man who led them to us. I'll NEVER forget it. Let me see him."

The sergeant stood looking out through the open window with his back to the room, when the prisoner was brought in. As the man came forward, glancing furtively about, obviously wondering why he was being brought from the stockade, Sergeant Harder turned slowly and looked him full in the face. The fear, the absolute terror in Ortega's face was confession enough. No words from the sergeant were necessary. The heart attack which followed might have been the result of Ortega's fear or it might have been his way of covering his guilt, but was neither convincing nor effective if he hoped to gain sympathy. It was to be a long time before he would have either his freedom or a chance to redeem himself.

It was good to see the commander's enthusiasm, for he had been very bitter when he left for the North. Being so close to those he loved and still denied the privilege of seeing them, when he had been away so long, was hard to take, even though he was fully aware that one of the primary reasons for his being chosen to head MISSION ISRM was his wide acquaintance in the city. An example of his value in relation to economic developments, particularly in banking in Manila, came on the trip. He hurried the information he had acquired back to ISRM to be relayed to GHQ:

> ROWE RADIOS FROM NORTH JAPS BELIEVED HURRYING NEW CENTRAL BANK SETUP TAKING ADVANTAGE OF SECTION NINETEEN ACT NUMBER ELEVEN QUOTE: ALL CURRENCY RESERVE FUNDS SHALL BE TRANSFERRED TO THE CENTRAL BANK ON THE DATE SAID BANK SHALL COMMENCE BUSINESS UNQUOTE: HE ALSO SUGGESTS THAT PRESIDENT OSMENA BE REQUESTED TO MAKE SPEECH AGAINST IT AS PEOPLE WILL REALLY GET BURNED THIS ONE. GOVERNMENT ALSO ISSUING LONG AND SHORT TERM BOND ISSUES ALL OVERSUBSCRIBED BY JAPS AS HEAVY BUYERS.

Commander Rowe came back to THE TOWER to a really bare mess kitchen. Two days before he arrived, Captain Hernandez called in the guerilla sergeant in charge of the procurement detail. "Double the detail of Mangyans searching for food," he said. "We don't want the commander to come back and find NO FOOD AT ALL."

"There are already two details at work, Sir. That was Captain Dodson's order yesterday."

"And they haven't found anything YET?" asked the lieutenant, wondering how long men could hold out without food and where they could go to get food in sufficient quantities to really help.

"You know, Sir, we've been feeding a lot of men. The little guys have stripped these mountains of just about everything but the monkeys."

"We won't do that unless—well, unless we're really starving," said Hernandez, turning a little sick.

"I think even Mang Pedro's old Parsons knows how serious it is, Sir. That old goat has been hiding out for two days."

"Now that I think about it, I haven't seen him. You don't suppose that any of the . . . ?"

"If you mean have any of the guerilla villages caught him, Sir, the answer is NO. Some of the men have gone out looking for him. They didn't want Mang Pedro to think . . ." "OK," interrupted Hernandez smiling, "I just didn't want that done without his consent, and it had to be for everyone, if it came to that."

They were well into the second day without food—they had not found Parsons—and Rowe and Hernandez were preparing the report on the commander's mission to the North, which was to be picked up by an Australian-bound submarine three days later at Barahan. By the time the high, staccato notes on the bamboo flute had stopped both men were on their feet, heading for the Radio Room where an intercom connected with the Crow's Nest.

Through his high-powered lenses, the lookout had spotted a ship approaching the coast near the Asis River Delta and Lieutenant Alvarez, had reported simultaneously from his Coast Watch station JRH, that a Jap corvette had arrived there. He was trying to determine what the vessel was doing.

Rowe and Hernandez leaned over the radio man's shoulders to read what he wrote on the small yellow message pad.

CREW APPEARS TO BE PREPARING FOR LANDING. LOWERING LANDING CRAFT OVER THE SIDE.

"Ask him if the alternate radio man is there to take over for him," said Rowe.

A moment later the operator wrote, "Yes."

"Tell Alvarez to take the stand-by detail there and proceed to the landing area. Offer any possible assistance. Have them keep JRH informed if they have to get out of his range of vision."

The radio man was writing again:

TWO LARGE LANDING CRAFT BRINGING MEN AND MATERIEL ASHORE. OUR MEN FILTERING IN TO OFFER HELP. CAN STILL SEE ALL OPERATIONS.

"Alert Dodson, Al," said Rowe. "He may get some action here."

The radio operator was writing again:

OUR MEN CARRYING JAP OFFICER PERSONNEL ASHORE PIGGY BACK. APPROXIMATELY TWO HUNDRED MEN ASHORE AND COMING ASHORE. SECOND LANDING CRAFT COMING IN ON SECOND TRIP. BEACHING BOAT. APPARENTLY NOT RETURNING TO SHIP NOW.

As Hernandez stepped out through the door, Dodson raised up from a log where he had been sitting. He had come up as soon as he heard the signal. Quickly Hernandez filled him in on the details, then said, "Alert your men, Bill. Find out just how many you have available and report back to George's office."

Dodson took off on the double. Rowe came out of the Radio Room and down the path. Hernandez fell in step with him. "This looks serious, Al. We've got a lot of important material that can't be radioed to GHQ. This report's GOT to be on that sub."

"It's a two-day trip to Barahan, if the trails are dry," said Hernandez. "We'll have to move fast."

"Meanwhile we've got to keep an eye on those sonsa-bitches on the beach—that's all we CAN do now. We can depend on Alvarez to keep us up to the minute on what they're up to."

"And if it comes to a fight," said Hernandez, "we can depend on Dodson."

A harmless-appearing bunch of native boys attracted to the beach by the enemy landing, gave the Japs every possible assistance. They carried the enemy officers ashore, piggyback to keep their shiny boots clean and dry, and set them down high on the narrow, sandy beach. With the personnel ashore, they carried in the equipment and helped establish a HQs back under the jungle trees. The sharp eyes of the native boys were open to every move, every word, and to the placing of every piece of gear brought from the ship to a large *nipa* house they appropriated to their use. Along toward evening, with HQs established, the commanding officer announced his plans to the men.

He assigned non-coms to details for reconnaissance patrols next morning—one to the north, one to the south. The guerilla standing near listened breathlessly for a patrol to be ordered to the east, but no such order came, and a large number of men were still unassigned.

One by one the native boys drifted away, each reporting back to JRH. Finally only Alvarez and two of the local boys remained, trying to make themselves useful so they would not be dismissed before they could find out more about the enemy plans and his reason for being there. Too many men remained unassigned!

The Jap CO was sitting at a folding table, studying a large map spread out in front of him. His boots had gotten dusty in the sand. Now that the more important details of establishing the beachhead were out of the way, he pushed back in his chair and characteristically, ordered one of the local boys to polish his boots. The boy knelt down obediently, and as he polished, he caught sight of the details of the map of western Mindoro. There he saw the reason for no detail to the East.

The next message from JRH said:

LANDING PARTY IDENTIFIED AS CRACK OUTFIT JAP MARINES REPORTED LANDING MANILA FEW DAYS AGO. RECON PATROLS ORDERED NORTH AND SOUTH. NONE ORDERED EAST. DO NOT KNOW WHY. SOME MEN STILL THERE. ALVAREZ HELPING JAPS SET UP THEIR RADIO IN HQS ESTABLISHED IN *NIPA* HOUSE NEAR BEACH. TWO OTHERS STILL THERE.

Rowe read the message and stood for a moment with his lips pressed tight together. The last four days had brought deep furrows to his brow. "This could mean ANYTHING, Al. God, what a time for the men to be hungry!"

Doggedly he went ahead, working on the report while Hernandez compiled those received from Luzon, Mindoro, Marinduque, Maricaban, Ambil, and Lubang Islands. They were working against time, and trying to keep in touch with what was going on down below, at the same time.

Just before twilight came the report that changed everything—except that they had a rendezvous to keep with a submarine.

Rowe had pushed back from his work for a moment and Hernandez came in from outside. "Al, have they found any food yet?"

"None," said Al, "but Mang Pedro is fixing up something for evening mess. There's not much nourishment in it, but it will help."

"Why bother, if there's no nourishment?" asked Rowe, sounding more worried than he realized.

"Ever hear of the '*kuru* tree'?" asked Al.

"I don't think so," said Rowe.

"It has a peculiar bark that can be stripped off and pounded and boiled. It's pretty insipid that way, but the guerilla boys say it tastes pretty good salted and peppered and fried in cakes."

An orderly came in from the Radio Room with a message but he waited for the captain to finish. "Mang Pedro says when the natives have no food at all, they eat the *kuru* bark to keep off hunger pains and keep down the belly-bloat that comes from prolonged hunger."

As Rowe's eyes fell on the message from JRH, he sprang to his feet. "Corporal, get Captain Dodson ON THE DOUBLE." At the tense tone of Rowe's voice, Al reached for the message and Rowe said, "ISRM is all through, Al. We've been here too long."

Al laid the message on the table and the two men read it through again together.

NOW UNDERSTAND NO PATROL TO EAST. MAN POLISHING SHOES OF CO SAW RED CIRCLE SURROUNDING TOWER POSITION ON MAP. OFFICERS DISCUSSING PLAN TO TAKE OFF

FROM HERE AT 0430 TO ATTACK ISRM APPARENTLY NOT SURE OF DISTANCE TO TOWER.

By being friendly and playing dumb the boys had learned that the enemy troops had come to track down and destroy an American force known to be operating a radio station somewhere in the mountains inland from Sablayan.

Their conversation indicated that they intended making the attack early in the morning, which proved that they did not know the rough terrain, the deep jungle, and the intervening valley and mountain range between their position and THE TOWER. One thing was certain. They would not know the trails and shortcuts ISRM runners and couriers had worked out.

Again Dodson was waiting nearby. "You sent for me, Commander," he said.

"Yes, Captain, come in. ISRM is all through, Bill. The Japs know we are here—and just about where we are." "The corporal just told me. You said there were about two hundred of them, Captain," he said, turning to Hernandez.

"Right," said Hernandez. And they intend taking off from there at 0430 to wipe us out."

"We'll have to get there first," said Dodson. "I wish I had more men. Funny how important that food detail seemed before we knew this. But my men can take care of them if WE make the attack."

"I know the men are hungry, Bill," said Rowe grimly, "but Al says Mang Pedro is fixing up some *kuru* bark for mess. I don't know how much good it will do, but..."

"Fighting on an empty stomach isn't easy, Commander, but my men have done it before and they'll do it again. If only we had some.. He hesitated.

"Some what?" asked Rowe.

"*Tubá,* Sir. If my men had some *tubá,* I KNOW they could handle them." He laughed. "You know that 'I-could-whip-anything' feeling."

Rowe smiled and nodded, "Yes, I think I do."

"But you're probably not familiar with our *tubá.*"

"A kind of coconut wine, isn't it?" said Rowe.

"Yes, Sir, but a pretty potent wine."

"Captain," said Rowe, looking steadily into the face of the rugged, young fighting man he had come to know he could trust, "Do you HAVE any *tubá*?"

"Not a drop, goddammit, and you've no idea what a hell of a job it's been to see to it that we didn't. Sometimes my boys forget that this is not a combat unit. When reports come in about some of the things that happen, I have to be pretty rough to keep the men under control. I couldn't take a chance on them getting liquored up some night and taking care of things on their own."

"Can you get some?" asked Rowe.

"With enough money in the right hands, Sir, I could have enough by this time tomorrow to whip the whole Jap army."

"Well, we don't have till this time tomorrow—but then we don't have the whole army to whip. More to the point, can you get enough to carry your men through this scrap tonight?"

"If I haven't been too rough on their sources, yes. I'll get the right men on the trail right away."

"OK, Al, fix him up with whatever he needs. Bill, tell your men not to haggle. JUST HURRY. And Al, stop at the Radio Room on the way back and tell Alvarez to stand by there to answer any questions and to guide Bill's men in."

At exactly 2200, Dodson was shouting commands to the thirty liquid diet boys he had picked to attack approximately 200 of the enemy's crack Marines. Standing in formation, in a steady rain, they passed the bamboo canteens of *tubá* along the line to give them a good start. At the foot of THE TOWER mountain they had another and again as they reached the summit of the lower range. Then to assure their being in really good fighting trim, they stopped about half an hour's march from the beachhead for one more generous drag on the *tubá*.

Arriving at the beachhead before any activity had begun, they took the enemy by surprise, and in true guerilla fashion, disposed of the sentries without a sound. Alvarez slipped in under the house, some four feet off the ground in that low area, and set a bomb just under the radio he had helped to install. Others placed bombs at points he indicated, and dashed back to their lines. The enemy troops who had not found sleeping room on the floor of the big *nipa* house, were sleeping in the clearing in front, directly between the two columns of guerillas, fanned out among the trees.

Six deafening explosions in quick succession sent splintered bamboo, bundles of *nipa* and human bodies hurtling through the air. Red flames shot up to stain the blackness of the jungle night as they licked at the quick flaming walls and the grass roof. The astounded men inside the house who survived the explosions staggered out through the single flaming doorway and Dodson's men picked them off neatly as they cleared the door. To add to the panic of the men awakened by the explosions, two of Alvarez' men from station JRH, dashed out around the lines, firing at intervals of ten to twenty feet a bamboo cannon, a noisy, gasoline-powered instrument of the devil, which depends upon the breath of the gunner to vaporize the fuel. It was totally ineffective in the way of inflicting any actual damage, but for creating the impression of a much larger force and much larger guns being used, it could not have been better.

In their confusion, the men who had been sleeping on the ground outside the house were incapable of any coherent action. Fifteen minutes after the first bomb, ninety of the men trapped in and around the house by Dodson's right and left flanks of rifle fire, were dead and seventy were wounded, with hardly a return shot being fired.

With little Pablo standing proudly beside him, Dodson gave the order to CEASE FIRE! His Guerilla Fighters withdrew without a single casualty.

"Let us finish them, Capitan," begged some of the eager *tubá* boys.

"NO MORE," ordered Dodson. "They've got a ship out there. We've got to leave enough to find out what they're likely to do next."

Dodson's force withdrew farther back into the jungle. Great clouds of sparks billowed out as the walls of the house fell in and the *nipa* roof collapsed. All that was left was a mass of hot, red ash when the men who had helped the landing force in the afternoon, came back. Some of the survivors huddled in the grey dawn beside the dying fire. Others were busy separating the dead from the wounded and giving first aid.

One of the guerillas approached an officer and said, "We hear shooting and see fire, Sir. We very sorry. Could we do anything to help?"

The ranking officer among the survivors thanked him and said he would be grateful for their help. The guerillas went to work helping to get the wounded men, their weapons and small equipment which had been left outside the night before, into the landing craft and back to the ship. As they worked, Alvarez asked innocently in a beautiful Tagalog-English-Japanese jargon, "Will you come back to get *americanos* and their radio station?"

"We will be back," said the young Nip officer in good, stateside English. "Next time we will not fail. In three days we will be back with a force of Marines and WIPE THEM OUT!"

"You like us to help you when you come back?" asked one of the detail from JRH.

"Do you know the trails to the mountains from here?" asked the acting CO.

"Oh yes, Sir. We know river trails and the best and shortest trails to mountains. We need work too, Sir. We have no money and no work long time now."

"You watch for our ship on the third day," said the young officer. "If you lead us to them in the mountains, we will pay you—pay you well. But for THIS, the smart Americans will pay," he added bitterly. "We know where they are and how they got there. They went in by the river, but they will not find it so easy to get out that way. We will leave men to guard the river to see that they do not. They will answer to the Imperial Navy and Marines for this."

So the Japs had done it again. They had to brag about what they would do and how they would do it. Now Alvarez and his men could go back to their post. This particular job was finished.

After what seemed endless waiting to the men working at THE TOWER, the first message came in from the battle zone. It read:

TRAPPED TWO HUNDRED OFFICERS AND MEN IN AND ABOUT HOUSE. NINETY DEAD. SEVENTY WOUNDED. NO CASUALTIES MY MEN. LEAVING SMALL FORCE HERE TO HELP GET WOUNDED BACK TO SHIP AND REPORT TO US ON FURTHER ACTIVITIES. STARTING BACK NOW.

Signed/DODSON.

22

» » OPERATION RIVERBOAT

Now the months of planning and hard work which had gone into THE TOWER OF ISRM, those convenient quarters, classrooms, underground tunnels and warehouses, the excellent position for air and sea observation, and above all, a perfect site for the transmitter to Australia, would revert in time to a desolate mountain waste.

From the moment it was established that their position had been compromised, every available man was assigned to some pre-arranged detail. They had taken time out only to see Captain Dodson off with his thirty *tubá* fighters. There had been the usual hearty slaps on the back—Good luck—Good hunting, and *Bahala na's,* as they took off down the slippery mountain trail. The spirits of the fighting men were much better than those left behind in the much less spectacular job of tearing down all they had built up in months of labor.

It was truly a bad time for the men to be hungry. But in September 1944, hunger was not new to the fighting men in the Philippines. In February 1942, the Surgeon General at USAFFE (USAF FAR EAST) HQs on Corregidor, reported that among the men on Bataan, only 55 per cent were fit for combat duty because of disease and malnutrition. They were slowly starving. Offshore from Mariveles, soldiers in *bancas* had set off dynamite and returned with the boats full of fish, if the boats were not sunk by enemy fire. Men on Bataan (without the natives' knowledge of the jungle) died from eating the *nomia,* a poisonous tuber resembling a potato, and the jungled hills were stripped bare of bananas, coconuts, papayas, wild pigs and deer. Then the service *carabaos* went for food and after that the horses. Came the day when the monkeys no longer chattered in the trees, and at last—the dogs no longer howled at night.

Now in September 1944, on Mindoro Island, the men of MISSION ISRM would eat Mang Pedro's cakes of *kuru* bark another night. The men Captain Dodson had left for duty at THE TOWER and those who had returned from the unsuccessful hunting detail, reported to Captain Hernandez. They were dispatched to round up the *carabao* tenders who, with their animals had made possible the rapid penetration of the area, and hurry them to THE TOWER.

Before the technical men could begin to dismantle the sensitive radio equipment and pack it for another move, final messages had to be sent informing GHQ of their situation and warning all substations to cancel their codes and be prepared to use new ones when they returned to the air. A detail began unearthing the buried supplies. Remembering the buffeting on the rocks, boxes floating in the sea, and the days of maddening uncertainty which followed, the men were meticulous in packing the equipment.

Accumulations of records had to be properly disposed of and as Hernandez went through the file of messages sent from ISRM to substations he could not suppress an occasional chuckle as he read those typical of the commander's pungent humor, for example:

> YOU REPORT SINKINGS BUT FORGET TO STATE SHIP TYPE. YOU ARE NOT CERTAIN WHEN LOVE CHARLIES SEEN. QUERY: WASSAMATTER YOUR EYES JOE?

or,

> PAPPY TO JUNIOR: WHATINHELL IS MATTER WITH YOUR CRYPTO MEN? THREE DAYS AGO WE RECEIVED A MESSAGE IN SINGLE TRANSPOSITION. QUERY: ARE YOU TIRED OF LIFE?

Apparently oblivious to all the activity and confusion attendant to dismantling the hub of their existence, wondering how Dodson and his men were making out and although for the moment pushed to the background, the vital question of which way to move—George Rowe sat quietly working to complete his report to GHQ. Whatever was happening down below, or whatever lay ahead, he had a deadline to meet. A submarine could not wait.

The major thought in the mind of everyone other than the commander, even though it was not their responsibility, was "Where will we go?" Running a close second and one that could hardly be called "minor," was "When do we eat?"

Several times as the night wore on, Rowe and Hernandez discussed momentarily the various possibilities open to them.

To go farther inland as originally planned was automatically eliminated. The first prerequisite of an Intelligence unit would be violated. The enemy would know they were there and it would be only a matter of time until they would be in exactly the same position. Then, should they go north or south. There were many valid reasons for not going south. They would be going away from their ultimate goal, and the reports Captain Hernandez had just compiled from all the outlying islands, confirmed Commander Rowe's theory of the air-funnel to Manila. Going south, then, would put them on the trail with a long caravan of animals and men, directly under the enemy air lane.

Finally the commander stood back from the map spread on the table. Hernandez waited. He knew George had come to a decision. In a moment he would say, "I'll tell you what we'll do, Al."

Looking back at the map again before he spoke, Rowe missed the smile that flickered over his companion's face as he prepared to trace their projected course, saying as he did so, "I'll tell you what we'll do, Al. They'll expect us to run away from them—probably to the south. We'll fool 'em. We'll move right into 'em. We'll go north and get that much closer to Manila."

"George, you're a genius," said Hernandez enthusiastically. "We could go all the way up to the north coast. Why we could eliminate that six-day march from here to Abra de Ilog, and back again."

"Sure we could," said Rowe, happy that the decision was made. "Think of it—12 days cut from every mission to Manila! Why Al, it's a natural. Why didn't we think of it before?"

The corporal stationed just outside the door came in and said, "Captain Dodson is here, Sir."

"Come on in, Bill," said Rowe pushing back from the table and walking toward Dodson with outstretched hand.

Bill Dodson gripped his hand firmly. He was tired, wet, hungry, and covered with mud, but the gleam in his eye unmistakably was that of the conqueror.

"We've been expecting you," said Rowe simply. "I guess the trails are pretty slippery," he said, thinking of the day he had come up that trail with the first caravan.

"Yes, they are," said Dodson, "and of course we couldn't start back right away. We wanted to get all the dope we could. They know we followed the river in. The CO—that is, the ranking officer, we GOT the CO—said 'The Americans found it easy to get in, but they will not find it so easy to get out.' They are coming back in three days to avenge the Marines they lost. They're leaving a squad to guard the mouth of the river so we can't get out while they go back for reinforcements. They never seemed to realize that we were local men."

Suddenly aware of the full significance of what Bill had just told them, Rowe said, "That means their guards will be between our boats and the open sea. We'll have to get a detail out to round up those guards and keep a close tab on them until we get out."

"I did that before I left, down there. My men won't lose them," said Dodson with a long, weary breath.

"Good," said Rowe, "we've got to get this gear out of here. If we lose it, THE MISSION is lost—and we've got to get the heavy gear out by boat, as far as possible."

"My men could easily put those guards out of the way," said Dodson.

"I'd rather sneak past them and let them hunt us while we make our getaway."

"That's probably the smart way to do it," Dodson agreed. "If we finish them off the reinforcements will take it for granted they got it trying to stop us on the river."

"Right," said Rowe. "I think our chances are a hundred per cent better if we don't have to get rid of 'em. Now then, Bill, you know your men better than anyone else does. Do you think they could get the heavy gear down the river in the *batels* after dark—and get past those guards?"

"That's quite an assignment, Commander, taking a heavily loaded *batel*, even an outrigger, downstream under sail. But if anyone can do it, they can. I don't believe better boatmen live than some of my men."

"To get away with it, we've got to know where those guards are every minute—what they're doing. We may even have to decide for them what they're going to do. Those men you have tailing them, Bill, do they speak Japanese?" "One does, that is, one does well. The other one's not so good. I'll get a replacement for him right away."

"We've got to be sure of every move. If worse comes to worst, let me know. I might surprise you, but we've got to know what those bastards are doing and saying—yeah, and what they're thinking. Of course, if they spot us getting out, then we'll have no choice."

"Right," said Dodson. "I'll go and line up my key men and let them decide who they want to work with them."

"Fine," said Rowe. "Al has a detail out now rounding up the *carabaos*. They should begin showing up here some time this morning." Turning to Hernandez he said, "Now then Al, this report HAS to get under way. I'd like to stay here and see this operation through."

"OK, George, just say the word. You know I'm ready. It's a good two-day trip to Barahan with good weather and dry trails. The trails are already bad and if this storm keeps up, we'll be heading into the wind and rain."

"OK, then," said Rowe, "You take Willie, Zamora, Mang Pedro, your Cut Throat Squad and a platoon of Mangyans—and no matter what happens—you've GOT TO GET THROUGH!"

"We'll get through," said Hernandez quietly. "Those men are all fast on the trail, and you couldn't do better than Jerry and Bill at this end."

"How soon can you leave?" Rowe asked.

"Within the hour," said Al. "Zamora and Mang Pedro have everything ready. I thought you'd want to handle it that way."

Rowe got up and started toward the door, then stopped and gripped Hernandez' shoulder firmly. "That's what I like about working with you, Al. You're always..."

He was interrupted by someone calling out, "Commander, would you give us a word of advice here, Sir?" From that hour forward, to Al and Willie Hernandez, and Mang Pedro, THE TOWER was to remain forever but a vivid page in the history of MISSION ISRM. As they started off down the slippery mountain trail, George's orders, always quick and to the point, were cracking out like rifle shots, muted only by the steady rain which was going to double the effort required for everything they had to do.

By mid-afternoon of the second day, equipment and supplies had been unearthed, the various installations dismantled, and packed on the backs of the *carabaos*, and the first contingent of the convoy was on its way. With all possible planning complete, and alternatives worked out for any foreseeable changes in plans, Commander Rowe, his bodyguard, Del Rosario, a platoon of guerillas of Dodson's choosing, and a platoon of Mangyans set out for the North.

Captain Berg was left in charge to bring up the rear with responsibility for matériel and men. This time, however, he had the support of Bill Dodson and his men, their courage, strength and loyalty.

That night, the small outrigger *batels*, loaded with tons of radio, weather equipment and other supplies, with Dodson's men in command, eased out of their moorings and Operation Riverboat was under way. Every hand was on the alert. In the operation of the heavily loaded boats there was no margin for error. A single wrong move, however slight, could be disastrous. The river, swift and swollen from the heavy, two-day downpour, swirled about the small craft lying dangerously low in the water as they moved out into midstream and started on their precarious way down to the sea. Every floating log was a potential hazard.

A final check with the guerillas tailing the enemy guards indicated that they were still divided on opposite banks of the stream and had not stationed a single man on the small delta island. With the first boats about a mile from the wide mouth of the river, a sudden, brisk breeze stretched the sails taut and whipped the boats up to an alarming speed. Rapidly approaching the point where the enemy guards had been reported last, Dodson's men hauled in their sails, nosed their craft into the swift current close to the mid-stream island. Lying low in the water, they skimmed by in the darkness and the shadow of the heavy, overhanging branches of the trees on the banks and the priceless cargo drifted safely out into the open sea.

The failure of the enemy platoon to post an island guard had permitted the evacuation of the vital heavy gear which, considering the time allowed, almost certainly would have been impossible by overland transportation. Dodson's men literally had staked their lives on doing the very thing the enemy platoon had been left there to prevent. But those unlucky devils could not have won in any case. Their numbers had come up when they drew the assignment, regardless of which way it went. As it turned out, they had a few more hours before they had to bow in prayer and follow in the suicidal footsteps of other military failures of their breed.

At Asis Outpost, everything that was to be moved was ready and waiting when the first contingent arrived from THE TOWER. Lieutenant Logan's phony maps were left to adorn the walls of the Orderly Room, and the Radio Room was littered with meaningless code messages, leaving the impression that the place had been evacuated in great haste.

23
» » TOP SECRETS AFLOAT

Darkness overtook the captain and his party on the downward trail near the *nipa* hut where he and the commander had taken refuge from the storm on their first reconnaissance. They stopped for a few hours' rest out of the rain.

As that midget task force left the hut in the foothills before dawn, still in the driving rain, it was not particularly encouraging to realize that two full days of sodden trails lay ahead and all possibility of communication behind. At the final sign-off of Station ISRM, just before they left THE TOWER the night before, KAZ had also left the air (for them) until subsequent contact and positive identification could be established with an alternate set of codes.

Throughout the entire mission, their only physical contact, and now their only contact with GHQ was the submarine. Accomplishment of a rendezvous with a submarine in enemy waters required a great deal of planning, scheduling, and communication, with luck playing no small part.

From January 1942 until December 1944, submarines were the only Allied craft operating in those waters. So effective was the enemy blockade established during the first seventy days of the war that it forced a complete reversal of the Allied sea and air routes to the Orient—around the other side of the world. Some of the water routes stretched out to 72 days from port of embarkation to destination and many thousands of miles of uncharted air lanes had no facilities for servicing supply planes. Small ship owners in Timor, New Guinea and Java were neutral in their sympathies. They were ready and willing to take the risk of running the Jap blockade for a fee commensurate with the risk involved, but cash was the only language they understood. U. S. Government funds in Melbourne, paid by check, were not acceptable.

So as the position of our troops on Bataan became more and more desperate, Allied HQs had to start over again. Cash was sent by plane from Washington to Brazil, across the Atlantic Ocean, Africa, Arabia, India, the Bay of Bengal, South China and the South China Sea to Java. It was little wonder that in those long heartbreaking months, desperate, defiant, young Americans sang out across the wild, jungle-covered hills of Bataan a song of frustration and disillusionment that went:

"Were the battling bastards of Bataan
No mammy, no pappy, no Uncle Sam
No aunts, no uncles, no nephews, no nieces
No rifles, no guns, no artillery pieces
And nobody gives a damn."

Now as Captain Hernandez and his party strove to make contact with the submarine scheduled to pick up their reports for GHQ, their luck too seemed to be running out. The storm had slowed them down to a maddening pace. As they pounded along the trail, their shoes and clothing heavy with water and covered with mud, every now and then a low-hanging branch or rain-drenched liana slapped them in the face. For more than 48 hours, the only food in their stomachs had been the *kuru* bark. The first retreat along the trail was on the outer side of the second range of mountains. There they took long enough to have food and change to dry clothing offered them. Depending upon the circumstances of the particular post at the moment, they might have thin rice soup and tea or a piece of fine roast pork with the rich tang of the open, wood fire and perhaps a sweet potato from the embers. Whatever they had now, had to be carried with them. There was not time to stop.

At nightfall of the second day, they passed out of the storm belt. The trails were dry and the night clear and starlit. All that night, they hurried along carrying the two heavy, metal cannisters containing the reports, stopping only minutes to rest and pick up food. They had lost too much time in the storm.

Through the third morning they kept hard to the trail, nerves on edge from the lack of sleep and the ever-lessening margin of time left to make their rendezvous. With minutes to go before noon of the third day, the hour scheduled for the rendezvous, they were welcomed by the guerillas at a post just outside Barahan.

By that time, the captain, Lieutenant Willie Hernandez, Mang Pedro and Zamora were all well known to this post. Their mission was explained quickly and two trusted guerillas volunteered for the hazardous task of sailing back and forth in a small fishing boat identified by a small American flag (which had to be hauled in every time a plane or boat approached), to make the contact with the submarine.

The metal cans and several demolition bombs were placed under the fishing gear and the volunteers were furnished with high-powered lenses. The captain gave final instructions.

"I know I don't have to impress upon you the seriousness of your undertaking, but let's go over it once more. In those cans are TOP SECRET reports from Manila, Southern Luzon, Maricaban, Marinduque, Lubang, and Ambil Islands. The families of almost every man at this post are somewhere in those islands.

"I don't have to tell you that being caught by the enemy with them in your possession would be much worse than sudden death, not only for you and your families but for many others. See to it that you DON'T get caught. The cannisters are designed to sink on contact with water. If you see that you actually are about to be captured, dump them and use the bombs to blow up your boat. You will be close enough to swim ashore. Are you clear on all details?"

"It's all clear, Sir," said one.

"We understand, Sir. Leave it to us," said the other.

As they shoved off, the rest of the party watched from the shelter of the thick jungle trees and plants growing down to within twenty yards of the sea.

Through the long afternoon and evening the men on shore as well as those in the boat scanned the surface of the sea for sight of the periscope. Enemy planes flew over occasionally, apparently taking no notice of the fishing boat. Night came and still no signal had been sighted. A night rendezvous had not been anticipated nor planned for, but before dawn the men were out again—just two men, fishing.

In the early light, Captain Hernandez and Mang Pedro stood under the trees, scanning the sea through powerful lenses. Once the captain lowered the glasses and stood silently waiting and wondering, Mang Pedro said, "You are very quiet this morning, Capitan."

"I was thinking, Mang Pedro, of another morning," Hernandez replied.

"Of another boat, maybe—with an old man and two little boys, fishing?" asked the old man.

Hernandez nodded.

"I was thinking of that too, Sir, and that I was very lucky man that it was you watching on shore."

Hernandez laughed lightly and shook his head. "No," he said, "You were lucky that you didn't give Sergeant Balleras reason to believe you were doing anything but fishing. He was the one following you with the gun."

"Maybe you right—but I still very lucky."

The day wore on with no sign of the submarine. Night came and the boat put into shore again. At dawn the fishermen went back to sail back and forth while they fished and waited for a periscope. A patrol plane flew over and went on his way, but he turned and came back again. That time he circled the boat, flying very low before he went on.

"I have a feeling he's spotted us," said one of the men uneasily.

"He looks like the one that looked us over yesterday," said the other. They were in a very bad spot by that time.

"I wish that sub would show up and let us get rid of this damned stuff," said the first. "We've been here too long." But the sub didn't show up and the men stood by, hoping and praying that the vigil would end soon. Back in the jungle, the first caravoy from ISRM had arrived and set up a perimeter of defense, to wait for the rest of the expedition. Eventually several sections were dispersed over an area of probably two miles.

Commander Rowe arrived with the second contingent. He was frankly worried over their failure to contact the submarine. "What time did they go on watch?" was his first question.

"Twelve hundred hours," replied Hernandez, "exactly according to instructions."

"Are you sure that nothing happened that our men failed to see the signal?"

"I'm positive," said Hernandez. "We've maintained a constant watch on shore. They've been on the alert every minute. We could see them from here, could almost tell what they were saying."

"I don't understand it—unless. We won't think about that. We'll just have to wait and keep watching."

"We could try to query GHQ," suggested Hernandez.

"It's too soon. They wouldn't answer," said Rowe, his face tense. "We'll just have to wait."

It was months before they learned that the sub had developed trouble while submerged. Her commanding officer had finally discharged the crew and then blown up the ship to keep her modem equipment from falling into enemy hands.

At about 1000 on the third day, the high staccato notes of the bamboo flute cut sharp and clear through the jungle air. Instantly the camp was alert. Men were ordered to battle stations as an enemy patrol vessel came up over the horizon. Rowe and Hernandez stood with binoculars frozen in their hands. About 400 yards from their boat the patrol vessel opened up with her 75's. The shells fell short of their mark. "God, I hope they don't get those boys," said Rowe, "and the REPORTS! They'd know EVERYTHING."

"Our men know what they have, and what to do in an emergency," said Hernandez. They won't let the reports be taken—unless they're hit first."

"Let's hope they don't get the men, even if they have to dump the reports. And incidentally, that's pretty goddam lousy marksmanship they're showing right now."

"They're doing something in the bottom of the boat," said Hernandez breathlessly. "The cans are in that end, under the gear."

"One has a bomb in his hand and the other one has one of the cans," said Rowe.

"There go the cans—and all that work. Three days and nights of walking and three more of waiting," said Hernandez, sick at heart.

"And there go the men," said Rowe.

Almost simultaneously, the boat was blown to bits by the bomb the guerilla had held in his hand and another enemy shell hit the water probably thirty feet from the sinking boat.

"They didn't forget a thing," said Hernandez, "but where are they?"

"NO—OH GOD NO!" cried Rowe in mental agony, "Al, one of those goddam cans is floating."

"It CAN'T be," groaned Hernandez.

"But it is," said Rowe hopelessly, "and we can't send a boat out—we can't fire a shot—we can't do a goddam thing." "There is one of the men," said Al, "off to the right. They're both there, swimming ashore."

"Thank God for that, but look, just look at the reflection from that goddam can. They couldn't miss it if they were deaf, dumb, and blind."

"There goes a boat over the side after it," said Hernandez. "God, I wish we could blast it out of the water."

"And say, 'Here we are. We sent those reports. Come and get us.' We'll be damn lucky if we get out of here without a full scale attack."

He was right. There was nothing they could do but stand there and watch two men in a rowboat pick up the container of TOP SECRET reports, then turn and row back to the patrol vessel, accomplishing probably the best day's work they ever had or ever would do for the Imperial Navy.

In addition to the commander's very comprehensive report on

conditions in the north and what we were doing about them, together with suggestions for future action, there were many local maps and reports from agents in the surrounding islands and a map showing the entire network of Radio, Coast Watcher, and Radar Detector Stations. Also in accordance with Geneva Regulations, there were receipts signed by local farmers for money paid them for cattle and supplies, together with one of the very few packages of mail ever to leave THE MISSION, addressed to wives, sweethearts, and families of perhaps every man who hoped he still knew the whereabouts of those he loved. They had no way of knowing which of the cans had been picked up.

The patrol boat would turn in their report, and that on top of the defeat the Marines had taken at the beachhead, would send the Japs out beating the earth for them from THE TOWER to Barahan and up and down the coast. Runners were sent back to warn the farmers. Their names might not be known but they would have to be on guard.

Two weeks later they learned, from Tokyo Rose, that the cannister retrieved from the sea had held the package of mail, the signed receipts, and the map of the network. That meant all locations would have to be changed, and no longer were they protected by the anonymity of THE MISSION. Every man who had sent out mail would become a hunted man.

Later, one of the men who was identified through the mail, the only letter he had ever written home, was caught while on a mission. Another agent taken with him succeeded in keeping his identity secret, but saw his friend unbelievably tortured. The survivor, a boy of nineteen, came back with tragedy in his eyes and hatred in his heart, to report that even in the agony which at last, mercifully brought death, his friend had refused to reveal his mission or its source.

The night before the TOP SECRET fiasco at Barahan, a party of guerilas came into the camp there. All were ragged, some ill, others obviously half-starved. One, a little paler and a little thinner than the others began to identify himself to the Sergeant of the Guard as Lieutenant Ruben Songco, and claimed to have been with the Philipps Party and said he was, to the best of his knowledge, the only surviving commissioned officer. After a moment the sergeant said, "Would you know one of the survivors, if you saw him?" "There were not many survivors," he said. "Any one of them would know me."

The sergeant turned and spoke to a corporal and after a short conference the corporal took off on the double. "Just wait here a few moments, Sir," said the sergeant. "It isn't that we doubt you, it's—well, we have to be careful."

"No one knows that better than I," said the lieutenant. "I've been a long time getting here. A few more minutes won't make much difference."

He dropped down on a coconut log to rest, and the corporal came back shortly with Sergeant Harder. Lieutenant Songco recognized him at once, but waited for the sergeant to speak. For a few seconds, Harder looked at the pale, emaciated face, then they rushed together. Throwing their arms about each other, they laughed and cried and slapped each other's shoulders. "It's good to see you, Lieutenant—GOOD to see you. I didn't think we ever would again—but God, Sir, you're thin. What happened to you?"

"I had a badly infected leg from a gunshot wound that night, and then going into malaria didn't help. I tried to find my people in Pampanga, but they had gone somewhere to the mountains. A poor family took me in but they weren't even able to feed themselves and I had no money. Have you heard from any of the others?"

"Sergeant Alberto is here," said Harder. "He joined up with this party in August."

"That's wonderful. I wondered about all of you. Did anyone else escape?"

"I heard that one of the technicians got away, but I've never seen him. But, Sir, who do you think they're holding prisoner here?"

Songco shook his head and said, "Who?"

Sergeant Harder gave the true name of the one they called Ortega, and a cold, hard tone came into his voice. "Not that one—not HIM?" said Songco in amazement. "Yes, Sir, the one that led the Japs to us. I identified him here. Some of the local guerillas got word that he probably was the one."

"What was he doing here?" asked Songco, feeling sick at the memory of the treachery of the prisoner and the slaughter it had brought about.

"Trying to do the same to this party," said Harder, bitterly.

"And he's still ALIVE?"

"Yes," said Harder, "Commander Nicholson has some theory about letting him have a long time to think about his crime."

"Whatever the reason, I wouldn't want to be in his shoes," said Songco.

Then, suddenly realizing how long they had been talking, Sergeant Harder said, "I shouldn't be keeping you here all this time, Sir. Commander Nicholson and Captain Hernandez will want to talk to you."

They found both men working in the commander's tent where the corporal on orderly duty announced Lieutenant Harder and a visitor. Lieutenant Songco looked at Harder, but before he could speak, the commander called out, "Come in, Lieutenant."

Hernandez was on his feet instantly, his hand outstretched "Lieutenant Songco! You're alive! This is wonderful." Turning to Rowe, he said, "Commander Nicholson, this is my very good friend, Lieutenant Ruben Songco. He was with Major Philipps."

"So you're Lieutenant Songco," said Rowe, shaking hands cordially. "This IS a surprise. Glad to have you aboard, Sir." Turning to Harder he said, "I guess it was a surprise to you too, Lieutenant?"

"That's right, Sir. We could never find out what really happened to him. It's mighty good to see him, but he doesn't look like he's had too good a time of it."

"I guess I was lucky, at that," said Songco.

"Did you fellows know each other here in the Islands?" Rowe asked, looking at Songco and Hernandez.

Hernandez and Songco answered at once, "No," and Songco finished, "We met in California, right after I finished at the Academy."

"West Point?" asked Rowe.

"Annapolis," replied Songco.

"Great," said Rowe. "The Navy can stand a little more support in this outfit. Wait a minute—wait a minute. I thought the Philipps Expedition was all ARMY."

Songco smiled. "That's right, it was. But that was because there wasn't any Navy—Philippine Navy, I mean. I was called up in June '41. You're from the States, I take it."

"No," said Rowe, beginning to enjoy the whole scrambled situation. Manila's my home. I'm really NAVAIR."

Songco threw up his hands in a gesture of complete confusion. "Isn't ANYONE what he's supposed to be?"

The other three men laughed heartily. "Not many, Lieutenant, not many, I assure you. You've probably noticed that Sergeant Harder is called Lieutenant Harder. Captain Hernandez is really Lieutenant Hernandez and our Captain Berg is really Master Sergeant Berg."

"I don't get it," said Songco.

"There had to be some way to keep the rank of our technical men and the guerilla outfits on a workable basis. It was embarrassing when a Tech Sergeant, for instance had to get tough and say, 'That's an ORDER, Sir,' to a guerilla colonel. This was the only way I could see to do it."

Songco laughed again and shook his head in bewilderment, "What a way to run an army!"

By fortunate coincidence, they picked up a broadcast that night from

President Osmena, in Australia. He was speaking in honor of their late President, Manuel Quezon, who had died a few weeks before in New York. Osmena's message was one of encouragement, at the same time pointing out to his people that their only hope lay in patience, loyalty, and waiting a little longer for deliverance. The speech was passed on to the mission personnel and through Captain Dodson to his Guerilla Fighters, who had fought their undercover battle against the invasion of their country from its murderous beginning.

At times, since joining forces with MISSION ISRM, Dodson's men had rebelled against the restraint imposed upon them by their assignment to an Intelligence mission, when they felt the force of enemy oppression or saw the atrocities committed against their people—sometimes an entire village—as they went from place to place.

Only the deep understanding and sheer strength of character of a man of their own kind, kept them under control.

At such times Commander Rowe realized that to him and to MISSION ISRM, Bill Dodson truly was worth his weight in gold or anything better they had to offer.

Timing of President Osmena's speech could not have been better, for it was almost exactly 12 hours later that the TOP SECRET reports fell into enemy hands and once more they were forced to run. The guerillas would have liked nothing better than to make a try at recovering the reports and then fight it out later with the Japs, who undoubtedly would have sent a force ashore.

Minutes after the top secrets had been picked up, the *carabao* tenders of the first contingent of the convoy were alerted to prepare to move out. The others followed in succession ahead of the usual time lapse between contingents. There probably would be no other place at which they would be in greater peril than right there where the reports obviously originated.

Rowe, Hernandez and Dodson agreed that the original plan of moving the heavy gear by boat should be adhered to. The Marine incident on the coast near Sablayan and now this incredible piece of bad luck at Barahan, undoubtedly would step up enemy patrol activity. Wherever and however they went, the move would be hazardous. The move by boat seemed most logical. Three flotillas of three or four boats each moved along the coast to the north, spaced as well as possible, considering the urgency of getting out of the immediate area. Several times there were narrow escapes in which part of the boats slipped in unnoticed, to hide in narrow inlets under cover of overhanging vines, mangrove roots and branches as enemy patrols passed by, apparently not concerned over one or two boats which might be traveling together.

A few hours after his arrival at Barahan, Lieutenant Songco had alternately burned and chilled his way into a miserable malaria attack and after watching one of the most heartbreaking experiences of the entire expedition, Captain Hernandez had followed suit. Because of the severity of their respective malaria attacks, Lieutenant Songco and Captain Hernandez and the small task force which had come from ISRM, remained in camp until the last contingent was ready to move out. Unable to move on his own power, Hernandez was strapped to the back of a *carabao* once again, and as they went out onto the trail in the driving rain, he lapsed into unconsciousness—delirium would probably be more accurate—from which he did not recover until they were nearing their destination.

Later, Zamora said to him, "What is her name, Sir, the girl you talked to while you were sick?"

But the words "What a man doesn't know can't be bayoneted out of him" came into his mind before he spoke. It was a temptation sometimes to talk of the ones they loved, but his very impersonal tone told more than his words when he looked at the man who was his almost constant companion and said, "You must have been mistaken. There is no one," and the soft-spoken, intelligent young man never spoke of the girl again.

Those were dark, discouraging days for everyone of MISSION ISRM, weary and heartsick over the compromising of their position and the almost superhuman effort required for the hurried evacuation. All were working against time, many were also struggling against illness. Hardly a rest stop was passed after they left Barahan, without one or two dropping out, to follow when they were fit for the trail again. And now the uncertainty of what might be the consequence of the reports falling into enemy hands.

Passing out of the storm belt once more, they traveled as hard and fast as the clumsy, sled-like carts would permit. The time out for the inevitable water stops for the *carabaos* was sheer torture as the men waited in an agony of suspense, expecting runners from the rear guard momentarily, to say that the Japs were in pursuit.

24
» » JUNGLE CITY

Unlike the top-of-the-world position of THE TOWER OF ISRM, the new post snuggled at the very edge of the sea, under shelter of thousands of tall, straight, coconut palms. Atop the rugged mountains rising almost straight up from the back of the campsite, was a perfect location for the transmitter. Earlier, Sergeant Berg had established the first substation here in incredibly short time and had named it accordingly, PDQ.

Immediate access to the sea, a panoramic view of Verde Passage, and a mountain-top transmitter beamed out to Australia, provided PDQ with every prerequisite for Radio, Coast Watch, Radar Detector and Weather Station. As a point of contact with Allied submarines, and for leaders of the pre-invasion operations arriving by PT-Boats (the first Allied surface craft to return to these waters) their value to GHQ would be infinitely increased.

All this they found in a beautiful, old copra plantation, offered for their use by its owner, Mang Salizar, a man of unquestioned loyalty and an indefatigable worker in the Resistance Movement.

Fully aware of GHQ's need for their daily reports, the time required for unpacking, testing and setting up the equipment seemed interminable. Actually, they had accomplished almost the impossible. Within one week from date of arrival, they had put the radio gear into operation, substituted new codes for the old ones, and identified themselves with GHQ. Already the 12 days of jungle travel clipped from every mission to Manila, reduced the hazards and increased the effectiveness of every agent in the field.

Among the first steps in activating the new camp was the establishment of a small Base Hospital, under the supervision of the guerilla doctor, with Mrs. Collada as Head Nurse. The six remaining nurses were doing double shifts. Half their number had been called to other units by that time. With only a *buri* roof over their heads and pitifully lacking in medical supplies, they began receiving the many patients suffering from malaria and dysentery. The first week in the new location, they lost two fine, young guerilla fighters with malignant malaria.

The new post, laid out approximately in an ellipse, included the permanent HQs, Radio Room, Club House, a Watch Tower overlooking Verde Passage, several barracks and the Guard House. Eventually a baseball diamond, Willie's Well, Rowe's Landing, and Hernandez Park were added and Captain Berg's greatest morale builder, la Barberia (the barber shop), the first service of its kind since Brisbane, offered haircuts at one peso per head. Soon after that, the dentist's office, near the hospital, neat and clean if not too well equipped, offered a thorough examination and whatever work the dentist could complete in the one visit, for five pesos.

Shortly after the activation of the main station at PDQ, two weather specialists, Sergeant Caswell and Sergeant George, came up from Australia via submarine, bringing with them the newest ideas and weather equipment available. The pastel-colored, hydrogen-filled balloons they sent up from the new weather station atop Snob Hill, high above the tops of the coconut trees, played hide and seek with enemy reconnaissance planes and became a source of delight to many of the Guerilla Fighters. Completely incongruous with the background, the balloons added nothing to the sense of security of many others at the main HQs below, regardless of the Argus-eyed weather men, also with a normal interest in survival.

Weather had become one of the chief concerns of the Army, Navy, and Air Force and stations had been set up from the North Pole to the Gobi Desert and points east, south and west. A study of long-range weather patterns and coordinated reports from isolated spots from many parts of the globe, provided GHQ with a well integrated service. Techniques developed by use of new electronic devices, resulted in long-range forecasts of 48 hours, ten days and thirty days, of sufficient accuracy to permit planning for future operations. Due to expert weather service in the China-Burma-India area, where a gallon of gas probably was worth more to Allied Forces than any other place on earth, by taking advantage of predicted winds, a pilot could make the gasoline usually consumed in ten missions over the Hump, stretch out to do eleven.

In their immediate area, the prediction of impending storms was vital to air success as well as landing operations scheduled by the Navy. So the Weather Group remained on the hill. The balloons, looking like inflated Easter eggs, continued to please (or plague) the men below, and weather became an important part of the daily reporting to GHQ.

Twenty-four hours in the new HQs, a converted plantation warehouse of galvanized sheeting, under a tropic sun, convinced all concerned that something more appropriate to the climate should take top rating on the priority list. A few days later with the combined efforts of supply officers Berg and Mang Salizar, architects Rowe and Hernandez, and Dodson & Company, builders, a very comfortable and adequate two-story HQs was finished.

The main Post HQs, above stairs, surpassed in efficiency and completeness many offices in much more pretentious military establishments under far more favorable circumstances. In one wing was the Map Room and Communications Center and in the other, the General Office, Commander Rowe's and Captain Hernandez' private offices. The lower floor furnished quarters for Commander Rowe in the wing overlooking the Passage, "Rowe's Nest," with a small but pleasant breakfast room, and one or two rooms for storage of vital or highly classified material. In the other wing the Marine Dining Room faced the water and Captain Hernandez' quarters, at the rear, commanded a view of most of the other buildings of the post.

Tempo at the new location increased steadily. More and more trained men were required. A Troop Training School was opened at Estrella, Naujuan, and under the command of Lieutenant Songco soon became Little Annapolis. Several weeks later a report came in which saddened the entire post and at the same time roused the fury of every man there. It read:

> 3 DECEMBER 1944: NAUJUAN, MINDORO PROVINCE: APPROXIMATELY 150 TROOPS LANDED AT ESTRELLA COMING FROM CALAPAN. THEY RAIDED THE GUERILLA TROOP SCHOOL HEADED BY CAPT REUBEN SONGCO, AUS, AT SAN AUGUSTINE SCHOOL BUILDING. CAPTAIN SONGCO THE FIRST REGULAR OFFICER THIS COMMAND TO BECOME A CASUALTY WAS KILLED IN ACTION. THREE GUERILLA OFFICERS AND SIX ENLISTED MEN WERE ALSO KILLED. THE JAPS RETURNED TO CALAPAN WITH ESTIMATED 80 DEAD.
>
> THEY COMMANDEERED PALAY (unprocessed rice), PIGS, COWS, AND OTHER FOODSTUFFS ON THE WAY TO CALAPAN LOADING THE SUPPLIES INTO CARTS PULLED BY FILIPINO CIVILIANS.

The search for food still occupied a large detail of Mangyans. Large garden plots were planted at the new location and more variety began showing in the mess as off-shore contacts with submarines became more frequent. Many a treasure was brought out, looked at longingly, and in the end, like the birthright of Esau of old, traded for what seemed more important at the moment, food from the ship's galley. A flag from a sunken enemy ship brought a good return in food. A magnificent samurai sword was surrendered as the price of a ham. It was this kind of bartering with submarine crews that finally gave the new post its permanent name— CAMP NIMITZ—in honor of the hand that was feeding them.

One constant drain on the food supply at the new site was a POW camp. This operation was a costly one from the standpoint of personnel required, as well as the limited food supply, but was one which their moral philosophy (and Geneva Regulations) demanded. Often they were hard-pressed to feed themselves and their agents who sometimes had marched a hundred miles and schemed and contrived their way through a dozen sentry posts to get there. Still they shared what food there was with the enemy POW's, enemy sympathizers, and collaborators who could not be allowed their liberty to menace the Allied cause, and specifically MISSION ISRM.

The POW camp was situated perhaps five miles up the river and at the end of a mountain trail of perhaps two or three miles. They made no secret of the existence of the camp and its being there sometimes had a very salutary effect upon local citizens, who were not inclined to be co-operative when their help was needed. One such incident had to do with a boat owner at Abra de Ilog. The man was doing a flourishing business transporting cargo, obviously enemy war matériel. Captain Berg had serious need of such a boat to transport some lumber and other necessary supplies. He explained his problem as well as possible, considering the necessary security regulations, and tried to rent the boat for a few days. The owner refused. Then he offered to buy it, but the owner refused to sell. A few weeks in the POW camp gave the supply officer the use of the boat while he needed it, brought the owner to a more co-operative state of mind, and eliminated further trouble of that kind in the village.

Due to their close proximity to the sea, an alternate radio station had to be established in the event of an attack on PDQ. Time for the re-invasion was getting closer and closer. They could not start over again and still be of any use to GHQ in that operation. The site of the POW camp seemed also a logical site for the alternate station and served the purpose of keeping the personnel required for the two activities to a minimum.

With the wider scope in the operation at Camp Nimitz, there were inspection trips and other necessary local travel which consumed much time. This brought about the activation of a cavalry platoon of the quick, sure-footed little horses of the Philippines, a cross between the Malayan and Arabian animals.

As early as 21 September 1944, the Third Fleet began carrier-based air attacks on Manila and other points on Luzon. Soon after the activation of Camp Nimitz, the guerillas began fishing American aviators out of Manila Bay and the South China Sea. When enough of the birdmen had been brought to Nimitz, and before the Navy was ready to undertake their evacuation, baseball games were scheduled between the fliers and their rescuers. Those games might not have been the world's greatest exhibition of skill in the sport, but they served a great purpose as morale builders, easing taut nerves and releasing the inevitable tension which at one time or another everyone felt. With seven-eighths of the personnel being Guerilla Fighters, there were plenty of rooters for their team, but a dearth of rooters for the fliers. Commander Rowe hit upon the idea of bringing some of the Nip prisoners down to root for the aviators, and the games took on a more cosmopolitan air. In the beginning the POW rooters fell somewhat short of the Dodger and Giant fans in enthusiasm.

On Philippine soil, and in a military camp, they were the direct responsibility of the guards of that camp, who, in this case, in spite of personal preference for the "Browns," cheerfully accepted the added responsibility of acting as cheer leaders. With proper inducement, the "Yellows" did their duty noisily, if not eagerly for the "Whites," while the "Browns" cheered lustily for their own.

At Camp Nimitz, often called the "Main Street of the Pacific," their nearness to the sea lanes became a matter of grave concern. They lived almost in dread of the day when the success of Allied air and sea forces might be their undoing. An enemy troop transport sunk in Verde Passage might send hundreds of enemy troops upon them, for they were well within the range of a good swimmer, with his life at stake.

With the first days of December, Dodson's men began to feel a nostalgic urge for a church for the Christmas season. In the absence of any religious service, this large group of native men, many lost from their families, all suffering under the hand of a cruel, heartless enemy, sorely needed the comforting spirit of Christmas and a place of worship.

About the end of the first week in December, the Christmas season seemed upon them. Captain Dodson walked into Captain Hernandez' private office one day and said, "Captain, I have a request to make. I don't know how you and the commander will feel about it, but—well, I feel it's important to my men."

"If it's important to your men, Bill, it's important to all of us," said Hernandez. "What is it?"

"A church, Captain. We just can't seem to face another Christmas without a church."

Hernandez looked puzzled. "A church," he repeated mechanically. "Tell me, Bill, what have you in mind?"

"The men have been talking it over. They think there's enough native material right here, out in the jungle I mean, to build it. Mang Salazar has told them he will get anything they can't find."

"Then what you mean is, that the men want the time to build a church."

"That's about it, Sir," said Dodson. "With enough men working, maybe twenty or thirty, they could do it in short order."

"How long?" asked Hernandez, stalling for time to think of the ramifications of such a project.

"I wouldn't like to say exactly," said Dodson. "It would be pretty much of a guess—but I'd say they could do it in a week."

"You think they could build a church in a week, Bill?"

"I think so. Of course if anything urgent came up on the outside, it might take a little longer, but every time anyone had a free hour, he could be working. It would go fast."

"But what good would a church be without a padre? There isn't a padre even in Abra de Ilog."

"That's right," said Dodson calmly. "But there's a man in Batangas just home from a seminary the Japs have closed. We'll send a couple of men over to get him."

Hernandez chuckled. "Well as usual, Captain, you seem to have thought of everything. I'll speak with George and let you know."

All hands fell to and almost like magic, there, deep in the jungle, stood a truly handsome little structure of bamboo, *nipa* and *buri* leaves, neatly bound and strongly fashioned, held in place by wooden pegs and abaca twine. The famed Tabernacle of Salt Lake had nothing on Little Town Cathedral. Not a nail had been used in its construction. Instead of a year, in one week their church was finished.

On the last afternoon, teams of four and six were carrying in coconut logs for benches, when a great cheering and hand clapping was heard down on the main street of the camp. A group of guerillas were following a *carabao* cart with a cover over the load. Mang Salizar was heading the procession which went directly to the cathedral of the jungle.

Hearing the noise from their offices in HQs building, Rowe and

Hernandez met in the outer office, going out to see what it was all about. Mang Salizar looked a little embarrassed, but very happy.

"Good afternoon, Mang Salizar," said Rowe. "You seem to have quite a following."

A little flustered, but with great dignity the older man replied, "Good afternoon, Commander. Is getting very near to Christmas time?"

Rowe was really enjoying the situation. If Mang Salizar was sponsoring it, it must be good. "Yes," he replied. "It's only a little while now. We have much more to be happy about this year than we did last."

This was very true, for in the interim between the beginning of the construction and this procession on its way to the church, General William C. Dunckel had led his forces ashore at San José and Mindoro had been liberated.

"Yes, Sir," said Mang Salizar. "Everyone very happy. Everyone want to thank *americanos* for liberation of our island. People of Abra de Ilog want to make little gift to CAMP NIMITZ."

It was Rowe's turn to feel embarrassment as Mang Salizar pulled the cover from the cart—and the bell from the church in Abra de Ilog. The commander felt very humble and he said, "This is a wonderful gift, Mang Salizar. I know the men are very happy. They have worked hard from dawn till dark to build the church and I know you have done a great deal to help."

"Oh no, I help only little bit, Sir. The boys, they do all the work," said the older man glowing with pride.

"I wish Captain Dodson were here. He's gone across to Batangas for the padre. The boys weren't able to get him to come."

"Don't worry," said Mang Salazar confidently, "Captain Bill bring him back all right. Captain Bill very fine man."

"A fine man and a fine soldier," said Rowe with deep sincerity.

Soon the bell was installed in the open belfry, below the cross atop the structure. A brilliant, red-gold sun was sinking into an almost purple sea, when Dodson's white-sailed *batel* put in at Rowe's Landing. Following the captain was a young man in the white clerics of the tropics, and several guerillas. One of the men carried a small, basket-weave bag. In it were the padre's vestments and communion vessels. As they walked down the palm-lined road, through the camp, the padre was frankly astonished at what he saw—including the church. But it was Captain Dodson who stopped in wide-eyed amazement as the bell rang out in tones clear and beautiful in the stillness of the evening, calling the men for the Angelus.

Later that night, when Dodson, Rowe and Hernandez sat together having a good night cigarette, Rowe said, curiously, "Tell me, Bill, how did you manage to get the padre to come when the others said he wouldn't?"

"It wasn't too difficult," said Dodson with a wicked grin and a twinkle in his dark eyes.

But Rowe was insistent. "How did you break him down?" "Well, you see, Commander, he was—well I think he was afraid."

"Afraid?" echoed Rowe. "Not of YOU?"

"Oh no," said Dodson, "Maybe the Bishop—maybe the Pope. I couldn't really tell."

"I don't get it," said Rowe.

"Well, when I told him we wanted him to come—that we had to have him, he said, 'I have already told your men, Captain, I cannot come to your church.' 'But WHY, Padre?' I asked him. Then he told me."

The young priest had not been actually stubborn. It had been a more serious problem with him. "Because," he said patiently, "I am not padre. I am only student. I have no authority to say the Mass. No authority from the Bishop, no authority from the Pope. You see, Captain, I CANNOT hold the Mass."

But Dodson too was persistent. "Tell me this, Padre, do you know how to say the Mass?"

"Of course," said the man, plainly annoyed. "I have been in the church all my life—first as choir boy, then as an acolyte. I was at seminary four years, but I have no authority to say the Mass."

Dodson had spent all the time he could afford on this project. "Look, Padre," he said, looking straight into the eyes of the hesitant one, "I am a very busy man. I have many things to do. You too have work to do. Now go and get ready. You are coming with me to serve with my men. You are a padre with everything but authority. We have a church with everything but a padre. Bring what you need to stay a long time, and don't forget your communion vessels."

"But Captain, you cannot.. the student priest began, but wilted under the gaze of the strong fighting man.

"I cannot WAIT," said Dodson, finishing the sentence for him. "You come along and do the job you're trained for, and let ME worry about the authority."

So they had their priest—and if Dodson's authority did not merit the full approval of the good padre, it remained a matter between him and his conscience, for he stayed with them until the closing of CAMP NIMITZ, after the full scale invasion at Lingayen Gulf in January 1945. With their mission there accomplished, his blessing followed them as they sailed away from Rowe's Landing into the bright morning sunlight. He waved goodbye as they pushed off and stood watching from the tower as long as they could see his white cotton robe against the deep green shadow of the jungle.

25

» » CAPTURE OF A TREASURE SHIP

The Japanese Navy had gone a long way down the scale since their bold, successful strike out across more than four thousand miles of ocean at the beginning of the war. November 1944, however, found the hulks of the once mighty Nippon Fleet strewn from Luzon to Leyte. Japan had begun to feel her first real defeat in 350 years—since Japanese Admiral Hideyosho, a would-be invader, had been defeated by Korean Admiral Ye-Sun off Korean shores in 1592. Even with the battle for Leyte lost, the only Allied craft yet to venture into the waters off Luzon and Mindoro was the submarine.

With that area constantly patrolled by sub-chasers, the enemy seemed to feel himself still in full possession of both islands. Having failed to locate the radio stations indicated on the map retrieved from the sea at Barahan, he apparently decided that the points marked were proposed stations. At least there was no indication that he knew what lay behind a very thin fringe of jungle along the north coast of Mindoro, only a few miles from Luzon, his own main stronghold in the Philippines.

The situation for the men behind the jungle fringe was becoming desperate. They were perilously near to closing down their main radio station for lack of supplies. In reply to their urgent request for supplies from GHQ, they had received this message:

ARRANGING FOR SUBMARINE TO CALL SAME RENDEZVOUS ONE EIGHT REPEAT ONE EIGHT NOVEMBER WITH YOUR REQUIRED SIGNAL SUPPLIES. SAME SIGNALS AND PROCEDURE AS OUTLINED. IN CASE SPOT COMPROMISED AND YOUR RADIO GIVES OUT BEFORE ETA (Estimated Time of Arrival) DISPLAY SIGNAL DURING SAME HOURS IN PROMINENT POSITION

ON BEACH CLEARLY VISIBLE FROM SEAWARD. UPON SIGHTING SIGNAL WILL PROCEED TO ALTERNATE SPOT WHICH YOU WILL DESIGNATE IN URGENT REPLY ACKNOWLEDGING THIS MESSAGE. PLEASE CHANGE YOUR STATION INDEX NUMBER TO READ ZERO THREE SIX REPEAT ZERO THREE SIX. WILL BE WAITING TO HEAR FROM YOU.

This was fine, but the eighteenth was almost two weeks away. They needed supplies now! Then on a bright sunny afternoon the Jap subchaser *Higu Maru* rounded Point Baeto and steamed into the sparkling blue water of a peaceful little cove. The *Higu Maru* dropped anchor, unaware that every move on her decks was under close observation by a U. S. Intelligence station. Certainly the men on board were not aware that even before their landing operation had begun, a welcoming party headed by a U. S. Naval commander and a keen, experienced guerilla captain was on its way down to take a hand in whatever shore action they had in mind.

Rowe and Hernandez had heard the signal from the bamboo flute, in the HQs office. They dashed to the Radio Room to see what the Coast Watcher had to report. Through his binoculars, the CW man observed the action taking place on deck and relayed it to the operator at PDQ.

"CORPORAL!" shouted Rowe, and turned to see the man probably three feet behind him. Lowering his voice, he said, "Call Captain Dodson. Tell him to alert a squad for immediate action at the beach. ON THE DOUBLE, Corporal."

George Rowe had trained for many months for the post of Lieutenant Commander in the U. S. Navy and there were times when got more than a little fed up with NICHOLSON LINE sailing. Battling ships was his meat, even if it had to be done with a few land-based Guerilla Fighters.

Fastening the belt on his holster, Rowe said lightly, "They've probably come to bring the supplies we ordered from GHQ. Maybe the batteries and oil. Just mention anything you need, Captain, and we'll try to bring it back with us."

Hernandez went out to see them off and as the squad went out of sight under the heavy jungle roof over the trail, he returned to the Radio Room. The Coast Watcher was furnishing PDQ with all but a ringside seat for the show. Over the radio operator's shoulder, Hernandez was reading every word as it came in.

ENEMY VESSEL SUB CHASER TYPE. TWO .50 CALIBRE ONE 75 MM. GUNS.

PREPARING FOR LANDING PARTY.

LOWERING LANDING CRAFT OVER THE SIDE. 25
OR 30 MEN GOING OVER THE SIDE.

Ten minutes later he came in again and Hernandez was back reading over the operator's shoulder.

ONE – TWO – THREE – FOUR – FIVE – SIX – EIGHT –TEN – TWELVE – FIFTEEN – EIGHTEEN – TWENTY-TWO – TWENTY-FIVE – THIRTY – THIRTY-FIVE – FORTY MEN ASHORE.

By the time he had gotten to twenty, Hernandez had called out to the corporal standing outside the door. "Corporal, alert another squad. Have them follow Commander Rowe and Captain Dodson ON THE DOUBLE. They're going to need more men fast."

As the captain came back from ordering the second squad to action, the radio man said, "He says our men have arrived, Sir."

Suddenly a cold shiver ran down along the captain's spine. He remembered a moonlit night a few months before, when he and his two men had jumped out of a tiny boat and run for the shelter of the trees.

Fighting enemy troops on land had long since become commonplace to Bill Dodson and his Guerilla Fighters, but attacking an enemy subchaser and its crew—from the beach—with Army rifles and one Browning Automatic was a new kind of warfare, even for him.

Taking positions in the shelter of the jungle trees, Commander Rowe called the orders. "Bill, it will be up to you to knock out the ship's guns. With a few lucky shots, they could knock the hell out of us."

He continued, "Carillo, you see to it that none of them gets away with any idea of heading back to the ship with that landing craft. We'll need it to bring back what we need from the ship."

"You mean we're going out to the ship, Sir?" asked the astonished man.

"Right," said Rowe. "With that many men coming ashore, there can't be more than eight or ten left on board, if there are that many."

"Now then, the rest of you men. We're outnumbered about three to one. OK—every one of you pick your three men and take care of them."

The CW was back with more news:

CHANGE THAT FORTY MEN TO FOURTEEN. THEY MOWED THOSE YELLOW DEVILS DOWN LIKE DUCKS IN A SHOOTING GALLERY.

The second squad lost no time getting down to the beach. By the time they had reached the others, they had taken care of ten of the sailors who had gotten by the first squad. With the landing party routed, Rowe and Dodson and several of the Guerilla Fighters set out in the landing craft for the ship.

There was no sign of activity as they approached the ship. "You must have done a good job with those machine guns and the 75, Captain," said Rowe.

The commander's assurance did not fool the captain. He had been fighting this enemy too long to expect a straightforward approach—and he didn't like the looks of this. "Maybe they didn't leave enough men on board to fire them," he said.

"They wouldn't leave her unguarded," said Rowe as they pulled alongside. "But whatever they did, here we are!"

One after the other they scrambled up the ladder and on to the deck. Still no men in sight. The one man left on deck had hidden in a lifeboat. The others had huddled together in the captain's quarters. Two guerilla guards were left to keep watch on the prisoners while Rowe and Dodson began a systematic search of the vessel, working their way from cabin to cabin, opening a door, then backing away, guns drawn. They took searching parties through every compartment, searching for what they needed or could use. The galley was bare.

Hunger had driven those poor devils ashore and they had picked a bad spot—but there on the ship, with most of its crew lying out there in the jungle, were all the things Rowe's men had asked for, waited, and even prayed for. All the things he had joked about bringing back were there—all kinds of batteries, oil, gas—the ship's radio now dismantled. They carried down to the landing craft all they could take back. There were enough supplies to keep Station PDQ on the air now until the sub came from GHQ.

With the supplies all transferred to the small boat, Rowe and Dodson returned to the captain's cabin to question the survivors of the crew. Commander Rowe began to question the prisoners. He spoke first in English. No answer. Perhaps they did not speak the language. The same questions in Japanese still failed to bring a reply. They were just not talking. Looking into the face of a crewman he had been sure understood him in both languages, Rowe said in English, "You, Sailor, I think you understand me. Ask your buddies if they want to go ashore as our prisoners or go down with the ship. We're going to blow her up."

His face utterly devoid of expression, the man turned to his fellows and asked the question in Japanese. With the same mask-like expression, the self-condemned men answered him. He said quietly, "They say go down with the ship."

Looking once more at the men who knew they had only minutes to go, Rowe called out to his squad, "All right, Men. Let's go."

As he turned toward the doorway, he caught a flicker of satisfaction pass over one man's face. Suddenly he realized that the man had not moved since they had entered the cabin. He had stood there like a statue the entire time. Part of his men were already on deck when Rowe called out, "Hold it, Men." Turning to the crewman he said, "Stand aside, Sailor," then to Dodson, "Captain, see what you can find there. He's covering up something."

An almost imperceptible slump of his shoulders was the only outward evidence of the disappointment, the regret for his failure as the man moved aside, revealing a panel in the bulkhead. Dodson slid the panel to one side and lifted out a metal box, several books, and a letter file.

Picking up a small volume from the lot, Rowe examined it carefully. A glow of satisfaction came over his face. "If this is what I think it is," he said, "here's the REAL treasure of the *Higu Maru*."

"What is it?" asked Dodson.

"I think it's the crypto code of the Imperial Navy," said Rowe, awed by his good fortune and the narrow margin between that and missing it.

He looked at the heartbroken boy who had gambled his life to protect the book. "Too bad, Fellow. You almost made it."

Two of Dodson's men appeared at the door. "All ready, Sir. All bombs in place. We'd better go."

The time was short. Rowe said simply, "Let's go."

They filed out of the captain's cabin and quickly went down the ladder to the landing craft. Rowe was the last man to leave the cabin. Closing the door behind him, he stood silently for a moment. With an odd little shake of his head, he turned and followed the others. About half way back to shore, they heard a series of explosions and as they watched, the *Higu Maru* keeled over and plunged forward into the sea.

That evening they sent a message to GHQ which read:

FROM SUB CHASER DESTROYED HERE TODAY WE HAVE THE FOLLOWING: COMPLETE SET JAP NAVY CRYPTO SYSTEM WITH CODES, ETC. SHIP'S LOG, MAPS, STACKS OF TECHNICAL BOOKS MARKED SECRET AND VARIOUS TECHNICAL EQUIPMENT.

Realizing at once the importance of such a find, to the invasion operation ahead, GHQ answered at once:

LOOKING INTO MATTER OF ASSIGNING SUB TO PICK UP JAP CRYPTO SYSTEMS AND OTHER MATTER. ADVISE BY URGENT REPLY WHAT RADIO EQUIPMENT YOU NEED MOST IMMEDIATELY, AND WE WILL MAKE EFFORT TO SEND WITH SUB. OTHER EQUIPMENT WILL COME WITH SCHEDULED SUPPLIES.

As soon as the rendezvous could be arranged, the code books were on their way to GHQ and a few days later, the radio man laid a message on the commander's desk. It read:

> NAVY ADVISES THAT ENEMY DOCUMENTS YOU SENT LAST SUBMARINE WERE OF GREAT VALUE. YOUR ACTION WAS COMMENDABLE.
>
> SIGNED/DOUGLAS MAC ARTHUR

It was still some weeks later, early in December, that the final entry on the log of that day's business went forward to GHQ. It said:

> ALL OF THE CREW OF SUB CHASER HIGU MARU FINALLY ACCOUNTED FOR. THUS JAPS DO NOT KNOW CRYPTO CODES WERE COMPROMISED.
>
> SIGNED/NICHOLSON

26

» » THE COCONUT PATROL

As the bitter struggle for the Philippines advanced through the mountains and rice paddies, the mud and the typhoons of Leyte toward Ormoc, the Chiefs-of-Staff began to look toward Luzon. On 20 November 1944, one month after the Leyte landing, this message came through from GHQ:

> URGENTLY WANT LOCATIONS OF ALL EXISTING RADIO STATIONS OR STATIONS THAT WILL SOON BE OPERATIONAL CALL SIGN OF ALL STATIONS AND DISPOSITION OF ALL CRYPTOGRAPHIC SYSTEMS HELD BY YOU AND THIS HQS.

Later the same day another message came direct from General MacArthur.

> MACARTHUR TO ROWE: IT IS OF UTMOST IMPORTANCE THAT ALL STATION PERSONNEL BE THOROUGHLY BRIEFED ON AIR WARNING PROCEDURE AS THIS INFORMATION AND INFORMATION ON ENEMY SEA MOVEMENT IS VITAL TO OUR PRESENT OPERATION. QUERY: HAVE YOU INFO ON WHETHER APO ISLAND IS OCCUPIED AND WOULD IT BE POSSIBLE TO PLACE COAST WATCHER POSITION AT THAT POINT? ALSO DESIRE INFO ON ENEMY ACTIVITIES ON MAESTRE DE CAMPO ISLAND. WITH THE PHILIPPINE CAMPAIGN NOW UNDER WAY THE IMPORTANCE OF YOUR POSITION AND THE FLASHING INFO YOU CAN GIVE ME OF ENEMY TROOP MOVEMENTS CANNOT BE OVEREMPHASIZED. AYE SHALL DEPEND ON ITS COMPLETENESS AND ACCURACY IN PRESENT OPERATION AND THOSE PROJECTED FOR THE FUTURE.

Rowe replied to these messages that day as follows:

YOUR NO. 13: NOVEMBER TWENTY: RADIO SENT TODAY TO LUBANG ISLAND CALL SIGN SKIP. RADIO SENT TODAY TO MARICABAN ISLAND CALL SIGN PSC REPEAT PSC. AS SOON AS ATR BATTERIES AND TUBES AND ADDITIONAL RADIOS RECEIVED INCLUDING OTHER SUPPLIES REQUESTED IN OUR NO. 27, WILL ESTABLISH STATIONS AT SAN JOSE REPEAT SAN JOSE— BATAAN REPEAT BATAAN—APO ISLAND REPEAT APO ISLAND— DEL MONTE POINT BATANGAS REPEAT DEL MONTE POINT BATANGAS. RADIO WILL ALSO BE ESTABLISHED ON MAESTRE DE CAMPO ISLAND WHETHER OCCUPIED OR NOT IF YOU DESIRE. EYE CAN AND WILL PLACE RADIOS ANY PLACE YOU DESIRE BUT MUST FIRST GET THE RADIOS. THEREFORE PLEASE INCREASE THE NUMBER OF TWO EIGHT EIGHTS OR ATR'S REQUESTED TO TEN WITH SPARE PARTS AND EYE WILL GIVE YOU COMPLETE AND ACCURATE COVERAGE ALL PHASES. ALSO INCLUDE SOME GAS AND OIL AND A POWER SUPPLY UNIT FOR TARE FIFTY SET. IF THESE ARE TO BE SENT PLEASE ADVISE AND WILL SEND COMPLETE LIST OF BARE ESSENTIALS NEEDED TO AVOID REPETITION OF SUPPLY ERRORS.

NO. 231: ROWE TO MAC ARTHUR: SIR, SINCE COLONEL WHITNEY LEFT BRISBANE MY SUPPLIES HAVE BEEN RIDICULOUS: LIKE YOUR GOOD SELF IN PAST HAVE TRIED MY BEST BY IMPROVISING BUT SOME ITEMS CANNOT BE IMPROVISED. EYE HAVE ALWAYS REALIZED IMPORTANCE OF MY ASSIGNMENT AND ASSURE YOU HAVE DONE ALL AND WILL CONTINUE TO DO BEST TO ATTAIN YOUR OBJECTIVES WHICH INCIDENTALLY ARE MINE QUOTE TO GO HOME UNQUOTE. QUERY: REQUEST ONE SHIPMENT SUPPLIES WHICH WILL ENABLE ME TO ASSUME FULL RESPONSIBILITY FOR SUPPLYING YOU WITH INFO EYE KNOW YOU NEED FROM THIS AREA. LIST OF SUPPLIES AND MONEY NEEDED WILL BE SENT ON YOUR REQUEST.

The invasion plan was to intersect the Philippines about mid-way between the north and south. The lower tip of Mindoro was the most likely spot for the first American landing. Meanwhile at the northern shore, every type of craft available was pressed into NICHOLSON LINE service. As coconut traders, Dodson's guerillas patrolled the Batangas, Cavite, and Manila Bay areas, searching for downed American fliers. As our carrier-based aircraft increased their activities, the Coconut Patrol rescued one American flier after another shot down by anti-aircraft guns and enemy planes. One guerilla, named Julian, made so many daring rescues and miraculous escapes with the men he went after that his name became synonymous with fabulous rescues. Another who excelled in this activity was Benny de Guzman, ex-Featherweight champion of international note. Because of these men, many an American aviator lived to fight another day when, according to all the conventional rules of the game, he should have been at the bottom of the ocean with the wreckage of his plane.

There were those who were not so lucky, who fell where no Coconut Patrol boat was near to pick them up. Two such were reported to KAZ.

> BODY OF UNIDENTIFIED AMERICAN PILOT FOUND ON SEVENTEEN NOVEMBER FLOATING IN MANILA BAY WITH HANDS TIED BEHIND HIS BACK. ANOTHER PILOT CAPTURED AND KILLED BY JAP KEMPI NEAR MAKIKINA. IF YOU APPROVE PLEASE ASK ARMY NAVY TO BRIEF THEIR PILOTS TO TRY TO LAND NEAR BEACH JUST EAST REPEAT EAST OF WAWA REPEAT WAWA IF THEY CAN MAKE IT.

As to the courage and resourcefulness of the following men evacuated from CAMP NIMITZ, the record speaks for itself.

MILLER, William E., LT. (jg.) USNR-Pilot—Shot down over Cavite. Engine hit, oil gauge going down. Glided down, hit water outside Corregidor. Paddled to Fortune Island on rubber raft. Stayed there 17 days with emergency kit and fishing kit. Raft damaged on rocks.

FULLER, BERT C. CRM US—POW Radio Electrician, escaped from Corregidor 12 May 1944. (The following is an excerpt of the Intelligence report on Bert C. Fuller. 2910084).

> Attached to Patrol Wing 10 PBY at beginning of war, planes destroyed by Japs on Bataan on Christmas evening; Communication Chief of Patrol Wing 10, aide to Commander Bridgitt, Patrol Wing 10, Operations Officer under General Pierce, Commander of Left Wing, 2nd Army Group stationed Mariveles. Formed Naval Battalion, Marines, Navy, Filipinos attached to Navy, given mixed arms.
>
> As POW was in charge of all Jap radio equipment on the fortified islands and in Bataan. After two years of careful bowing and working his way into Jap confidence, executed an escape on 12 May 1944, with three others, using rafts made from 12" powder cans, paddled to Cavite. Six months in Cavite Province organizing a guerilla unit, the Liberators, consisting of 1800 guerillas, well armed, equipped with cal. .50 MGs, air and water cooled BARs and Enfields bought from smugglers from Bataan.
>
> 1 September 1944, held a meeting of all guerilla agents of Cavite Province and proposed plans for the rescue of American pilots. From the first bombing of Manila on 21 September to November, six American aviators were rescued and delivered to Allied Command.

(See photograph of these pilots at CAMP NIMITZ awaiting

evacuation.)

HUMPHRIES, RAYMOND, POW, Corporal—Enlisted 8 December 1941. Escaped Corregidor 12 May, 1944 with CRM FULLER. Proceeded to Cavite, then to Mindoro.

As the plans for the full-scale invasion progressed midget task forces from MISSION ISRM were assigned to a starting point below San José, Mindoro to furnish daily reports on roads, tracks, and trails—on rivers, bridges, mountain roads, and even small creeks. Details were needed on exact location of any concentration of enemy troops, their defenses and activities, which kept Station PDQ on 24-hour duty receiving information from the sub-stations.

General Yamashita had been convinced by his own General Staff and Intelligence Service that the Allied invasion forces would move through Verde Passage, from the east, attacking Manila from the south. American Guerilla Forces did their utmost to confirm that belief. As the Nips began moving troops, ammunition and supplies to meet the Allied attack, their transportation needs became tremendous.

Motor trucks acquired through some influential guerillas in the Manila area and manned by Dodson's men, were put into service carrying enemy troops, equipment, ammunition, supplies, AND—ISRM Mobile Radio Units.

Enemy officers gratefully put their men and material aboard those trucks and the white-sailed boats of the NICHOLSON LINES, and eagerly signed the travel papers, unaware that they were consigning most of the men and virtually every ton of cargo to destruction.

The crews helped the troops store their supplies and matériel safely away, and as soon as they could open up on their radio, notified demolition squads of the location and matériel to be destroyed, or they would beach their boat or hide their truck and go back after dark and take care of the situation themselves.

After the exchange of messages between ISRM and GHQ—and between Rowe and General MacArthur personally—the officers and men of THE MISSION waited, hopefully at first, then desperately for the radio gear Commander Rowe had requested to take care of the increased traffic between PDQ and the sub-stations, also between PDQ and KAZ.

More than one man went into Little Town Cathedral to say a prayer that a submarine would bring the supplies soon. Without them, PDQ could carry on only a few more days. Finally, in desperation, Commander Rowe radioed KAZ:

THE WORK TO IMPROVISE THIS STATION SETS NEW HIGH IN

RADIO HISTORY—BUT WILL WORK. EYE NEED OIL AND GAS. CAN YOU PARADROP ONE DRUM EACH AT MAIN STATION IMMEDIATELY? IF YOU HAVE NO PARACHUTES DROP IT INTO WATER. IF YOU CANNOT SUPPLY SO ADVISE AND WILL MAKE RAID AND GET SOME LEND LEASE FROM THE JAPS. PLEASE GIVE ME A BREAK ANSWER YES OR NO AS MY BATTERIES WEAK AND WHOLE NETWORK IS ENDANGERED.

The break the commander asked for did not materialize. No oil—no gas—no answer. Now the radio men had to have batteries. Rowe was sitting at a bamboo table in his office. A corporal came through the door in answer to his call. "Corporal," he said, "ask Captain Hernandez and Captain Dodson to come up right away."

"Yes, Sir. Right away," said the corporal and hurried out. The two men came in together. Rowe looked serious. "Sit down, Fellows," he said. Then, "You probably know what's on my mind—those goddam supplies we haven't got. It's too damn bad Whitney's left GHQ. Those bastards down there now can't get the lead out and get anything done." "Looks like they could at least say they weren't going to send them," said Hernandez.

"That's what I mean," said Rowe, "Whitney would have sent the stuff or given a goddam good reason why. Not that the reason why is going to help now, but . . .

"Looks like we're going to have to get it ourselves," said Dodson.

"And it SOUNDS like you've got an idea," said Rowe. Dodson and Hernandez glanced at each other. Dodson said, "Captain Hernandez and I were talking about it when you called us. My men are just about ready to go after the things you need."

Hernandez didn't quite manage to suppress the smile that came when Dodson began, a little dubiously, to explain his plan. Dodson had no doubt of the plan, but he wasn't quite sure of the commander's reaction to it. "Here in the Islands," he began, "we have an old custom. In America it might be called a good will gesture."

"And I suppose you think GOOD WILL is going to get the gas and oil and batteries we need, Captain?" asked Rowe with a strong touch of sarcasm in his voice that disturbed Dodson, an element that never before had entered into their relationship.

Some of the usual sparkle went out of Bill Dodson's eyes as he said very deliberately, "Let me finish, Commander, before you make up your mind."

Rowe recognized the storm warning and said simply, "Go on."

Dodson continued, "The young men and women from one village or island dress in fiesta costume and become, for a day or an evening, strolling or sailing *troubadorés*. They go from village to village or from island to island serenading—singing and dancing. Then the village people give them gifts in return."

"Like oil and batteries, for instance?" Rowe kidded. Dodson spoke carefully. He was trying to ignore the sting of the commander's earlier remark. "If the *troubadorés* are professionals, the villagers give them money. If they are just friendly visitors, they give fruit and flowers."

"Very interesting and very nice—if you have nothing to do but sing and dance for fruit and flowers. Where do you intend to get the girls to make your party look like the real thing?"

"Oh we've taken care of that," said Dodson smiling. The tension was gone now. "Don't ever let it be heard that I said so, but some of them are real beautiful, when Captain Hernandez gets them fixed up."

Obviously skeptical, Rowe said, "I still say if you fellows can sing and dance your way into a Jap garrison, which is the only place in this neck of the woods you're going to find what we need, and come back with the stuff—well, you'll have to be damn good. How long will it take you to get ready?"

"We're ready now, Sir. You remember some of the boys reporting the Jap garrison east of here being restocked a few days ago?"

"Yes, I remember. It's down the coast a few miles." "Right," said Dodson. "We plan to sail in there in three hotels just before dark, stroll around the village serenading until we have the lay of the land. We have a map of the place and our people there have arranged to give us any last minute details."

The commander smiled as Dodson went on. "We'll work our way to the market place. They've set up their supply depot there. We'll get a good lively dance going. Julio and Manuelo will take their game cocks and get a cock fight going—maybe get some of the Japs to betting on it—and then we'll get what we want and get out."

"Just like that, huh," said Rowe, knowing that these daring fellows knew exactly what they were letting themselves in for. "And you think the goddam Japs are going to let you carry off their supplies while you strum your guitars, sing a few songs and put on a cock fight? Suppose they decide to search you for weapons."

"They've prepared for that, George," said Hernandez. He had let Dodson carry the ball long enough. "They know they'll probably have to shoot it out. They know too that we've got to have—well, anyway Bill has devised a screwball guitar. Funny thing is, the damn things play, even with an automatic or a tommygun stashed away inside."

"OK," said Rowe, with a wave of his hand. "I see you've thought it all out. Can you go tonight?"

"That's what we'd like to do, Sir, if it suits you," said Dodson—and the Coconut Patrol went into action.

A moment later Dodson and Hernandez were on their way down to the Guerilla Village. The platoon had been getting ready to give the commander a preview, to try to sell him on the idea. The seriousness of the undertaking was forgotten for the moment in the less commonplace business (to them) of making up some of the smaller, and finer featured guerillas as pretty native girls.

Dodson had sent out an SOS a few days before and in response, the men had brought in a number of colorful fiesta costumes. With these, a few silk scarves, and a kit marked "Camouflage," Hernandez, the showman, was soon working the miracle of make-up.

Zamora, with his slight build and fine, regular features was the real glamor girl of the outfit and before the show was over, was called upon to prove that he was not.

The party was chaperoned by a father and mother with one or two young sons and one little girl—small Pablo dressed in a lovely little embroidered party dress, licking a sugar-cane candy-stick. He had been overjoyed at the thought of being allowed to go, for until someone came up with the idea of the party dress for him, he had expected to have to stay behind and miss the fun.

A runner came back to the main camp to inform the commander that the party was off—with Captain Hernandez in command. Then Rowe realized how quickly Dodson and Hernandez had taken off, allowing no time for his grounding Hernandez.

Furious at the moment that his exec had taken advantage of his silence, Rowe shouted orders to alert Captain Berg and the cavalry platoon. As the *troubadorés* moved along the coast at a speed calculated to bring them to the garrison village about sunset, Rowe and Jerry, with the cavalrymen hurried along the jungle trail in the same direction. At least, if the *troubadorés* got into any real trouble and needed reinforcements, they would be there. They could not afford to have anything happen to Hernandez and Dodson and other trained and valuable personnel.

The cavalry platoon arrived at the edge of the village with its inevitable jungle backdrop, in time to see the *troubadorés* tie up two of the boats. They hid their horses and, leaving guards to look after them, moved in closer and watched the serenaders stroll leisurely from the beach up along the main street, to the music of their strange looking guitars.

They saw with relief that the Nips were accepting the *troubadorés* at face value—and obviously the faces were acceptable, for one after the other of the soldiers tried to make friends with, or passes at, the beautiful dancing girls. Even little Pablo, with his party dress and his candy-stick, came running after his indulgent "mother," bawling at the top of the high falsetto he had been rehearsing all day, about something "that nasty soldier" had tried to do. The *Troubadorés* were not concerned with the conduct of those they were serenading so long as it involved only insults to their womanhood.

Some of the more spectacular dances the men had been rehearsing, were in progress by torch light in the street. A little farther on, the game cocks with razor-sharp "spurs" strapped to their legs, were attracting some of the more sporting type, who picked their favorites and placed their bets.

In the early darkness, the third boat came in and the procurement detail, with some local assistance, found its way to the stalls of the marketplace. There the supplies stood neatly arranged as though set up for inspection by the two men designated to walk about and indicate by a turn of the hand, rubbing of the nose, or pulling at an ear, the location of things the team following them should try to pick up. Two men took positions on a kind of mezzanine overlooking the main floor. Two other teams got set in strategic positions to get away with the loot. Before the search for batteries and a few other necessities got under way, several metal, five-gallon containers of oil and gas, conveniently stored at the back of the building, were already being hurried down the dark, unguarded back lane to the boats.

They knew that getting away with the supplies was almost certain to involve shooting it out with the troops; but they hoped to call the signals and start any fighting that had to be done in their own time. The street show had succeeded beyond their wildest hopes in attracting the enemy personnel away from the supplies stored on the shelves in the marketplace. However, an alert MP walking back inside to check the stores, spotted one of the procurement detail carefully selecting the batteries. The MP's one shot before he fell under the man who sprang upon him from the mezzanine, was the signal for the melee that followed.

The cavalry platoon stood by in the darkness, machine guns ready for action. They watched Dodson's *Troubadorés* smash the fake guitars and pull out their tommyguns to cover their men making off with the supplies.

Most of the enemy troops were too stupefied to offer any resistance to the fighting-dancing-girls who had just been playing a lively Latin tune on those strange looking native instruments.

The raiding party made a run for the boats, with the priceless supplies, and carrying two of the men who, though not seriously wounded, were unable to make it back on their own power.

One who missed seeing the finish was the Nip sergeant who had been openly on the make for Zamora. Irked by the fellow's amorousness, the glamorous Zamora smashed his guitar over the head of his would-be lover, as the man turned, inadvertently to see what was causing the commotion at the market-place.

Now they could establish the Coast Watcher station on Apo Island, as the commander had indicated in his reply to General MacArthur, "whether occupied or not." The Apo group of three or four small islands off the southwest coast of Mindoro, near San José, where the first landing in the Western Philippines was to be staged, and on the projected route of the major assault force to Lingayen Gulf. A single enemy Coast Watcher on one of those small islands could defeat the whole invasion strategy, the essence of which was surprise. It was unlikely that a small, isolated area with no economic or apparent strategic value to the enemy would be occupied. However, if GHQ wanted a CW station there, ANYONE without a good logical reason for being there would have to be removed.

Lying to the south and west of Pandan Island, where MISSION ISRM had first touched Philippine soil, the Apos were familiar ground to Mang Pedro. Next morning, after the lend-lease batteries had been installed and other supplies checked and inspected, a radio team and a squad of guerillas, with a very proud old man acting as guide and counsel, set out for the islands to establish the CW station and report on whatever conditions they found there.

27
»» THE Q-BOAT MENACE

For several days, almost every agent coming in from Luzon brought information on a small, fast, and deadly, motor-powered, torpedo craft called the Q-boat. One of these toy-sized, wooden boats with a two-man suicide crew, was capable of destroying a good sized warship.

Darting out from the countless small creeks and Hogs along the island coastline, they could constitute a major hazard to Naval operations in the invasion. More insidious than the Kamikaze, these pilots could lurk unseen beneath the overhanging mangrove trees along the river banks, in the tall reeds and grass in the marshes or under the stilted grass huts, sitting like huge baskets on poles in the swamplands.

With precision timing and without orders, they could dart out individually, to hurl themselves against an Allied convoy, with disastrous results.

About the same time an inquiry came from GHQ about another device which apparently was being reported from other areas. That query read:

IT HAS BEEN REPORTED THAT NIPS ARE USING SHORE BASED TORPEDO LAUNCHING MECHANISM IN SOME SECTIONS OF THE PHILIPPINES. INFO IS URGENTLY REQUESTED REGARDING LOCATION WHERE SUCH DEVICES MAY BE INSTALLED. QUERY: ARE TORPEDOES LAUNCHED FROM TUBES OR RACKS? DIMENSIONS OF TORPEDOES: CAN TORPEDO LAUNCHER BE TRAINED OR IS IT FIXED? WHAT IS MINIMUM DEPTH OF WATER IN WHICH TORPEDOES CAN BE LAUNCHED? ALSO REQUEST INFO ON CONDITION OF SUBMARINE CABLES FROM MANILA TO GUAM, HONG KONG, CEBU CITY, SORSORON, ORION REPEAT ORION, AND CORREGIDOR. ALSO CABLES FROM MARIVELES TO CORREGIDOR. ARE NIPS USING CABLES?

Lieutenant Willie Hernandez set out with a party to Batangas, to check the Q-boat menace. They came back just ahead of a tropical storm on which the weather man had issued warnings to surrounding towns.

Willie's party had found large concentrations of the Q-boats in the inlets and deep rivers emptying into Balayan Bay, Batangas Bay and other strategic points along strategic Verde Island Passage. They brought back a description of the small craft, which were of light wood construction with hardwood bows. The boats were approximately 13 feet long, and powered by converted automobile engines, inboard, with a steering wheel at the center of the cockpit against the deck line. The deck, roughly two and a half feet from the center planking of the hull, extended aft from the bow, six and a half feet, leaving the rest of the hull open.

Painted a dull, olive-green, the Q-boats were almost invisible against the jungle background. They carried no armor and no armament—just a full load of explosives, directed by two men who stepped into the boat—said goodbye to this world—and headed for their target and the next.

The thoroughness of the enemy in distributing the deadly little craft was apparent on the map of the area, which indicated six main targets. In Janao Bay, near the town of Anilao, lay 100 of them and another 100 across the peninsula at Talaga. Between Mabini and Bauan were 50, and on Batangas Bay at Tabangao were 50 more. Crouching under the dense, trailing vines and mangroves overhanging the Wawa and the Cuta Rivers were 20 each and along the banks of the Santiago River in central Calatagan, an additional 200 were counted.

At the first warning of the approach of an Allied task force, by a single Jap Coast Watcher, a minimum of 500 of the deadly little craft with their tons of explosives and a thousand human sacrifices, could be hurled against the sides of an unsuspecting convoy within minutes.

Commander Rowe and Captain Hernandez were deep in the evaluation of this new threat to Allied shipping, and trying to determine if these boats could be the launching device referred to in the query from GHQ, when the storm with its howling wind and pouring rain came roaring in from the sea. As the storm increased in violence, with coconuts and hard, wing-like palm fronds zooming along on the wind, a runner from one of the guerilla villages down the coast, came running in to the main camp. A corporal came in from the outside and said, "A runner from East Village is here, Sir."

"Send him in," said Rowe.

The runner spoke excitedly, "Sir, enemy ship putting in to shore, 'bout 300 yards below East Village. Look like she drop anchor. Much lights on deck, like she getting ready for landing. *Teniente* OD say he keep close watch. He let you know quick, anything happen, Sir."

"OK, Juan, tell him to keep me posted, and thanks. It's a bad night," said the commander as he returned to the demanding work at hand.

In a few moments the corporal was at the door again. "The runner from East Village again, Sir."

"Bring him in and wait here," said Rowe.

Almost before he was through the door, the agitated runner burst out, "Sir, I get back almost to East Village and hear shots—many shots. Japs must have landed while I gone."

Instantly Rowe and Hernandez were on their feet. Reaching for his jacket hanging on the wall, Rowe began with an angry, "Leave it to the goddam Japs to attack on a night like this. Corporal, sound an alert and Juan, you report to Captain Dodson and take your orders from him."

"Yes, Sir," said the runner and turned to follow the corporal on the double.

Strapping on his automatic, Rowe said, "Al, get all the maps and records ready to destroy them if we have to." "Don't worry about things here, George. I'll take care of everything," replied Hernandez.

The high notes of the warning flute sounded as Rowe started for the stairway. Stopping for a second at the top of the stairs, he said, "Fire the building, Al, if they attack in any great number. We can't have another Barahan."

"OK," said Hernandez. "Good luck out there, George." Rowe dashed down the stairs and out into the pouring rain. Guerillas with rifles, automatics and tommyguns were running into the open quad from every direction. "Man battle stations!" shouted Rowe. "Captain Dodson, send runners to warn West Village. Alert the nurses at the Base Hospital for evacuation."

As Dodson turned to look for his runners, Pablo inadvertently stepped in front of him. Dodson almost bent double in his tracks to avoid stepping on the little fellow. "INTO YOUR FOXHOLE, PABLO," Dodson stormed at him, "and don't come out till I tell you to."

Off went Pablo as fast as his short legs would go, and with a powerful leap, went into his foxhole, which in the semi-blackout he had failed to notice was full of water. Bobbing up to the surface, he was sputtering and shouting for help when a guerilla nearby dragged him out of the hole.

Above stairs, Captain Hernandez prepared for immediate evacuation of the Map Room and the Radio Room. Secret documents and some of the experimental devices on which they were still making tests, would have to be destroyed if attack seemed imminent.

In Hernandez' quarters, directly under HQs office, a sub-machine gun had hung on the wall since the day he moved in. The gun could be seen from the outside when the door was open. A guerilla who had been intrigued by it since the day he came to the post, had often passed that way just to look at it. He had often dreamed of holding it in his hands, but had never had that opportunity. Now with all the excitement he could not resist the temptation. He had opened the door, looked about, then taken the gun from its peg and darted outside. His first experimental effort with the weapon resulted in the wild shots which had added startlingly to the confusion.

Hernandez cleared the steps just as Dodson roared at the man, "Put that gun back where you got it, you blasted idiot, before you kill somebody—and surrender yourself to the guardhouse, before I use it on YOU."

Taking the gun from the trembling hands of the bewildered man, Hernandez took it back inside, where he picked up a few things he would want to take with him in case of an evacuation. As he stepped back outside, a runner was coming across the quad, heading directly for Dodson. Seeing the runner, Rowe and Hernandez both walked quickly toward the guerilla leader. All listened anxiously as the runner began, "Capitan, Sir, *Teniente* OD, he say he hear shots in main camp. He say, 'What is trouble—anything wrong here?'"

"Is anything WRONG here?" exploded Dodson.

"Yes, Sir," continued the runner, intent upon delivering all of his message. "And *Teniente* OD say you not worry 'bout shots in East Village. He say he forgot to tell Capitan that Village Commander order practice alert tonight. He say hope not any im—unconvenience to officers in main camp."

A ghost of a smile flitted across Hernandez' face as his mind went back instantly to Old Bertha, Mang Juan's crocodile. It quickly disappeared when he heard Dodson boom out in a tone he had never heard the captain use to or about one of his men, "Go back and tell those goddamned idiots to surrender their arms. Put them in the guardhouse—IN IRONS—and give them half rations of rice and water till I'm ready to see them."

Terrified at the anger of the usually calm, soft-spoken captain, the runner said, "Yes, Sir, me tell them." Throwing a salute to the captain, he took off at a speed for which "on the double" would have been a masterpiece of understatement.

Standing there soaking wet, mud to the neck, his hat gone and a trickle of muddy water down his forehead, Rowe looked at Hernandez, clean, dry and comfortable, and said with magnificent sarcasm, "WELL, Captain Hernandez, what the hell issue of *Esquire* did YOU just step out of?"

A moment later Dodson and Rowe, looking at each other with that look of something important suddenly remembered, said simultaneously, "Who the hell SAID East Village was under attack?"

Apparently the enemy ship had put in near the coast to ride out the storm, but a sharp lookout was maintained until she pulled up anchor and went on her way.

Rowe's momentary anger was soon dissipated by relief that they were not faced with another evacuation—too late to start over again. At his suggestion, Captain Dodson occupied himself with an active cooling-off period before going down to East Village to reprimand the unfortunate Guerilla OD, who had unwittingly touched off the pyrotechnics.

28

» » EYES AND EARS OF GHQ

One day in November 1944, Coast Watchers and other sub-stations scattered along the south coast of Luzon and the north coast of Mindoro suddenly came alive. In quick succession from west to east, they reported a large convoy of cruisers, carriers, transports, and escorts of the Imperial Navy out of Manila, heading through Verde Passage. They carried reinforcements to bolster an already lost cause on Leyte. The convoy was reported within the ten-minute limit required to be of operational value. Shortly after the last of the vessels had cleared Verde Passage, U. S. Navy carrier-based planes came roaring in to bomb and sink a large percentage of the vessels.

Three days later, massing all available ships, another and still larger convoy sailed out of Manila over the same route, on the same assignment. The situation of the enemy on Leyte was desperate. He MUST get reinforcements there; but the Coast Watchers flashed the movement of the second convoy to PDQ. Again GHQ alerted the Navy planes.

Those were tense, crucial days at CAMP NIMITZ. Commander Rowe and a large party were away on a mission. Captain Dodson and most of his fighting force had been dispatched to the northeast coast near Calapan. A large enemy force had landed there and had to be cleaned out. Most of the men who were left at the post were in the hospital. Medical supplies were exhausted and malaria was playing havoc with the men. The radiomen flashed the report of the second convoy to GHQ and waited for the planes they knew would come—praying as they did so that they would not get there until those ships had cleared The Passage. There were not enough able bodied men available to defend their position against an accidental invasion by men who would swim ashore from that many sinking or disabled vessels. It is doubtful if the position of CAMP NIMITZ was known to Navy Air, but it was nonetheless gratifying to receive the "passing" report from the last CW station on the northeast Mindoro shore. The convoy was well out of The Passage and heading toward Sibuyan Sea when the squadron struck and destroyed an even greater number of vessels than in the attack three days before.

While on that mission, Commander Rowe learned that Major Ramsey and his men in south central Luzon were carrying on under tremendous difficulties. Being a combat unit as well as Intelligence, their requirements were infinitely greater than those of MISSION ISRM, as indicated by Ramsey's radiogram to GHQ:

> RAMSEY TO COMMANDING GENERAL SWPA: SITUATION INCREASINGLY DESPERATE. HUK BALAHAPS WITH SUPERIOR ARMS EVIDENTLY GIVEN BY NIPS STEADILY CUTTING RANGE OF OUR OPERATION AND INTELLIGENCE NETS. UNLESS FUNDS AND AT LEAST TEN THOUSAND ARMS AND RADIO EQUIPMENT TO CONTROL BULACAN AND MANILA AREA DROPPED WITHIN FIFTEEN DAYS AT HACIENDA REMEDIOS INTELL WORK WILL BE DISRUPTED IF NOT STOPPED. HAVE BEEN OPERATIVE ON QUOTE BORROWED UNQUOTE WAR NOTES: CANNOT OBTAIN ENOUGH TO MEET EXPENSES DUE STEADY INFLATION. REQUEST FOUR DAYS WARNING AND AMOUNT OF EQUIPMENT BEING SENT IF THIS REQUEST GRANTED.

Only the constant efforts of the technical men of MISSION ISRM kept Station PDQ on the air and furnishing the necessary flow of information to GHQ from their own agents and Major Ramsey's outfit.

Area maps sent to GHQ from the guerilla cartographers trained at ISRM, drawn to scale and dated and timed as to observation, conveyed a vast amount of intelligence information to keep GHQ and General MacArthur aware of changing conditions in and around Manila.

With the full complement of three thousand agents stemming from MISSION ISRM, the loyal men, women, boys and girls of the Philippines did all but perform miracles to aid in the liberation of their country. Sometimes a single error cost a life, but on the whole they were remarkably successful in keeping channels clearly defined and identities secret.

A complete collapse of the national economy followed close upon the destruction of the city of Manila by the invasion forces. Most of the men were either in prison camps or fighting in the hills and jungles with guerila outfits. Many girls were left to live in whatever way they could in a city overrun with enemy personnel. Whatever the cost to many of those girls in suffering, humiliation and heartbreak, the service they rendered their country and ours could not be measured by any yardstick commonly applied to the profession into which they had fallen.

Enemy officers and non-coms undoubtedly would have been amazed, had they known how much priceless information they dropped and how quickly it was relayed to GHQ through whatever channel of communication the girlfriend reported to.

When the Navy began bombing attacks on Manila, it was very important to General MacArthur that he have a photographic record of the effectiveness of the attack and the defensive tactics employed by the enemy. He ordered a motion picture to be made of the projected bombing. At the last moment, something happened, maybe a camera shutter failed. Maybe the film was too old. Whatever the cause, when the film was hurried to the dark room and processed, there were no pictures. The accommodating Room Service boys at the Manila Hotel knew every officer and high-ranking government official by rank, name, and serial number. If they could take such infinite pains to serve General Yamashita and his staff with delicious food and refreshing drinks, surely they could oblige General MacArthur, when all he wanted was a few rolls of exposed movie film.

The Nip general and his staff also had been interested in their defense effort. As those planes came roaring in over the city, a young sergeant on the staff, who was an excellent photographer, dashed to the roof where his camera was set up and waiting for just such an opportunity. He remained throughout the attack, picking up every possible bit of action of enemy (ALLIED) planes, and their own anti-aircraft guns—anything he thought would be of value to his superiors in their defense against Allied air attacks in the future.

When his film was developed and edited, he had what he proudly described to his commanding officer, in the presence of one of the Room Service men, an excellent and very comprehensive record of the attack. The Nip general and his staff assembled to see the effectiveness of their anti-aircraft defense. The lights went out and they waited eagerly to see the film. A murmur went over the room. Then a sharp order from someone in authority to start the picture.

The delay had occurred because the sergeant, who was also the projectionist, heard his name called from the inner office. The voice, he was sure, was that of the general himself. That was a summons no one could ignore. He dashed down the hall to answer and found no one there. He hurried back to the projection room, perhaps ninety seconds later—ninety seconds too late. Through the teamwork of an unusually efficient

Room Service man and a pleasant, accommodating elevator operator, his film was on its way to ALLIED HQs PROJECTION ROOM.

After the fury of that assembly of imperial torturers, hari-kiri probably was a welcome, if ignominious end for the unlucky non-com who had done his best, but his best had not been quite good enough.

In mid-December 1944, as Major General William C. Dunckel and his invasion force bore down upon San José, in southwest Mindoro, a daring triangle of radio stations were in operation on Luzon, one practically under the shadow of the enemy high command; DMAC-4 in Grace Park, Manila, DMAC-5 at Mariveles, on Bataan Peninsula, and DMAC-2, farther to the south near Magelanes in Cavite Province. In addition, 11 well placed CW stations, ten active Channels of Communication throughout the area, four Weather Stations, and three Radar Detector Stations were in full time operation.

With his unprecedented losses in men and ships in the lost Battle of Leyte, and the devastating uncertainty as to time and place of the coming Allied invasion, enemy efforts to combat the inevitable reached a frenzy.

At that point, with the invasion almost upon them, a situation in Manila required Captain Hernandez' immediate and personal attention. Since the Batangas jail incident, the Nips had not given up the search for him. Reports indicated that they thought him to be still active on Luzon. As a security measure, they followed the usual alternate party plan, with Captain Berg and Baker Party eight hours ahead of Hernandez and How Party.

Both parties had crossed Verde Passage and were once more moving through the Jap-infested region of Batangas fighting their way through a blinding rain, on muddy, slippery trails. Captain Hernandez found himself slowing down, no matter how hard he tried to maintain his normal pace. His teeth began to chatter and the wet clothing clinging to his body felt as though it had been dipped in ice water. He could not walk. Soon he could not move and at that moment he felt he could not even go on living. The party had to keep moving. Captain Berg's party had fallen back in order to keep closer touch with How Party. When Captain Hernandez could not go on, two men were sent to bring a *carabao* to carry him. Mang Pedro and several of the men sat near him, waiting for their return. Zamora went looking for something to make a hot broth to warm him. The temperature dropped and the rain grew colder. As he lay there surrounded by thin-faced, anxious men, runners came back from Baker Party. One went directly to the captain and said, "Sir, Captain Berg say you must hurry—get away from here—but be very careful. He say Japs beating earth for someone. Just one man they look for. He think you that man"

Hernandez motioned the men to him. "Men," he said weakly, "you heard what he said. I cannot go on, but you certainly cannot stay here."

"Sir, we cannot leave you," said one of his Cut Throat Squad.

Another said, "Sir, you wouldn't stand a chance alone with those dirty bastards."

"Attention, Men," said Hernandez. "We have no time to talk. I cannot go on. Quick now, dig a trench beside one of those logs, put me in it and bank it over with leaves. If you hurry, we may all live. If you are caught here, some of us will surely die."

The men began digging furiously with their bare hands, in the soft leaf mould accumulated on the jungle floor. Gently they lifted his thin, malaria racked body and placed him in the trench. With his canteen in one hand and his automatic in the other, they banked the leaves over in a natural-looking drift. As they were ready to cover his face, the youngest of his Cut Throat Squad looked down at him, almost in tears and said, "Sir, I will not leave you."

For the only time in his career, Hernandez, helpless and almost hopeless, raised a weapon at one of his own men. "Corporal," he said, "that was an ORDER. Go NOW." With grief and anguish in his voice, the boy said, "Yes, Sir. I go. I cannot help you if I am dead."

"Go on—all of you. On the double," said Hernandez as his hand dropped heavily back into the leafy camouflage.

Some of the men disappeared into the jungle while others climbed trees nearby, stretching along the limbs, their weapons drawn, waiting. Hardly were they settled when a party of Japs, including three or four officers appeared. Some were content to look for the object of their search, with only an occasional prod into a suspicious-looking spot here and there.

Two particularly vicious officers (Could they be remembering a Batangas jail?) slashed and hacked at everything in sight. Approaching the log where the captain lay, one of them stooped and slashed horizontally through the pile of leaves with his bayonet, so fast and so sharply that the leaves fell back undisturbed. In spite of the fever that burned through his veins, Hernandez felt a chill of horror go through his body as he heard the words of his pursuer. The bayonet sliced through the leaves. In tight, breathless silence, he felt the weight of one and then the other as the two men stepped up on the log for an instant, crushing it against his body—and were gone.

Satisfied that the Jap party had left, the men came down from the trees to find the captain unconscious. Some of them had filtered into the village and steered the enemy patrol back into the area they had just left. Some of the enemy squad had questioned them and they admitted having seen such a party near the village, trying to find food, but that they had found none there and had gone on south.

The *carabao* detail came in and brought the animal to where the captain lay beside the log. Blankets were arranged and the unconscious man lifted up and strapped to the animal's back, and they were on their way.

Many hours later, he regained consciousness as they plodded on through the jungle. He opened his eyes and looked about. To Zamora, who was walking beside him, he said, "What happened? How long since you hid me in the leaves?*

"That was yesterday afternoon, Sir," replied Zamora. "What happened—is every one all right?"

Seeing the captain awake, several of the men came in close to speak to him. Answering his question, Zamora said, "Some of the men went to the *barrio* to meet the enemy patrol and give them phony information, Sir."

"You are very weak, Sir. Maybe we stop and get something hot for you," said Mang Pedro, trying to change the subject.

"Later, thank you Mang Pedro," he said; then, "What did the others do? Hernandez insisted.

"We started away," said the young one, who had wanted to stay with him. "Then we think we hear the Japs coming, so we have to climb trees and wait for them to pass."

Hernandez had been unconscious by that time, but he had a feeling they had not left as he had ordered. "Don't you know you might all have been killed?"

"Oh yes, Sir, and we did start. Then we remember, we have made a promise, Sir."

"What was this promise?" asked Hernandez.

"You could not hear it, Sir, but we promise you that if one of those sonsabitch touch you, we kill every one of them. Then we HAVE to stay, Sir. We have given you our word. Maybe they kill us, but we take a lot of them with us." While the captain was on his way back, another emergency arose and certain vital information was requested by GHQ. Willie happened to be in camp and volunteered to make the trip. He took his aide, a Japanese mestizo who had been born and reared in Manila and trained at ISRM, along with a picked squad which often went on hazardous missions with him.

The situation was more complicated than they had anticipated and it was necessary to get the information "first hand from the Japs," he explained when he came back, meaning that they had gone into an enemy post, gotten their information and gotten out again.

"My God, Lieutenant, we didn't expect you to take such a risk as that," said Rowe.

"But you had to have the information," said Willie.

"Sure it was important, but so are you—very important to us. We don't want you dying for your country. We want you to stick around a while and LIVE for it."

"Well, it really was very simple. It just took a little while." "What do you mean, 'it took a little while'?" said Rowe. He knew this was going to be good, but he turned a little pale when Willie explained. His aide knew that it was a Japanese custom, that the enlisted men had to bow their heads as the high-ranking officers passed.

"So?" asked Rowe, when Willie hesitated.

"So—some of the men of my squad, volunteered to borrow some equipment for us, and . . ."

"What kind of equipment, Lieutenant," asked Rowe, determined to know how he had accomplished such a feat.

"Well, they borrowed a general's uniform for me, and one for a general's aide, and, oh yes, a general's car, so they would be sure not to look at us as we drove in."

"My God, Man," Rowe almost gasped. "How did you get back out?"

Willie laughed, "Just like the general would. We got back into the car and rode out."

Enemy personnel in the penetrated area quickly became aware of the crime and a little later, the identity of its perpetrator. Willie Hernandez had joined the list of hunted men.

Soon after that an agent brought in the word that the enemy knew the exact location and strength of Camp Nimitz. Only the lack of sea power to spare from larger operations had saved them from attack. Upon hearing that a force of Q-boats of a larger type were being readied to annihilate them, they radioed a request to GHQ for permission to close the camp and join the strong Allied force advancing toward Luzon.

The answer from GHQ was simple and to the point:

IMPERATIVE YOU HOLD YOUR POSITION THROUGHOUT LUZON INVASION OPERATION AT ANY COST. YOU AND YOUR CHANNELS OF COMMUNICATION ARE THE EYES AND EARS OF GHQ.

29
» » LANDING ON MINDORO

As the sun rose on the morning of 15 December 1944, American troops under command of Brigadier General William C. Dunckel, advanced through swamp lands and sugar canes, rice paddies and copra plantations, to take the airport at the city of San José, near the coast of Southwest Mindoro.

The radio men at Station PDQ worked first in relays, finally all together, throughout the day receiving, relaying and sending messages to and from GHQ and ISRM agents in that area, confirming the early morning flash reports on the landing. Up to that time MISSION ISRM had been responsible to GHQ only. On the day of the Mindoro landing, PDQ received this message:

> EFFECTIVE IMMEDIATELY YOU AND THE MEMBERS OF YOUR DETACHMENT ON DUTY MINDORO ARE PLACED UNDER COMMAND OF BRIGADIER GENERAL WILLIAM C. DUNCKEL, USA, COMMANDING GENERAL ALLIED TASK FORCE IN MINDORO. YOU WILL CONTINUE TO REPORT ALL INTELLIGENCE RECEIVED FROM LUZON DIRECT TO THIS HQS SWPA. SIXTH ARMY HAS COPIES ALL CIPHERS AND KNOWS YOUR CODES.

Commander Rowe's reply went forward immediately:

> ROWE TO GENERAL DUNCKEL: SWPA DIRECTS ME TO REPORT WITH PARTY TO YOU. EYE AM LOCATED NEAR ABRA DE ILOG. HAVE THREE HUNDRED MEN PARTIALLY ARMED. THEY ARE EXCELLENT GUIDES, ETC. EYE AWAIT YOUR ORDERS.

(Excerpts from) a report received from the captain of a special Intelligence mission in the San José area brought more details of the invasion operation as follows:

USAFFE FOURTH MILITARY DISTRICT, BOLO AREA REPORTS ENEMY INSTALLATIONS AT CAMINAWIT PT. DEMOLISHED BY AMERICAN PLANES BEFORE THE LANDING WAS EFFECTED ON THE MORNING OF 15 DECEMBER . . . SAN JOSE CENTRAL JAPS FLED TO THE MOUNTAINS BEFORE THE AMERICANS LANDED. MORE THAN TWO HUNDRED SHIPS OF DIFFERENT CATEGORIES STEAMED INTO THE BAY OF SAN JOSE . . . THE LANDING WAS EFFECTED FROM BARRIO ADELA TO CAMINAWIT, SAN JOSE . . . TOTAL STRENGTH OF THE AMERICAN FORCES LANDED SEVENTEEN THOUSAND. THIS IS ONE OF THE TASK FORCES OF THE SIXTH ARMY IN LEYTE UNDER COMMAND OF LT. GENERAL KREUGER.

SIGNED/GOHERSINDO DE LA TORRE CAPTAIN, INFANTRY

General Dunckel was not a stranger to Mindoro. He was, in fact, famed for his knowledge of both the geography and the climate of the Philippines. Also, as early as 20 November 1944, MISSION ISRM had been sending reports on every phase of enemy activity in the area in which he would penetrate. Before moving his men farther into occupied territory, however, he wanted to make his own reconnaissance. With a squadron of PT boats, the general set out on the evening after the landing and proceeded up the west coast from San José, arriving at CAMP NIMITZ at 0300, the hour which often had brought excitement and activity to MISSION ISRM.

On half an hour's notice, the guards were ready to stand inspection. Breakfast was waiting to be served in the small breakfast room, and the general's progress from Rowe's Landing to HQs, was along a very recently christened roadway. He could not suppress a smile of appreciation, and generously refrained from touching the paint on the road markers along "General Dunckel Blvd."

Since they were preparing for his arrival at such an early hour, they decided to show him the works. By the time he had finished his breakfast, every unit was in action.

As the party walked out of the breakfast room, they heard from somewhere out of the grey dawn a crisp, clear order for the change of a gun position. In the Intelligence Room, thirty men were at work on their maps, some new, some copying new information from maps received from agents in the field. Other men were preparing the daily list of contents of Manila Bay reported by observers throughout the bay area, to be forwarded to GHQ. In the Radio Room, men were receiving the dawn reports from scattered CW's. The general seemed amazed at the existence of such a post there in the midst of enemy occupied territory.

It was inspection of the Guerilla Fighters, standing Reveille, that brought out the great heart of the man. Looking over that company of men, ragged and tattered—at rigid attention—he called out a quick "AT EASE." Standing there with the men at his command, he seemed to feel the full significance of their being there. Abandoning the routine inspection, he walked among the ranks, touching a young boy's cheek, patting a thin, ragged shoulder, in sincere admiration for the splendid job they were doing and the heroic effort they were making for his country and theirs.

Completing his inspection, the general turned the men back to their leader and walked back toward HQs with Commander Rowe, Captain Hernandez and Captain Berg. "Gentlemen," he said, "I am proud of you. You have done a fine job. I had heard about your work here, but I had no idea that such an outfit as this existed here in the jungle—less than 150 miles from the HQs of the ENEMY HIGH COMMAND."

With the arrival of American troops, the people of Mindoro began to feel the first freedom in years. The hordes of civilians who lined the beaches of the towns along the west coast, shouting, singing, and waving their hands or an American flag, seriously hampered the task force assigned to attack enemy concentrations in those areas. However, within three days, General Dunckel's men, with sea and air protection from without and guerilla aid from within, pushed rapidly up the coast to take the town of Paluan.

A message from General MacArthur to Commander Rowe, received on 19 December 1944, read:

AYE COMMEND YOU AND THE MEMBERS OF YOUR DETACHMENT FOR SPLENDID SERVICE WHICH PROVIDED ME WITH PRECISE AND ACCURATE INFORMATION ON LOCAL ENEMY DISPOSITION ESSENTIAL TO THE LANDING AND EXECUTION OF THE MINDORO OPERATION.

For the people of most of the Island of Mindoro, THE WAR WAS OVER!

The Navy's PT boats were outstanding for dash and maneuverability. Immediately after the Mindoro landing, they went into action. General Dunckel scheduled a bold thrust into Philippine waters with his PT squadron, the first surface movement of U. S. vessels there in three long years of enemy occupation. His party was to proceed up the west coast of Mindoro, through Verde Passage to Calapan, which lies at the point where the north coast cuts sharply to the southeast. A route which paralleled the concentration of Q-boats on the north shore of the Passage. More reports on the Q-boats were coming in and like the General, Commander Rowe wanted to see for himself.

What the commander saw on that reconnaissance trip convinced him that something had to be done, fast. His radiograms to GHQ immediately upon his return read:

> NO. 331: HAVE CONFIRMED CONCENTRATION OF JAP Q-BOATS ALL ALONG BATANGAS COAST, BALAYAN BAY AND UP TO NASUGBU, TOTALING OVER FOUR HUNDRED BOATS, EACH MANNED BY TWO-MAN SUICIDE CREW FOR BLASTING TROOP SHIPS DURING LANDING OPERATIONS. WE BELIEVE NUMBER VESSELS DISPELS POSSIBILITY OF JAPS PLANNING TO USE THESE BOATS FOR LANDING TROOPS ON MINDORO ISLAND.
>
> FOLLOWING IS FOR YOUR CONSIDERATION: MAJORITY OF THESE BOATS ARE IN RIVERS AND ARE ACCESSIBLE TO LAND ATTACK. IF YOU CAN SUPPLY THREE HUNDRED THOMPSON MACHINE GUNS WITH TRACER REPEAT TRACER AMMO AND SOME PENCIL DELAY BOMBS OR DEMOLITION BOMBS MAJORITY THESE BOATS CAN BE KNOCKED OUT BY ONE PRE-ARRANGED SIMULTANEOUS RAID. WE WOULD LIKE CHANCE TO EXECUTE ABOVE.
>
> NO. 332: AS AN ALTERNATIVE OR IN CONJUNCTION WITH OUR NO. 331, EYE AM SENDING PARTY TO SURVEY RIVER CHANNELS AND MOUTHS OF RIVERS WHERE Q-BOATS ARE HIDDEN TO ASCERTAIN IF RIVERS COULD BE BLOCKED BY SINKING OF LARGE SAILBOATS OR LANDING CRAFT AT STRATEGIC POINTS. BELIEVE THIS ITEM OF EXTREME IMPORTANCE. WOULD WELCOME SUGGESTIONS FROM YOU. PHOTOGRAPHERS WILL TRY TO OBTAIN PHOTO OF Q-BOATS.

Once fully informed of the menace to any kind of Naval operation, GHQ lost no time in arranging for a joint sea and air attack. Meanwhile the PT boats continued to come up from the new base at San José, pick up Intelligence men who would orient them on target information and then, like wolves in the night, they would prowl the inter-island waterways. Covering in one night an area that would have required three days in a hotel, they picked up much additional information, disposed of enemy craft that came their way, picked off enemy gun installations, ammunition dumps, and other targets located by agents of MISSION ISRM. Then, before dawn they would strike out for home base. Combining the skill of the PT boat crews with the up-to-the-minute information furnished by ISRM Intelligence agents, plus Commander Rowe's keen eye and zest for action, the Navy's PT squadron turned in a brilliant performance.

Coincidental with these activities, in late December 1944 Captain Hernandez was completely occupied with his final advanced intelligence class training at CAMP NIMITZ preparing the men for maximum efficiency in the invasion of Manila. Plans for the commander's proposed air and sea attack on the Q-boats, called for guerilla parties to land at scattered points and fan out to warn the fishermen and other civilians of the many small coastal villages, to evacuate the area adjacent to the targets.

In a two-hour inferno of bombs, shells and flame, coordinated Naval and Air forces reduced the Q-boat threat along the Luzon shore to a charred and splintered mass of wreckage. Two hundred and fifty men of the suicide crews also had perished with their craft.

From that time forward the days whirled by. There was so much to do and so little time! Rowe had an important mission to the East and Captain Berg and Willie Hernandez had gone on separate missions to Manila when the malaria bug caught up with Hernandez with a vengeance. The Base Hospital had long since reached the bottom of the barrel in supplies and when this, the worst attack of his entire experience came, there was no medication, no malaria shots closer than San José. With the PT boats operating in coastal waters, that would have been only one day's sailing time, but all available PTs were operating elsewhere momentarily.

Always on the alert for any symptoms of an approaching attack, Zamora had sensed this one before the captain, himself, realized it, probably because it was unlike any he had suffered before. During a session of his class, he said, "Take a break, Men. I'm going to be good to you this time. Take half an hour."

Zamora had come in and sat down on a stool at the back of the classroom, to see how the captain was getting along. As the others went out he said, "Sir, why don't you give up and get into the sack? When you get into a bout with malaria, you know who always wins."

"But I don't think it is malaria," said Hernandez. "I'm not chilling. I have no temperature. It's just my chest. That's why I had the men take a break—the pain in my.. He clutched his chest and sank down on a bench.

"It's malaria, all right, Sir. I've seen it too many times. Let's get you flat, so I can massage your chest."

"But my class, I can't just..." The words died in the groan that escaped him as another paroxysm of pain swept over him. The fever came and he drifted back and forth between consciousness and unconsciousness.

They carried him to the hospital and Zamora sat by his cot, as his temperature rose slowly but steadily for hours. The nurses did what they could, but there was no medication, even aspirin to relieve the pain, as the cramps in his chest alternated with those in his legs. Each time, Zamora massaged the cramped area until the patient relaxed or fell asleep. In a moment of consciousness the captain heard the guerilla doctor say, "Without medication there's nothing we can do. It's only a matter of hours. No man can stand that temperature for long."

The doctor left after that discouraging pronouncement, which undoubtedly he had not intended for the patient to hear. Hernandez opened his eyes for a moment and looked at the white-clad nurse—one of the few who had a white uniform left—and said weakly, "Please, Nurse, will you and the others say a prayer for me?"

Zamora sprang to his side and the nurse whispered to someone, "Send for el Padre."

A wan smile played over the flushed face and Zamora bent low to hear the words "can't die with his absolution" and then, "Dodson's authority," before he lapsed into delirium. There was nothing to hold him now, save the prayers of his friends and the student priest who was still young enough to pray for his life as well as his soul—and perhaps the faith of the beautiful, dark-eyed girl who had said, "You will come back to me. I KNOW you will."

El padre came with his prayer book and a small reed basket of communion vessels. Hernandez opened his eyes again as the priest began intoning the last rites of the Church. The girl in white was kneeling beside him. Her uniform had changed to a white satin gown and a long wedding veil reached the floor—and floated out to become the chill fog of a San Francisco night. They were standing at the sea wall, and he lost her again. A breeze stirred in the palms outside the *nipa* roofed shelter and with the sound of the wind in the palm trees, the girl was there again, a lovely warm night on the beach at Miami. He could hear music—José at the piano—and she was dancing on a platform of two Army trucks, back to back. The cramps in his legs began again and Zamora's hands turned automatically from the benevolent attitude of prayer for his soul to the more immediate necessity of easing the pain in his body. Then he slept.

The sun streamed in bright and warm across the open air infirmary when the captain opened his eyes again, and Commander Rowe got up from a stool nearby and walked over to him. Smiling down at the sick man, he said, "Well, Fellow, is this the way you act when I turn my back? The camp doc says you're going to be all right for now, but I have a medic coming up from San José on the next PT with some shots for you. These attacks are getting too serious and coming too often. We've got to do something about them."

"I'm all right now," said Hernandez. "It was just..."

Rowe stopped him. "Don't try to talk. Better get some sleep. You've had a pretty rough time of it. I'll go up now and see if I can't get some work done. I've been neglecting it."

Finding the captain in serious condition upon his return from his mission, George had sent a message to the base hospital at San José, saying:

> MY EXECUTIVE OFFICER IS DYING OF MALARIA. PLEASE SEND ON NEXT PT BOAT COMPLETE FACILITIES AND MEDICINE FOR INJECTIONS AS HE COULD NOT KEEP PILLS DOWN.

A few days later a medic arrived from San José. By the time he got there, Al was on his feet again, but as the crew put a landing boat over the side to send the doctor ashore, George Rowe was being carried to the hospital.

Hernandez walked down to the landing to meet the doctor and take him directly to George. As he introduced himself, the doctor looked at him with a puzzled smile. "I guess I'm confused, Captain," he said, "but I thought you were the one who was ill. The commanders message said 'my executive officer/"

"That was five days ago, Major. He's the one who needs you now."

One look at George and the visiting medic knew the exec was right. That put him in a bad spot. He motioned to Al to follow him outside, where they could talk. He had come all the way up the Mindoro coast to bring the malaria shots to Hernandez, and now... "Captain," he began, then hesitated, "this is really bad. It's just that too many of our ships aren't getting through, and too many men are needing the supplies that do. You see, I..."

"Major, are you trying to tell me that you have only enough shots for one of us?" Hernandez asked, directly.

The major nodded helplessly.

"Then there's no problem. He needs help now. I can wait for a few days. It may be in time to do him some good."

Before departure time for the next squadron bound for San José, George was feeling better and the major thought a few days at the Base Hospital would be good for him. Hernandez seemed fully recovered for the time being. His Intelligence class was still to be completed, and he had a mission to Manila on his immediate schedule. However, before the unhappy medic-without-portfolio had reached port at San José, Hernandez was out for the count in another serious malaria attack, and still no shots. It didn't seem to make any difference when his attacks came, nor where, he was never in the right place.

Came Christmas 1944, and CAMP NIMITZ invited the people of Abra de Ilog to attend Christmas Mass at Little Town Cathedral. They came, and stayed to marvel at the city that had sprung up in a few months and remained hidden among the coconut and banana trees, to become the island's stronghold of freedom. That day, CAMP NIMITZ was not a military camp. There were no soldiers drilling, no sound of clicking rifles. She had shed her uniform and donned the bright colors of the fiesta. The barracks and other buildings were bright with greens and Christmas decorations. Carols rang out to the accompaniment of native guitars. People knelt at the altar and at the coconut benches in the little church in prayers of thanksgiving.

A baseball game with Intelligence Service and Medics vs. Captain de la Torres' men, filled the little grandstand to overflowing. A tug of war came next and was followed by a coco-head carrying contest by the nurses, won by Miss Silvia de Leon, after trailing from the start. Miss Felicia Manfesta was second at the home stretch, with Miss Anguid third and Miss Gerense a fighting fourth.

The making of lanterns is something of an art in the Islands, and a very original entry by the medical section won first prize. Lieutenant Malaban's "B-29" and "1960 Rocket Ship" won second and third. The unconventional but highly appreciated prizes were packs of Kraft cheese, canned shrimp, and Phillip Morris cigarettes out of a Christmas gift to the camp from General Dunckel.

As evening came, bright lanterns were hung. A campfire leaped and flickered while gay, laughing Guerilla Fighters, nurses, and young people of the town danced in the open air. Older ones sat around the fire and at tables reminiscing and talking of what lay ahead, while the children watched the dancing, something most of them had forgotten or had never seen.

Scenes were not so festive in other parts of the Philippines that day. On the rain-soaked east coast of Leyte, an assault force convoy was assembling for the invasion. They planned to cut straight through the heart of the Philippine Archipelago, recapture Luzon and Mindoro (the speedy liberation of which no one had anticipated), and set up air fields overlooking the South China Sea, in striking distance of Tokyo.

Nip warlords sat stiffly around a table in their secret HQs at Santa Mesa Heights, a suburb of Manila. Still convinced of their racial and military superiority, they sought some strategy to recoup their staggering losses in men and ships in the Leyte operation. The Japanese had dreamed (and boasted) of turning the Leyte Invasion into a fiasco, but they had underestimated the teamwork of MacArthur's Army, Halsey's Fleet, and Kenny's Air Force.

A mad effort to transport troops from Manila to Leyte, six times the distance from CAMP NIMITZ to Manila, in sailboats, resulted in further losses and left General Kataoka to take his last stand on Ormoc Highway with less than five hundred exhausted, hungry, already defeated men, remnant of the famous First Division. Once the cream of the Japanese Army, they waited now with no other hope than a glorious end in the service of their emperor. Unknown to the masterminds at Santa Mesa Heights, the last of the First Division had made up their minds to wait for the glorious end in some place other than MacArthur's direct line of attack. On the night of 21 December 1944, they had deserted the Command Post at Kilometer 79, and fled to the south and west.

Now, whatever strategy the imperial brass had planned on the fragile fabric of a defeated army and a phantom fleet now at the bottom of the Pacific, it was doomed to failure. Hardly had they cleared the conference room, that Christmas evening, when Corporal George Herrerria, 978th Signal Unit, USA, entered from a side door, went to the conference table and quickly removed from under the table a sound recording of every word spoken at the conference, to be rushed away to GHQ. (See: Philippine Free Press, 15 October 1945.)

A few hours after the meeting at Santa Mesa Heights, Field Marshal Count Terachi, who controlled the combined military force as well as the entire Empire of Conquest of the Japanese, realizing that the fall of the Philippines was inevitable, fled with his entourage to Saigon in French IndoChina, to establish new HQs.

Early in January 1945, with the PT-boats furnishing transportation between CAMP NIMITZ and San José, Commander Rowe and Captain Hernandez, set out one evening for the new base, BM-5. The commander was going to deliver an Intelligence report and pick up material for PDQ. At last, Hernandez was to see the medics. They had arranged to take turns with the PT-boat captain, on the bridge of the flagship of a five-boat squadron. George had already put in a rugged day at the post, and the night ahead gave little indication of being any easier. Hernandez took his turn first, while Rowe went below to get some rest.

It was a beautiful, warm, summer evening just after the New Year. Hernandez had taken off his shirt to fully enjoy the fresh, sea breeze as he stood on deck, Intelligence report in hand, watching the setting sun. As they moved out of Verde Passage, into the South China Sea, a convoy of perhaps thirty enemy trawlers enroute to Ambil Island, came into view.

After a quick ship-to-ship communication, the PTs separated and maneuvered into position for an attack. They were to do a half-circle and come in two at a time, one from the north and one from the south, firing rockets, shells, anything that would damage the trawlers.

The flagship took the lead and was heading in at full speed, probably fifty miles per hour, when with a screeching, grinding, crashing roar, the fore part of the boat shot upward, out of the water. She hung there impaled upon a sharp, jutting point of rock barely below the surface of the sea and began see-sawing crazily up and down, threatening to capsize with every crashing wave.

Clutching desperately at a protruding bar, Hernandez caught and clung to it. Every other man he could see had a life belt. He was NOT a sailor—and those who were, seemed to be having a bad time at the moment. Finally a crewman with a Mae West in his hand, shouted, "Captain, here you are. Catch it."

He tossed the life belt in Hernandez' direction at the precise instant that George's head appeared from below and he shouted, "What the hell happened?" In the next breath, and with absolute terror in his voice, he said, "Al, where's the REPORT?"

With a sickening shock, like a blow in the solar plexus, Al realized that he hadn't the foggiest notion as to what had happened to the report AND that he had looked away, just in time to miss the life belt the sailor had thrown to him. For a moment the thought of the lost reports at Barahan, blotted out everything else; but a devastating sway of the boat pushed that to the back of his mind. Clinging to the bar, getting sicker by the moment from the swaying of the boat, he watched the life belt slide back and forth, stopping just out of reach at the end of every tantalizing slide. Maybe he could catch it next time, if there WERE a next time before one of those goddam waves dumped them into the sea.

Then suddenly, George Rowe was a Naval officer—on board a vessel in distress. "They're trying to put a boat over the side, Al. If they get it away, I want you on it. I'll stay here and try to find the report before they have to blow her up. My God, we can't TAKE another Barahan."

The width of the deck stretched between Al and the lowering boat. His matter of fact statement of the obvious, "I'll have to get TO the boat, first," was lost on the next wave.

Having let go of the bar to start, just as a wave struck, aft, he skidded along the deck on his bare arms and elbows, his hands in front of him. As he slid under an overhead vent, he saw or felt something falling from above. Involuntarily, his eyes closed and into his outstretched hands plopped the report. The impact of the crash had thrown it from his hands into the vent and, like the elusive life preserver, it probably had slid back and forth until the force of the big wave dislodged it.

Neither Commander Rowe nor Captain Hernandez could have given a really satisfactory report on the PT-boat attack but they hadn't started out to do battle with enemy ships. They were on their way to deliver an Intelligence report to a passing submarine, and they DID.

# 30
» » MISSION ACCOMPLISHED

With the gathering of the tremendous, secret invasion force off Leyte, GHQ's demands for fast, accurate information were insatiable.

As 14 December 1944 dawned over the Philippines, a carrier-based task force from Admiral Halsey's Third Fleet roared in over Manila. For three days and nights, tons of explosives poured from the skies over Manila and the bay, maintaining complete control of the air locally, accomplishing tactical surprise for General Dunckel's landing at San José, Mindoro, and completely confusing the enemy as to the focal point of the coming invasion.

Destruction of 269 ships in the bay, rail facilities, and enemy planes on the ground and in the air worsened the enemy's already desperate transportation situation. Every effort was made in the next three weeks to encourage the belief that Southern Luzon would be the re-invasion battle

At General MacArthur's direction, every friendly guerilla band on Mindoro and Luzon concentrated on the destruction of railroads, highways and bridges in the southern provinces and the incessant harassment of General Yamashita's forces. For months, U. S. submarines had been smuggling in all possible arms and ammunition to aid the guerillas in fighting from the inside when the re-invasion got under way.

The myth of the superiority of the yellow fighting man soon dissipated when he stood face to face with the brown boy with a gun. When surrender became imminent and inevitable, Japanese troops held out wherever possible to surrender to American troops rather than to the native guerila bands.

Among the thousands of Filipinos who volunteered their services to MISSION ISRM, there were few failures. The one traitor to volunteer

(Ortega) was still being held at the POW camp for the betrayal of the Major Philipps' Party. Claiming to have been a guerilla, he was tried by a military court martial and found guilty. When General Dunckel ordered Captain Dodson to clean out a sizeable force of Nips which landed on the north shore of Mindoro, between Calapan and Santa Rosa, Ortega was given his choice of standing public trial at the end of the war or redeeming himself in combat against the enemy.

The enemy force was routed. Many enemy troops were killed and a number taken prisoner, but at a tremendous cost to MISSION ISRM. A sad-faced sergeant hurried back from the scene of battle to report that Captain Bill Dodson was being brought back on a stretcher, with a bullet wound through his body at the waist, from right to left. For handsome, courageous Bill Dodson, the war was over. He was taken to the base hospital at San José that night by PT boat. They never saw Bill again, nor Pablo, the remarkable little character who for months had been Bill's shadow, but it was said by one who came back from the base hospital that the little fellow could be seen running errands for the nurses day or night whenever he was needed.

From that same skirmish came the word that a number of Dodson's fine guerilla fighters had been killed in action. Traitor Ortega was among those who were buried where they fell.

With the radios and vital equipment supplied by the submarines during the first week in January, Commander Rowe radioed GHQ that they could now step up reporting in the Manila area. On 8 January 1945, the day before the Lingayen Gulf landing, they received this message from GHQ:

> TO ISRM FROM KAZ: GLAD TO LEARN RE YOUR NO. 320 THAT MANILA COVERAGE WILL BE IMPROVED. NO REPEAT NO OTHER STATION HAS OR CAN REVOKE YOUR ORDERS TO YOUR OWN OPERATORS. IT IS EXPECTED THAT YOU WILL CONTINUE OPERATING YOUR NET GIVING MAXIMUM COVERAGE LUZON AREA AT THIS CRITICAL TIME.

On 9 January, the day of the all-out invasion at Lingayen Gulf, ISRM's station PDQ was notified of the passing of command of certain areas to Lieutenant General Walter A. Kreuger, Commanding General of the Sixth Army, and that:

> ... ALL ELEMENTS SOUTH OF THAT LINE WILL REMAIN UNDER THE OPERATIONAL DIRECTION OF GHQ. ALL RADIO TRAFFIC WILL CONTINUE THROUGH KAZ WITHOUT CHANGE. DESIRE THAT YOU BE ESPECIALLY ALERT TO REPORT MAJOR MOVEMENTS OF ENEMY LAND, SEA AND AIR FORCES. NOW

THAT THE BATTLE FOR LUZON HAS GONE AHEAD, SUCH MOVEMENTS MAY BE OF IMMEDIATE COMBAT IMPORTANCE.

As American forces moved south from the Lingayen Beachhead, hundreds of reports went forward to alert them to hazards along the approaches to Manila. They were informed of the positions of hidden gun emplacements, fortifications, ammunition dumps, fox holes, public buildings turned into embattlements, and excavations in roads large enough to disable tanks and trucks, camouflaged with a cover of bamboo, banana leaves and earth.

Roughly two weeks after the Lingayen landing, Commander Rowe, miserably ill of malaria, led the first OFFICIAL Naval patrol through South Verde Passage. Burning with fever, he lay in the captain's bunk until notified that the PT's had picked up two or three enemy ships on their radar. The first PT driving in toward the target (in single file) got its torpedoes off, and away. The second with Rowe and party aboard, got their torpedoes off, scored a hit, but were caught in the spotlight of the big ship. One big shell after the other sent the water spouting into the air on every side of them. The pilot of the PT quickly maneuvered in close to shore to lose his silhouette from the light. "Throw smoke," called the captain, "throw smoke." The light, fast craft, made of wood and powered by Cadillac engines, was soon enveloped in smoke. With magnificent courage, ingenuity, and daring, they dashed in at full speed, back tracked, zigged here, dodged there—everything but somersaulted that bucking bronco of the sea, till at last the enemy fire ceased and the PTs went on their way to look for other targets.

A few nights later, the PT Squadron was proceeding from the recently liberated port of Calapan, toward Camp Nimitz when, from his position on the lead boat, George spotted probably fifty Japanese sailboats and native *curicannans* moving along the coast. Instantly he called out an order to man the guns. The PTs slowed down and opened up with all they had, from the .30 calibre machine guns to the 40-mms. Three times they moved along the length of the Nip convoy, each time with accurate and devastating fire. Within the next two days, ISRM agents reported that about ninety per cent of the targets were effectively hit.

As the PTs moved along about 1500 yards from the western tip of the island, a shell hit the water. A cry of "105's" went up, but the location of the Jap 105 was not news to Rowe nor the officers of the PT-boat. Agents had located the gun months before and their information had been confirmed by an odd little character taken prisoner by one of the guerilla bands about the same time. He obviously was Japanese and was wearing the remains of an enemy uniform. His reasoning was amusing if not entirely logical, when questioned by the guerilla officer in command.

The man had stumbled into the guerilla camp ragged, hungry, alone and broke. "You give me food," he said, "I tell you all about enemy fortifications—anything you want to know."

"Why you little yellow sonofabitch," said the guerilla officer, "you ARE enemy. Why should we give you food? Why should you tell us anything?"

"Oh NO, Sir," he protested, genuinely distressed, "I no enemy. I guerilla like you—see." He held out his ragged sleeves. "I ragged. I have no gun—live all alone in hills, long time, eight months, nine months—maybe year. I no enemy, Sir. I guerilla. I tell you all about guns you give me food."

So he told them about the 105's and others that were in the exact locations ISRM agents had charted them, and now, months later, the PT's were prepared to maneuver past the guns unharmed and proceed to Camp Nimitz, another victory for the PTs and the Navy.

Certain scarce and critical supplies still were difficult to get. The ways and means of doing so, as more outside forces arrived were something like this:

ROWE TO COUGHTRY: G-3: EYE HAVE BEAUTIFUL JAP PISTOL FOR YOU IF MY JEEP AND TWO BOATS FROM THE NAVY ARRIVE AT MAMBARAO WITH BULLDOZERS, ETC. PLEASE ADVISE.

SIGNED/ROWE.

Or,

13 JANUARY, TO COMDR. DAVIS: I HAVE REALLY BEAUTIFUL JAP OFFICER'S SABRE. YOU HAVE TWO LAUNCHES OFF TENDER WITH NECESSARY FUEL AND BOAT ENGINES WHICH I DESPERATELY NEED. IT IS YOUR MOVE.

SIGNED/ROWE.

A few days after the liberation of Mindoro was considered accomplished, Commander Rowe walked into the office where Hernandez was working and said, perhaps just a little too casually, "Al, let's take a walk."

Usually that meant he wanted to discuss something very confidential. They set out along the coconut-lined lane down to Rowe's Landing. Once again, as on that morning back at the TOWER OF ISRM, when he had been deeply moved, George found it difficult to speak. Finally he came out with a completely irrelevant remark as they passed the tower housing the crows nest. Looking up at the oversized basket, large enough for two men and a few pieces of equipment, he said, "Well whatever happens, so long as the tower's in operation, were still in business."

"Right," said Hernandez, "but considering the fact that we've both heard that sage observation a hundred times, what the hell did you come down here to tell me?"

Rowe tried again. "Well, Al, I never—I mean it just—well it never occurred to me that.. He stopped again and pulled a folded sheet of paper from his shirt pocket and thrust it toward the man who had been almost his other self for so many months. "Here, goddamit, read it for yourself." It was a message from GHQ. Somehow it had never occurred to either of them that they would not finish as they had begun—together. But there it was. The Commander had orders to report to GHQ, which NOW meant Manila and HOME!

"This leaves you in command, Sir. I guess there's nothing more to say." His message to GHQ next morning said:

IT HAS BEEN A PLEASURE AND A PRIVILEGE TO HEAD A PARTY WHERE NOT ONE SINGLE CASE OF DISCIPLINARY ACTION WAS NECESSARY AND WHERE EVERYMAN EXCEEDED MY EXPECTATIONS IN COOPERATION AND EFFICIENCY.
SIGNED/ROWE.

Jerry Berg stepped up to second in command. There were few questions he could not answer either about Camp Nimitz or about the many channels of communication throughout the network, but there probably have been few cases where the ARMY so sincerely regretted seeing the NAVY shove off. In those seven months they had shared a rare and unforgettable experience.

Only a few days before, Mang Pedro had asked permission to return home. He was weary from the long, hard struggle for the liberation of his own island and lonely for his people. There was little they could offer in return for the truly heroic service he had rendered. With a smile and a lump in the throat, George, Willie, Jerry and Al bade good bye and Godspeed to a true hero and a grand old man who had responded so valiantly to the call of his own country and theirs. In a sturdy, little NICHOLSON LINE sailboat he had always admired and which, beyond a doubt he had earned, he set his sails to the southward toward the tiny island of Pandan where months before he had said, proudly, "Sir, I am reporting for duty."

About mid-February this message came from GHQ:

LT. AL HERNANDEZ COMMANDING. YOU ARE HEREBY ORDERED TO CLOSE CAMP NIMITZ AS MISSION IS ACCOMPLISHED. ALL RADIO SPECIALISTS ARE TO BE TRANSFERRED TO SIXTH ARMY HQS FOR FUTURE ASSIGNMENT. ALL RECONNAISSANCE MEN TO REPORT TO GHQ UNDER YOUR COMMAND. SGTS. CASWELL AND GEORGE ARE TO ACCOMPANY YOU AND THE REST OF YOUR

UNIT. AIR WARNING AND RADAR BATTALIONS ARE TO CONTINUE IN PRESENT SITE UNTIL THEY REVERT TO THEIR OWN UNITS. SIGNED/GHQ

Lt. Hernandez replied at once:

GOING OFF AIR PREPARATORY TO CLOSING STATION. RADIO PERSONNEL TO EMA.

SKELETON FORCE REMAINING TO CLEAR OBLIGATIONS.

SIGNED/HERNANDEZ

Looking back over those days at Camp Nimitz was to bring more than a touch of nostalgia. Men who share danger, hunger, and success get to know each other. They had learned there, with pressure on every side, that in times of need, the best in their men went into whatever task was assigned to them, whatever demands were made of them.

There were many who deserved recognition and whose efforts went a long way toward the success of MISSION ISRM, towards shortening the long road back. Some have been mentioned only as part of a group while others, due to the nature of their activities, could be mentioned individually. Willie Hernandez was one of those. When construction of roads and other local projects put money into circulation, Willie served as Secretary and Treasurer of the Finance Committee of Abra de Ilog. Later he became mayor of the town and finally was made Honorary Governor of the Province of Mindoro, when a mediator was required.

From the TOWER OF ISRM to Manila was a hazardous ten day journey, on foot, with a minimum of twenty six Jap sentry posts between the Luzon coast and the city. A volunteer who made the round trip was considered a hero. Fully aware of the fate of a captured spy, Willie became a regular courier. He went with Al on dangerous missions to the heart of enemy HQs, and when their own mobile HQs were penetrated by the enemy he aided in the escape. Whatever Willie Hernandez went after, he brought back.

A few days after Willie's daring penetration of the enemy installation in the Jap general's (borrowed) car, he was on a mission with his regular squad of picked men from Dodson's force, when they met an enemy patrol sent to bring in WILLIE HERNANDEZ, DEAD OR ALIVE. Acting, for the moment, just a friendly native boy with no military experience, he had never seen an order like that. He asked if he might see it. He could—and did. He also brought back the enemy patrol, ALIVE, with their orders in his pocket.

To the native boys he was "the smartest guerilla lieutenant", to the unit, "the smoothest secret agent", but to Al Hernandez, he was "my cousin

Willie".

There were fighter moments too, such as the day when George received a gift from a friend, Stateside. It was a bottle of perfumed hair tonic, the only thing alcoholic that would pass postal inspection. After a sun-warmed shower, George applied some of the tonic before starting out on some duty that took him walking through the camp. He came back saying, "I guess I'll just have to drink the goddam stuff. Even the lousy lizards give me the big eye, with that on my hair."

To any man who was there, must sometimes come the memory of several hundred men standing retreat, thin, ragged, often hungry. Some had hats, others caps. Some wore GI shorts for trousers, and some had no shirts of any kind, but one thing they HAD in common, a determination to see their country FREE.

No mission was too dangerous, no trail too long as they pushed off into the dawn or the black of night always with the theme which Dr. Hayden had given them in Tagalog, at the blacked-out aerodrome in Australia, unaware that it was to become their aloha and their au revoir, BAHALA NA—Come What May!

Finally came the hour when the last piece of gear was stowed away in the sixty-ton *Doña Juana*, still flagship of the NICHOLSON LINES. Lieutenant Hernandez and Sergeant Berg (back to their actual status now that there was no more guerilla rank to be considered), together with a good part of the original Intelligence Unit of MISSION ISRM, Sergeants Caswell and George of the Weather Unit, Sgt. Harder and Willie Hernandez, said good bye to their good friend and host, Mang Salizar and the white-robed priest who had come against his will, but now was loathe to leave. With a backward look at their jungle hideaway, they pushed off in the sparkling freshness of the new day. Turning for a last glimpse, one of the men said, "Look! El Padre is in the Crow's Nest."

His white garments were silhouetted against the deep green of the jungle, where he had climbed to watch until the tips of their sails would drop down over the dip and be lost below the horizon.

They skimmed along in the bright, morning sunlight over a shimmering sapphire sea, their white sails billowing full before a brisk breeze. That color photographer's dream came to an abrupt end as they rounded Cape Santiago on the Luzon coast and slipped out into the South China Sea. The last message to be received before closing down station PDQ had read:

CRUMP TO HERNANDEZ: FIFTH AIR FORCE HAS BEEN INFORMED THAT YOUR SAILBOATS ARE MARKED WITH BLACK SQUARES

PAINTED ON EACH SIDE OF SAILS. THEY HAVE ASSURED ME THEY WILL AGAIN ORIENT THEIR PILOTS.

With their immediate destination, Nasugbu, some fifteen miles south of Manila virtually in U. S. hands, the message had seemed reassuring enough, at that distance. Approaching the port of Nasugbu, in the face of a vast convoy of warships, battlewagons, light and heavy cruisers, destroyers, transports, and landing craft, with Naval and Air Force planes and Marine Corsairs roaring overhead, it was a different story. It required some really high-test optimism to believe that one single *curicannan*, identifiable only by a small, black square high in the tip of her sails, had more than the proverbial snowball's chance of survival.

Two days after sailing away from the pier at Rowe's Landing, twenty very weary, very seasick young men with a boat load of military equipment were challenged by an American patrol boat carrying two 50 cal. guns in the harbor at Nasugbu. The rugged "WHO GOES THERE?" of the challenging non-com was met by Hernandez' reply, "Lieutenant Hernandez and force." The man made no effort to conceal his doubt as he waited for Hernandez to present his papers. These tattered men didn't look like any American fighting force he had ever seen.

From Nasugbu they headed on into Manila on foot. Jerry, Willie and Al set the pace. They had all come this way before, but this time it was different. This time they walked toward the final showdown between the last, frenzied efforts of an already defeated enemy, ready to destroy the city he would not surrender, and a mighty re-invasion force equipped with every scientific device known to modem warfare, determined to take that city, if only the bare, scorched earth on which it stood.

"I think I'd just as soon not make it to the top of the ridge," said the lieutenant.

"We probably all feel about the same," said Jerry. "We know what's coming and we haven't got the guts to face it." "It was bad enough when they came," said Willie. "I don't have to tell you, Jerry. You saw it. And now they've promised to bum the city to the ground."

"They'll do it too," Jerry answered grimly.

"We'll see in about ten more feet," said Hernandez as they walked the last few feet to the top.

These men who knew almost every foot of the city now, practically every slit in the rugged, old stone walls, thought they were prepared for anything; but as they reached the crest, they stopped as one man, numb with horror at the panorama stretching out in the distance below—the beautiful city they loved—Manila, Pearl of the Orient, aflame I As they stood there, the rain came but the raindrops fell unheeded on faces already wet. Some of the happiest hours of each of those young men had been spent in that lovely, old city, peaceful, friendly and gay. But there was no peace now, no gaiety.

Along the way into the city lay American boys, victims of Jap snipers who had ambushed them from the trees. It was no recompense, but a cruel sort of satisfaction, upon arriving in Manila and working their way through the piles of rubble, barricades and tank traps, to see the ground under the trees littered with the bodies of the would-be conquerors who, having gained their Shinto Heaven, had left their stodgy bodies to fall unheeded and unmourned beneath the trees that had sheltered them.

With every bridge over the Pasig River destroyed, the ISRM party set up their HQs on the south bank and began coordinating intelligence reports for the different units who required them. Days and nights blurred together in the smoke and flame, death and destruction, the roar of guns and the screams of dive bombers. Great gaping holes were torn in the Intramuros, the old Walled City that had withstood time and the elements for more than 300 years.

On 25 February 1945, organized resistance came to an end. Soon Allied ships occupied Manila Bay where, like Pearl Harbor, the rusting hulks of sunken ships reared starkly from the water, half buried in the mud and sand. Weeks of fanatical resistance from house to house, room to room in office buildings, the Post Office and the Agricultural Building ended with the order, "CEASE FIRE."

Then, weeks later, came the Regimental Parade at Camp Murphy where the Unit was presented with the Combat Infantryman's Badge, the Bronze Star and the SWPAC Campaign Medal with three stars. It was there that Lieutenant Hernandez received from General MacArthur the Citation for the Legion of Merit.

One evening at the home of the Philippine Secretary of Defense, General Basilio J. Valdes, the general presented him with the Philippine Liberation Ribbon and more than a citation, the deep gratitude of the people of the Philippines "for a job well done."

On the evening before Al sailed for home, he and Willie took their last, long walk together. It was sunset as they stood high above Manila's once fabulous Escolta, now a desolate street of ruins, wondering what would come out of all the struggle, illness, hunger, privation and grief.

Looking at a picture that would never be erased from either of their memories, Willie said, "Tell me, Al, what do you think you'll remember most as time goes by?"

For a long moment Al thought in silence. Then he said, "I'll remember many things, Willie, a yellow life raft and the moon on the water, the view from the TOWER OF ISRM,

Dodson and Pablo, the smell of blood in the Batangas jail, two white crosses on a mountainside in South Luzon—but the first time that you and I stood here, on this spot, at sunset, I'm sure I'll NEVER forget."

"Why that time in particular?" asked Willie.

"It was then," said Al thoughtfully, "that I actually realized, with a vague feeling, I guess part sadness and part pride, that now we could truly say 'Mission accomplished/ My Chief had kept his solemn promise to the people of the Philippines. He had said, 'I Shall Return'—and now—HE HAD."

CITATION FOR LEGION OF MERIT

First Lieutenant Al Hernandez 01324774, (then Second Lieutenant) Infantry, United States Army. For exceptionally meritorious conduct in the performance of outstanding services in the Philippine Islands, from 7 July 1944 to 26 June 1945. Lieutenant Hernandez of the 5217th Reconnaissance Battalion volunteered to serve as Assistant Commander and Executive Officer of an Advance Intelligence detachment, and with his group, landed by submarine on the enemy-held island of Mindoro.

Despite constant enemy opposition, he successfully maintained a highly effective intelligence net, composed of numerous stations widely scattered over the island. Concerned with the expansion of the system, he organized intelligence and radio schools and instructed inexperienced personnel in the exacting procedures of procuring and transmitting vital information on enemy activities. In addition to his regular duties, he performed highly successful intelligence missions to Manila and his accurate reports were instrumental in the expeditious and decisive defeat of the Japanese in that area.

Through his outstanding efficiency, sustained bravery, and boundless enthusiasm, Lieutenant Hernandez contributed much to the success of his groups mission which proved invaluable in the liberation of Mindoro.

OFFICIAL
U. S. ARMY FORCES, PACIFIC
SEAL

A true copy from
G-2, GHQ
AFWESPAC

www.ingramcontent.com/pod-product-compliance
Lightning Source LLC
Chambersburg PA
CBHW042112120526
44592CB00042B/2698